The Art of Time

The Art of Time

~

Levinas, Ethics, and the
Contemporary Peninsular Novel

NINA L. MOLINARO

Lewisburg, Pennsylvania

Library of Congress Cataloging-in-Publication Data

Names: Molinaro, Nina L., 1960– author.
Title: The art of time : Levinas, ethics, and the contemporary peninsular novel /
Nina L Molinaro.
Description: Lewisburg, PA : Bucknell University Press, 2019. |
Includes bibliographical references and index.
Identifiers: LCCN 2018059772 | ISBN 9781684481279 (paperback) |
ISBN 9781684481286 (cloth)
Subjects: LCSH: Spanish fiction—20th century—History and criticism. | Ethics
in literature. | Levinas, Emmanuel—Ethics. | Other (Philosophy) in literature. |
Generation X—Spain—Attitudes. | BISAC: LITERARY CRITICISM / European /
Spanish & Portuguese. | PHILOSOPHY / Ethics & Moral Philosophy. |
LITERARY CRITICISM / European / French.
Classification: LCC PQ6144 .M57 2019 | DDC 194—dc23
LC record available at https://lccn.loc.gov/2018059772

A British Cataloging-in-Publication record for this book is
available from the British Library.

♾ The paper used in this publication meets the requirements of the American
National Standard for Information Sciences—Permanence of Paper for Printed
Library Materials, ANSI Z39.48-1992.

www.bucknell.edu/UniversityPress

Distributed worldwide by Rutgers University Press

Manufactured in the United States of America

For Luis T. González-del-Valle—mentor, scholar, friend

For Robert C. Spires, "El Jefe," in memoriam (1936–2013)

For the Right Reverend Stephen Molopi Diseko,
bishop of the Diocese of Matlosane, South Africa

Contents

The Art of Time

1

Ethics, Alterity, and Levinas

Ethics, or the systematized set of inquiries and responses to the question "What should I do?," has infused both Western philosophy and fictional narratives for more than two centuries. From its inception, ethics has been closely aligned with the relational, the rational, and the religious. As a discourse, it addresses deep and abiding concerns about obligation, virtue, happiness, theology, and politics. And as one of the three conventional arms of philosophical investigation, ethics in the Western world is frequently conceived as normative and, as such, is organized around the articulation and analysis of binaries; these include good versus bad, right versus wrong, individual versus collective, human versus divine, reason versus emotion, subject versus object, and so on. Ethics is concerned with value judgments rather than judgments of fact. It remains a central feature of contemporary philosophical discussions because, far from achieving consensus, ethics has become increasingly—and perhaps even definitionally—irresolvable at the same time as it has acquired ever more urgency and complexity in the face of globalization, environmental pressures, political instability, and technological innovation.

As one of the foremost ethical theorists of the twentieth century, Emmanuel Levinas (1906–1995) has radicalized the discipline of philosophy by arguing that "the ethical,"[1] rather than the metaphysical, is the foundational position for human subjectivity and that conflictual human subjectivity underlies all of Western philosophy. Levinas conceives of ethics as at once idealistic and contentious, discursive and metaphysical; these and additional paradoxes place him in dialogue with the poststructuralist current that has infused much of Continental European philosophy since the second half of the twentieth century. Among such discourses, Levinas's voice is crucial because he grapples with the quintessential problem of alterity, or "otherness," and with how to articulate difference in relation to the competing and often violent movement toward sameness. His work is intimately relevant to the global resurgence of interest in ethics and, as I will subsequently contend, to the nexus between ethics, temporality, and narrative fiction in contemporary Spain.[2]

What is exchanged in the narration of otherness through time and how is such a relation realized? How can the intentional conscious perception of time surpass duration in order to broach alterity without reducing it to so many chronologies of the Same? Among the numerous (and ever increasing) manifestations of the contemporary Peninsular novel, I am particularly interested in the texts of a relatively recent cohort of novelists in Spain, provisionally grouped under the adapted moniker of Generación X [Generation X], or Gen X. Their fictional works have thus far defied easy classification—in part because these writers strive to communicate the exigency and timeliness of an ethics based in alterity and in part because they strenuously contest the notion that knowledge is power. Spain's Gen X writers are not philosophers, and they are not, in the main, philosophically self-conscious. They do not generally articulate their primary concerns as either ontological or ethical, but they do maintain, in varying ways and by various routes, that human subjectivity is fragmented and contentious and that it eschews both rationality and the so-called unity attributed to consciousness. Moreover, these writers uniformly explore and interrogate the fraught notion of humanity in relation to alterity and, I would propose, to time.

As one among many countries and national cultures with a long and disputed history of systemic violence against internally and externally perceived others, Spain is perhaps unusual in that during the first four decades of the twentieth century, it was the site of an embattled monarchy, two military dictatorships, and the Second Republic, which interrupted those dictatorships and was arguably one of the most politically and socially liberal phenomena in all of Europe. When General Francisco Franco Bahamonde's Nationalist forces defeated the Republican army at the conclusion of the Spanish Civil War in 1939, however, Franco governed during the ensuing four decades by publicly proclaiming, at home and abroad, Spain's mythic return to its former imperialistic glory. When the charismatic dictator died in 1975, the country eagerly surged toward democracy, membership in the European Union, and full participation in the global market—all of which reached a widely televised apex in 1992, when Spain hosted the Expo in Seville and the Summer Olympics in Barcelona and Madrid was declared the European Capital of Culture for the year. The final three decades of the twentieth century were accompanied by tumultuous economic recessions; terrorism; environmental disasters; the arrival of more than a million immigrants from Latin America, the Middle East, and the Balkans; constant political scandals; and growing calls for independence from the autonomous regions of Cataluña and the País Vasco (or Euskadi). These multiple threats to the image of unity, together with additional factors, continue to weigh heavily on Spain's role in the European Union and in global politics.

During the 1990s, many of the tensions stemming from the aforementioned events were condensed and refracted in novels by a heterogeneous assemblage of writers in Spain, writers who were successfully marketed to the reading public and critics alike as *la Generación X* and who sought to give voice and resonance to the demands and promises of ethical intersubjectivity. Their narrative fiction comprises the topic of the present monograph and offers a remarkably appropriate and diverse forum in which to examine the notion of time in Levinas's evolving formulation of the ethics of alterity. Because of the challenges and complexity of both Levinas's philosophy and Spain's history during the twentieth century, I have elected, here in the opening chapter, to briefly sketch the history of ethics, the status of Levinas's philosophy vis-à-vis that discourse, the key tenets of his ever-shifting theory of alterity, and the broad function of time in that theory. In chapter 2, I rehearse the history of Spain during the twentieth century, the emergence and consolidation of the Gen X, the convergences and divergences among the writers who were initially included that group during the 1990s, critical reception of the cohort, and why the concept of ethical alterity, as formulated by Levinas, is compelling and omnipresent in their novels. In the three succeeding chapters, I survey three distinct—and intertwined—narrative approaches to temporal alterity through a selection of novels published by Gen X authors in Spain during the mid-1990s. The first of these, chapter 3, examines the forceful reduction of intersubjectivity to the repetition of sameness and synchrony, together with the dire ethical consequences of this reduction, in Gabriela Bustelo's *Veo veo* [*I Spy*] (1996), Marta Sanz's *El frío* [*Cold*] (1995), and José Ángel Mañas's *Mensaka* [*Mensaka*] (1995). Chapter 4 tracks the temporary advent and enduring failure of ethical responsibility through Tino Pertierra's *El secreto de Sara* [*Sara's Secret*] (1996), Blanca Riestra's *Anatol y dos más* [*Anatol and Two More*] (1996), and Belén Gopegui's *Tocarnos la cara* [*Touching Our Faces*] (1995). And finally, in chapter 5, I investigate the startling diachrony of alterity in Juana Salabert's *Arde lo que será* [*Whatever Will Be Burns*] (1996), Sergi Pàmies's *Sentimental* [*Sentimental*] (1995), and Luisa Castro's *La fiebre amarilla* [*Yellow Fever*] (1994). In order to underscore the radical impetus of Levinas's philosophy of alterity and its applicability to Gen X novels, I offer the following outline of the history of Western ethics and Levinas's position within that history.

Always a constant in the energy of human interactions, conflict has, throughout the previous century and into the initial decades of the current century, assumed apocalyptic dimensions as technology moves us beyond the physical and mental boundaries of the human body, as globalization intensifies the material and political effects of consumerism and capitalism, and as visible and invisible distinctions among us translate into ever-more ideologically charged and traumatizing disparities—all of which provokes, in turn, more sophisticated strategies and tactics aimed at enforcing homogenization and conformity. Against the mounting tensions embedded in economic, cultural, and scientific changes, human beings continue to make decisions, we continue to assume and assign more or less responsibility concerning greater and lesser matters, and we continue to identify and passionately promulgate notions of good, bad, right, and wrong. We continue to anticipate, and in more instances require, action on the basis of certain interpretations of ethical distinctions. We continue to attach value and causation to our deliberations about such matters. And foremost, in the face of, or more likely because of, the insoluble disappearance of "we," ethics and ethical inquiry continue to generate escalating debate and tangible, even aggressive, consequences in all human societies, inevitably yielding an expanding array of discourses that intersect with the discourses of art, public policy, government, law, medicine, capital, and war.[3]

Ethics has ebbed and flowed throughout the consolidation and dissemination of the Western philosophical tradition, often rooting itself in the quotidian activities of many occidental societies. Metaphysics, epistemology, and ethics conventionally comprised the major branches of philosophical investigation during the prior three centuries, and they may be condensed, respectively, into reflections on the queries "What is there?" "How do I know?" and "How should I live?"[4] Although the terms *ethics* and *morality* are often conflated with one another, scholarly attention has increasingly focused on the ways in which the two are not interchangeable. Ethics derives from the Greek *ēthos*, meaning "character," while morality comes from the Latin *mores* and encompasses character or custom and habit.[5] It may be surmised that *ethics* is in fact the more expansive term, including much that exceeds morality, and Levinas's work confirms and enacts such expansion. According to ancient philosophers and their heirs, ethics may provide an alternative to the more narrowly envisioned concept of morality, and Levinasian ethics would undoubtedly constitute one such alternative, although probably not for the reasons articulated by early ethicists. Why does ethics continue to challenge philosophers, politicians, and the polis across epochs, cultures, and intellectual fields? Perhaps because it endeavors to enunciate and elaborate relationships between individual human actions and the social world in which such actions arise and by which they are constituted. Moreover, where there is human behavior, there is difference, and with difference inevitably arises the drive to evaluate and set the optimal values and conduct for societies throughout human history.

One of the most apparent features of Levinas's ethics lies in his attempt to conceptualize a position outside of the tripartite philosophical categories described previously. His work also stands in opposition to the premise, prevalent throughout the history of Western philosophy, that metaphysics precedes and makes possible both epistemology and ethics: according to the standard philosophical argument, only *after* establishing "what is" can we possibly theorize how and what we know and, consequently, what actions we should take. Using phenomenology as his methodological compass, Levinas turns such an assumption upside down by claiming that ethics anticipates and enables both metaphysics and epistemology. Our being and our knowing both depend on and come forward as a result of our a priori ethical debt to the Other:

> A calling into question of the same—which cannot occur within the egoist spontaneity of the same—is brought about by the other. We name this calling into question of my spontaneity by the presence of the Other ethics. . . . Metaphysics, transcendence, the welcoming of the other by the same, of the Other by me, is concretely produced as the calling into question of the same by the other, that is, as the ethics that accomplishes the critical essence of knowledge. And as critique precedes dogmatism, metaphysics precedes ontology.[6]

As is evident from the aforementioned citation, in which the "calling" indicates a present as an ongoing relation and/or an incipient future, notions of time and temporality are crucial to all formulations of Levinasian alterity. Tina Chanter notes, however, that "despite the fact that Levinas's notion of time is central to his philosophy, it is singularly neglected even by self-proclaimed Levinasians."[7] My current project seeks to partially redress this gap in the context of contemporary Peninsular narrative fiction.

In summaries of the Western philosophical tradition of ethics that Levinas simultaneously emulates, critiques, and revises, commentators often favor one of two approaches. The first, embraced by pre-1950s historians of philosophy and many authors of contemporary pedagogical texts, stresses the synchronic view and is committed to identifying universal (and therefore transhistorical) principles and topics. The synchronic strategy holds that ethics is and has always been linked to regulatory and concrete human actions, to producing and putting into practice answers to the protean questions of how one ought to live and how our actions and choices shape sociality. By contrast, the second approach, diachronic in method, considers changes in ethics over time. Specifically, contemporary historians of philosophy such as Alasdair MacIntyre argue that ethical concepts are altered as social life changes. These analysts arrange the story of ethics chronologically, frequently beginning with Homer or the pre-Sophists and concluding with twentieth-century Anglophone philosophers such as G. E. Moore, A. J. Ayer, Charles L. Stevenson, and R. M. Hare. The synchronic account tends to locate Levinas (if he is considered at all) within a specific subdiscipline of Western ethics,[8] whereas the diachronic perspective underscores his intellectual connections to his predecessors, from Plato to Heidegger and beyond. Both vantage points nonetheless emphasize the extent to which he engages and transforms the prescriptive tradition of Western ethics.

In the synchronic schematization, encountered in textbooks of Western philosophy, ethics is divided into several broad and hypothetically overlapping categories. One standard division, which is useful insofar as it generates three kinds of questions associated with ethical inquiry, delineates among metaethics, normative ethics, and practical ethics.[9] Metaethics considers the prerequisites and presumptions of ethical theories and encompasses most philosophies of ethics well into the seventeenth century. By contrast, although ethical inquiry has always proceeded from and enacted norms, in the seventeenth and eighteenth centuries, Thomas Hobbes (1588–1679) and Immanuel Kant (1724–1804), among others, formalized ethics as preeminently regulatory, and their work is often deemed to be the starting place for the subdiscipline of normative ethics. As for the third category of practical ethics, while philosophy has perhaps always incorporated a pragmatic component, some contemporary philosophers posit applicability as the determining characteristic of ethics more generally, and they conceptualize ethics according to its relevance for disputes produced within the disciplines of health care, business, law, biology, technology, and mass media, among others.[10]

To return to the three subdivisions of ethics, Levinas's work might be considered quintessentially metaethical in that it revises the premises that underlie the Western ethical tradition, it questions the potential separation between objectivity and relativism, and it places ethics at the center of all philosophical inquiry. His theories also intersect with normative ethics insofar as he stresses rules while at the same time concentrating on an atypical set of consequences. He is profoundly concerned with obligation, as is Kant, but he argues against rationality as the basis for the human understanding of duty.[11] Rather, for Levinas rationality is preceded by our ethical debt to the Other and to others, theorized as quintessentially different from the Same and from any perceiving subject.[12] And lastly, notions of practical ethics concentrate on social and individual performances and explore the following queries: how and when ethics can be most successfully applied, what kinds of ethical platforms are relevant to particular situations, and which situations are inherently ethical. Over the previous three decades, a constellation of interrelated topics has elicited intense attention from practical ethicists. Some recent foci include global and local poverty, the environment, abortion, euthanasia, animal rights, the penitential system, prostitution, child labor, epidemiology, terrorism, computer gaming, and genetic engineering.[13] A survivor of the Holocaust—or the Shoah, as it is known by Jewish thinkers and writers—Levinas was, until his death in 1995, keenly committed to the abolishment of suffering in all its manifestations.[14] To that end, he might have even gone so far as to contend that ethics is in fact always pragmatic because it determines human being, saying, knowing, and doing, all of which entail pragmatic consequences and effects.

If a synchronic view of his thought with respect to the Western philosophical corpus elucidates the ways in which Levinas's understanding of ethics does and does not illustrate the goals of metaethics, normative ethics, and applied ethics, then a partial review of the chronology of Western ethics in relation to his work will show how and why ethics as a general philosophical discipline developed, what Levinas inherited from his antecedents, and how his theory converges with and diverges from many of the prevalent conceptions of ethics. Levinas formulates ethicality both in consonance with and against mainstream Western ethics, and in so doing, he retains some of the historically specific demands and complexities of ethics so that his thought might remain germane to and coherent within philosophical discourse more generally. In this, he joins ancient and contemporary ethicists alike in addressing a familiar set of topics that encompass human nature, choice, value, psychology, science, divinity, and rights.

It is largely agreed that philosophical reflections on ethics in the Western world commenced some two and a half millennia ago with the pre-Socratics, Socrates, his disciple Plato, and Plato's successor, Aristotle, all of whom were instrumental in launching ethics in ancient Greece as a relevant and discrete intellectual pursuit.[15] It is significant for my subsequent discussion, which focuses exclusively on literary texts, that poetry preceded philosophy in ancient Greece by several centuries and that early Greek dramatic and historical texts produced in the second half of the first century BCE instigated the interdependence between nonphilosophical texts and philosophy, an interdependence that Plato would later question.[16] All of the aforementioned contributed to philosophical discussions on a range of matters that included what constituted *eudaimonia*, or "human happiness," and how it was realized and the most advantageous association between the individual citizen and society. As will become evident, Levinas, in keeping with many contemporary thinkers, exhibits definitive ties to ancient Greek philosophy, and his thought resonates especially strongly with that of Plato insofar as both are idealists and dialecticians. If Plato posited the Good as beyond Being, then Levinas will take up this tradition of transcendence and rework it to radically conceptualize the nature of otherness.[17]

From the outset, ethics in ancient Greece, at least as early as the Homeric epics of the *Iliad* (ca. 900 BCE) and the *Odyssey* (ca. 800 BCE), was understood as regulatory in that its purpose consisted of elaborating descriptive assessments of *arête*, or "human excellence," which was itself designed to complement a society organized around an accepted hierarchy of prescribed roles.[18] This early emphasis on the connection between exemplary citizens and their societies will infuse all ensuing formulations of ethics, including Levinas's theory. When, in approximately 500 BCE, views of citizenry, social arrangements, and the series of tasks associated with those arrangements came into conflict with the emergence of the city-state, the philosophical discipline of ethics was born as a way to teach people the rules of desirable behavior vis-à-vis their shared identity. Ethics thus began as a direct response to collective social changes and would continue, throughout the ensuing two thousand years, to dialogue with, contest, and foment the political, social, and cultural circumstances in which ethicists found (and continue to find) themselves. It is, for example, far from accidental that Levinas elaborated his own ethical theory in the wake of two world wars and as a drastic antidote to the horrors of the Shoah. As he observes, "Perhaps the most revolutionary fact of our twentieth-century consciousness . . . is that of the destruction of all balance between Western thought's explicit and implicit theodicy and the forms that suffering and its evil are taking on in the very unfolding of this century."[19] He will repeatedly return, in his philosophical writing and in his Talmudic commentaries, to the myriad ways in which his historical situation has informed his ethical position. Temporality is therefore not an abstraction for Levinas but rather lived experience.

Although Socrates is often regarded as the father of Western ethics, the writings of Heraclitus, who flourished around 500 BCE, in fact constitute the first substantial work on ethics. Heraclitus posited *logos* [natural law] as the origin and explanation for *nomos* [human laws and conventions], whereas Protagoras did away with the concept of natural law and Herodotus supplemented attention to human law with an awareness of cultural differences, arguing that laws may change from place to place but that the existence of such laws made possible sociality and civilized behavior. With the arrival of the city-state, a new class of teachers was charged with meeting the demands of an emerging group of students. These teachers, known collectively as the Sophists and aligned with the scholarly discipline of rhetoric, received two tasks, the combination of which engendered the intellectual relativism with which they are today associated: first, they were directed to develop for their students a coherent set of meanings for the reigning evaluative vocabulary, and second, they were charged with teaching their fellows how to live most effectively in dissimilar city-states, all of which were governed by public performance. One might even claim that ethics initially arose in response to a widespread push toward managing difference, a push that Levinas will, some two millennia later, attempt to reverse. It is crucial to note that, as an early example of the nexus between normative ethics and practical ethics, in ancient Greece and prior to Socrates, the ideals of virtue and justice, as well as all additional qualities, did not exist apart from their dominant practices in each city-state. Ethics therefore only attained significance in terms of its impact on human behavior and human lives. By contrast, Socrates and Plato would lobby for the transcendence or objectivity of ideal forms. While subsequent formulations of ethics, including those of Levinas, have often been targeted for their excessive abstraction, in its inception, ethics registered as the description of certain kinds of favorable human behavior.

The Sophists, together with their fifth-century contemporary Socrates, are among the earliest philosophers of ethics on at least two counts: on the one hand, they self-consciously pointed to reason as the ultimate determinant of optimal human behavior, and on the other hand, they formulated strategies that likewise employed reason to adduce the connections between how and why human beings act ethically.[20] From this moment onward, rationality would underwrite most formal ethical deliberations, and Levinas will radicalize the study of ethics precisely by theorizing the link between ethics and reason as imposed rather than intrinsic. Whereas the Sophists espoused a form of relativism, in that to live a good human life meant the ability to know and demonstrate the moral values of each civic community (ethics as *nomos*), Socrates sought to align ethics with the reasoning process itself, which in his estimation surpassed all cultural differences (ethics as *physis*): human beings were to preferably advance, through logical dialogue with one another, toward an understanding of what is good for us, together with the ability to evaluate what is more and less good and more and less bad.[21] In favoring discernable virtues as the highest human good over all other physical, material, financial, social, and political markers of success, Socrates attempted to steer ethics away from relativism and toward an early form of idealism that transcended public performance, a move that Levinas will match. Other equivalent terms for Socrates's notion of idealism include objectivity, universality, and formalism. At the same time, Socrates yoked all virtues, which were acquired jointly, to their applications, and he theorized that virtues were indeed synonymous with the knowledge of desirable and undesirable human actions. In sum, he set the stage for all successive ethical formulations by positing the following paradoxes: "Virtue is one, virtue is knowledge, no one does wrong knowingly and willingly."[22]

In the 380s BCE, Plato augmented his teacher's theories with the notion that one can only know goodness based on or caused by the Form of the Good (the Good-itself); because all forms are discernable, there is no distinction between the knowledge that gods might possess and the knowledge to which human beings can aspire. By the same token, Socrates's disciple also argued that certain kinds of human beings were more attuned to the acquisition of knowledge and that certain kinds of discourse were more appropriate to apprehending the Good-itself. So began a long-standing feud between philosophy and art, a feud that Levinas will continue by maintaining a characteristically Platonic distrust of literary language as derivative and manipulative. He will also imitate Plato in his belief in the humanly knowable Good-itself, but Levinas, as a phenomenologist, will locate the possibility of ethical knowledge within the purview of human perception. Transcendence will be transmuted into the act, rather than the object, of perception.

Several decades later, Aristotle rejected Plato's theory of ethical knowledge based on abstract forms in favor of knowledge that was centered on an analysis of the ends or purposes of natural objects available in nature: "When [Aristotle] proceeds to his definition of the good, he depends only on the view that rational behavior is the characteristic exercise of human beings, in the light of which any characteristically human good has to be defined. The good of man is defined as the activity of the soul in accordance with virtue."[23] As a successful response to the ensuing deity-centered ethics of the Middle Ages, and thanks to the eventual rise of the scientific method, the Aristotelian emphasis on natural objects and ethics as practical and therefore political would dominate much of the Western philosophical tradition from the fifteenth century onward. Although twentieth-century phenomenologists might loosely consider themselves to be scientists, Levinas's version of ethics is in direct opposition to Aristotelian philosophical methods in nearly every respect. Whereas Aristotle emphasized deduction and, to a lesser extent, induction, Levinas advocates the dialectic method; whereas Aristotle favored extrinsic objects, Levinas concentrates on intrinsic intentions; and whereas Aristotle organized his arguments around an analysis of the parts and the whole, for Levinas, any intellectual separation between the parts and the whole—any intrusion of reason—damages relationships, enables human suffering, and produces estrangement, violence, and solipsism.[24]

Although ethical reflection ebbed and flowed throughout late antiquity and into the medieval period, from roughly 1250 CE onward, Western ethics was primarily coupled in Europe to the consolidation of Christianity and to the dissemination of the Latin translation of Aristotle's *Nicomachean Ethics*, available in its complete version in 1247. It can certainly be posited that Levinas's ideas connect in a number of salient ways to the philosophical efforts of medieval thinkers such as St. Augustine (354–430) and Boethius (480–524) and to early Jewish philosophers such as Maimonides (1138–1204). Maimonides, as one example, fused an Aristotelian emphasis on virtuous behavior as the "Golden Mean" with a rabbinical emphasis on "the imitation of God's lovingkindness, justice, and righteousness after having achieved the highest achievable level of intellectual perfection."[25] It is during the seventeenth and eighteenth centuries, however, when—because of the political, intellectual, and religious ferment that infused the first half of the seventeenth century—ethics acquired a renewed relevance and ethicists attempted to forge a workable bridge between private and public morality. Instead of either substituting one intellectual justification of moral belief for another or reworking the available ethical traditions, during the 1600s, ethics involved nothing less than rethinking the extent to which human beings could direct and control their behavior and their choices. Indeed, it required a new view of what it was to be "human"—a scientific rather than a theological notion. When the seventeenth century commenced, it was generally agreed that human beings must receive guidance in moral issues from a source external to them, be it political or divine. By the conclusion of the following century, philosophers had commenced theorizing the possibility of moral autonomy, such that human beings could direct and control themselves and one another in moral matters without external intervention. Thus modern ethical philosophy was born.

As a result of this unprecedented shift in thinking, most seventeenth-century ethicists placed rationality or volition, as distinctly human capacities, at the core of their deliberations. René Descartes (1596–1650), for instance, lobbied for reason, self-knowledge, and self-control as the qualities that, along with generosity, would lead us to pursue a secular and practical notion of goodness. Although Levinas will, some three hundred years later, base his theory of alterity on the premise of moral autonomy, he will strenuously argue against rationality as the foundation for all Western ethics. Philosophers of moral autonomy during the seventeenth century may be separated into two camps: those who looked to rationality as the source for our innate self-directive abilities and those who claimed that sentiment provides the moral compass for our behavior. Levinas will refute the first position and modify, in accordance with the imperatives of phenomenology, the second position, which was promulgated by, among others, David Hume (1711–1776).

Hume is arguably the most eminent proponent in the eighteenth century of a so-called secular ethic of virtue, in which virtues were understood "not as habits of compliance with laws but as firm dispositions to respond to the needs of others."[26] Levinas will expand Hume's conception of virtue and his focus on justice while dismissing the companion component of social approval. Furthermore, whereas Hume concentrated on sentiment as the basis of the human drive toward serving the social good, Kant elaborated a theory of the duality of human motivation. Simply put, the only overarching principle for the latter's version of morality consists of the requirement that human beings not contradict themselves in their actions; he viewed rationality to be the foremost guarantee for consistency and intuition as the basis for apprehending duty. Kant inverts the notion that our knowledge of goodness determines our knowledge of rightness; rather, we must always decide what is right before we can know what is good. Levinas will imitate Kant insofar as both men argue for the internalization of the moral law and against an external agent, but he will attribute autonomy to the ontologically prior position of the human subject vis-à-vis the Other rather than to rationality, which perforce upholds the preeminence of the subject at the expense of the Other. Like Kant, Levinas will fasten on the duties of virtue, which promote justice and the social good, and he will also postulate that God exists as an effect of ethics rather than as the cause, but Levinas will resolutely unyoke duty, virtue, and divinity from rationality.

If Levinas emulates Kant in his defense of autonomy, then he adopts from nineteenth-century Continental ethicists their insistence that Kantian philosophy is excessively abstract. And he will likewise be drawn to their shared claim that sociality precedes rationality, as well as to their intellectual push for a superior human good that is not theistically derived. Moreover, nineteenth-century European philosophy generated the initial impetus for phenomenology, the philosophical method to which Levinas would adhere throughout his forty-year career. Edmund Husserl, the founder of phenomenology, lectured frequently on ethics at the University of Halle (1887–1901), the University of Göttingen (1901–1916), and the University of Freiburg (1916–1929). While a graduate student at the University of Freiburg, Levinas worked with both Husserl and Husserl's replacement, Martin Heidegger, and the young doctoral candidate subsequently published his dissertation, titled *Théorie de l'intuition dans la phénoménologie de Husserl*, on Husserlian phenomenology in 1930.[27]

In the early 1900s, Western ethical philosophy predictably aimed to revisit and restore earlier ethical traditions—such as Aristotelianism, Thomism, Kantianism, and Hegelianism—and to adapt them to the pressing moral issues of the day. Between 1900 and 1950, ethicists also contributed at least five original areas of ethical inquiry, four of which evince direct or indirect ties to Levinas's work. The first of these was value realism, pioneered by Franz Clemens Brentano (1838–1917)[28] and expanded upon by Max Scheler (1874–1928) and Nicolai Hartmann (1882–1950). Value realism attempted to "elucidate objectively apprehensible intrinsic values" and analyze "emotions—especially love and hate—construed as the medium through which such values may be discerned."[29]

Although Scheler and Hartmann were contemporaries of Husserl's, they rejected the latter's idealism, which Levinas will rework and retain.

The second area, associated with the efforts of twentieth-century French thinkers Jean-Paul Sartre (1905–1980), Simone de Beauvoir (1908–1986), and Maurice Merleau-Ponty (1908–1961), may be broadly categorized as an ethics of personal transformation and, at least in its primary manifestations, demonstrates substantial overlap with existential phenomenology. Like the value realists, these three philosophers initially sought to describe immediately given data using the phenomenological method, and like their peers, they rejected Husserl's key notion of the transcendental ego, whereas Levinas will apply this notion to the other. Moreover, they interpreted data in metaphysical terms and according to two central tenets: freedom constitutes the basis for all human aims and human beings bear responsibility for their actions and their lives. Levinas will eschew the first precept and modify the second in accordance with his distinct philosophical position.[30]

A third development in ethics emerged from philosophical responses to the two world wars and, more generally, to the rise of totalitarianism in Europe and elsewhere between 1900 and 1950. Some of the thinkers most often allied with this strand include Simone Weil (1909–1943), Albert Camus (1913–1960), and Hannah Arendt (1906–1975). Although Levinas's philosophy is not regularly considered among theirs, his ethical theory emerged and advanced, at least in part, as the result of his experiences during World War II, both as a French officer and prisoner of war and as a Jewish man whose parents and siblings were interned and eventually murdered in the Nazi concentration camps in Lithuania.[31] Much of his later writing will be directed toward questions of social justice, remediation, and peace activism.

The fourth field of ethical inquiry that surfaced during the first half of the twentieth century encompasses intersubjective theories of ethics and is associated with the work of Martin Buber (1878–1965) and with Levinas's own philosophy. Although the two men were roughly contemporaries of one another, were both deeply influenced by Jewish mysticism, and are often compared in light of their contributions to Jewish ethics, their ideas are far from synonymous. In his groundbreaking treatise, published as German under the title of *Ich und Du* in 1923 (translated into English and published as *I and Thou* in 1937), Buber distinguished between the I-It relationship, which manifests as isolation, history, partiality, and objectification, and the infinitely preferable I-Thou relationship, which produces joyful presence, reciprocity, community, and dialogue. While Levinas himself has recognized the potential affinity between his thought and that of Buber, he deems the latter's central concept of reciprocity to be unethical, narcissistic, and philosophically unviable: "Although Buber has penetratingly described the Relation and the act of distancing, he has not taken separation seriously enough. Man is not merely identifiable with the category of distance and meeting, he is a being *sui generis*, and it is impossible for him to ignore or forget his avatar of subjectivity. He realizes his own separateness in a process of subjectification which is not explicable in terms of a recoil from the Thou."[32] Familiarity, in the case of Buber's I-Thou relation, enables absorption of the second term into the first and the resulting erasure of alterity and ethical indebtedness. In Levinas's formulation, by contrast, the self assumes prior responsibility for the other, and the metaphysical debt only increases as our awareness of the debt increases.[33]

Trained as a phenomenologist, Levinas has consistently claimed the phenomenological method as his entry into ethics. By the same token, after dedicating the first decade of his philosophical career to generating extended commentaries on the ideas of Husserl and Heidegger, he subsequently moved beyond them and beyond what he considered to be the prototypical limitations of phenomenology. It may nonetheless be useful to outline the general contours of this branch of philosophical inquiry before explicating Levinas's particular theory of alterity.[34] Phenomenology is regularly defined as "'the study or description of phenomena'; and a 'phenomenon' is simply anything that appears or presents itself to someone."[35] At the risk of oversimplification, phenomenological approaches to ethics (and phenomenology more generally) might be divided into roughly two cohorts: transcendental phenomenology, as conceptualized by Henri Bergson (1859–1941), Husserl, and their colleagues, and existential phenomenology, as theorized by Scheler, Hartmann, Sartre, and Merleau-Ponty, among others.[36] As both a student and an avid follower of Husserl's approach, Levinas will initially cleave to the precepts of transcendental phenomenology in espousing philosophical idealism over the descriptive and eidetic approach practiced by the existentialists and their predecessors; whereas existential phenomenology maintains the existence of an external world separate from our understanding of such a world, idealism, influenced by Plato, affirms that ideas—or our understanding of the external world—in fact constitute reality.

Following in the wake of Brentano, Husserl sought, in the last decade of the nineteenth and the first decades of the twentieth centuries, to repudiate the intellectual dominance of scientific realism and in particular the widely disseminated confidence, common since the European Enlightenment of the seventeenth century, in the superior accounts of reality provided by the physical sciences. These scientific accounts were typically contrasted to the human perception of that same reality, which was itself inevitably equated to the inferior "appearance." Husserl and successive phenomenologists would attempt to dismantle the reification of external public objects over internal private experience in at least two ways.

First, Husserl endeavored to assign demonstrable certainty to human consciousness, or the transcendental ego;[37] in order for knowledge to be secure, the thinking subject must assume the reality of consciousness as primary and absolute. And second, phenomenologists argued that perception and experience, like the physical sciences, necessarily have an object; as Michael Hammond, Jane Howarth, and Russell Keat declare, "The description of experience shows it always to be experience *of* something. Experience, as it were, always refers to something beyond itself, and therefore cannot be characterized independently of this. . . . One cannot, for example, characterize perceptual experience without describing what it is that is seen, touched, heard, and so on."[38] Levinas will, as Eric Severson notes, engage the same phenomenological notion of intentionality, or the Husserlian *epoché*, but he will effectively substitute the primacy of the Other in the place of the Husserlian transcendental Ego.[39]

Transcendental or idealist phenomenology assigns to the self-aware Subject "a *constitutive* role with respect to the 'real world': the sense of meaning of the latter is provided by the former, the transcendental ego, which is not itself a part of that world, but rather is presupposed by it."[40] Throughout his career, Levinas will be drawn to the self-reflexive dimension of phenomenology; in *Ethics and Infinity*, for example, he distinguishes this dimension as "a radical reflection, obstinate about itself, a *cogito* which seeks and describes itself without being duped by a spontaneity or ready-made presence, in a major distrust toward what is thrust naturally onto knowledge, a *cogito* which constitutes the world and the object, but whose objectivity in reality occludes and encumbers the look that fixes it."[41] He thus shares with Husserl an interest in the object of intentionality, or what he terms "an opening of thought onto something present to thought and quite distinct from the lived experience of that thought,"[42] but he rejects Husserl's reliance on the concept of representation to capture the objective world. More germane to my argument, he will refute Husserl's intellectualism precisely because the latter situates consciousness outside of time, whereas Levinas posits early on that "time is not the achievement of an isolated and lone subject, but . . . the very relationship of the subject with the Other."[43] The multiple manifestations of this relationship within the context of novels produced by Gen X writers in 1990s Spain constitute the impetus for the current project.

In addition to his translation and investigation of Husserl's philosophical texts, Levinas also studied with Martin Heidegger after the latter replaced Husserl as the professor of philosophy at the University of Freiburg.[44] Indeed, scholars frequently acknowledge the distinctly Heideggerian dimension of Levinas's early work on Husserl, going so far as to suggest that his doctoral thesis "significantly opened up criticisms of Husserl from a distinctly Heideggerian 'historical' perspective, which he [Levinas] described himself as 'post-Husserlian.'"[45] Levinas insisted on the influence of both men in his initial philosophical texts, written during the 1930s and 1940s, although Heidegger's political commitment to Nazism proved decisive to Levinas's rejection of his mentor's work after the publication of *Sein und Zeit* [*Being and Time*] in 1927. Nonetheless, they both utilized phenomenological precepts to describe Being. For his part, Heidegger posited the following: "Dasein then revealed itself as that entity which must first be worked out in an ontologically adequate manner, if the inquiry is to become a transparent one. But now it has been shown that the ontological analytic of Dasein in general is what makes up fundamental ontology, so that Dasein functions as that entity which in principle is to be *interrogated* beforehand as to its Being."[46] As Colin Davis observes, Levinas also shares with Heidegger an understanding of Being as an event or process, as a becoming, and thus as inseparable from temporality and historicity.[47] The two philosophers likewise conclude, separately but in consonance, that conventional philosophy has neglected to conceptualize being in light of *time*.[48] Their interrogation of the temporal dimension of being is, however, fundamentally dissimilar because their interrogation of being, and of the objects and events that human subjects perceive, is radically divergent.

As with Husserl, even as he claims intellectual kinship with Heidegger's theories before World War II, so too does Levinas critique and unpack the implications of his teacher's ontological project, suggesting as early as 1935, in an article titled "De l'évasion," that there might be something that ineludibly exceeds ontology. "De l'évasion" was translated into English by Bettina Bergo, and the English-language text was published, together with supplementary texts, in book-length form as *On Escape* in 2003. As he moves further away from the formative influences of Husserl and Heidegger, Levinas grows increasingly concerned with how consciousness might encounter—and has in fact always already encountered—something beyond itself without erasing whatever might be different. He articulates and bases his own philosophical inquiry on the flaw that, according to Levinas, both of his former teachers evince: "Both thinkers subsume the Other under the authority of the Same, which is understood as consciousness in Husserl and Being in Heidegger."[49] And this authority is directly yoked to a specific, and specifically unified, notion of time. Because, from his earliest published texts, he binds his fundamental concept of alterity to time, "a progressively radicalized theory of time . . . unfolds in Levinas's work as a whole. Each of Levinas' works presents a distinct analysis of time, and each analysis is progressively more radical than the prior analysis, as the analysis of alterity is progressively radicalized."[50] Alterity and temporality become interdependent, and as he successively theorizes the former, he refines his understanding of the latter.

During the 1940s and 1950s, Levinas gradually reframes the concept of intentionality, a cornerstone of phenomenology, in order to underscore relationality and, more particularly, the foundational relationship between self and Other.[51] As a major component of his revision, he formulates the idea of *il y a* in direct opposition to Heidegger's *es gibt*. The two phrases might loosely be translated as "there is," but whereas with the French *il y a* Levinas signals impersonality and an anonymous existing, Heidegger's German phrase emphasizes the generosity and abundance of Being. Furthermore, Levinas replaces Heidegger's Being with the notion of consciousness as a "hypostasis," a term that he defines in *Time and the Other* as "the event by which the existent contracts its existing."[52] More significantly for my larger project, he asserts in 1947 that the present is *the* event of hypostasis in spite of (or perhaps because of) the fact that "positing hypostasis as a present is still not to introduce time into being."[53]

For Levinas—and at this point in his philosophical deliberations—consciousness, subjectivity, and identity proceed from the *il y a* as opposed to preceding it. His formulation thus supplies a potential alternative to Heidegger's *Dasein*, which appears to advocate solitude and the perceiving subject's self-sufficiency in the present, or synchrony. In overt contrast to Heidegger's work, however, Levinas posits temporal relationality as a key feature of alterity. He further appropriates from structural linguistics and Ferdinand de Saussure the term *diachrony*—as Severson summarizes, "the trace of the other is experienced in diachrony; the evidence of the 'passing' of the other is borne by a different time than the present of the self."[54] For Levinas, there first exists the anonymity of the *il y a*, followed by the hypostasis of consciousness, followed by the perceiving subject's encounter with the unassimilable and alien object, which perforce precedes it and for whom the subject assumes an infinite responsibility: "An 'internal consciousness,' [the protoimpression] will become consciousness through the temporal modification of retention, designating perhaps the essence of all thought as the reserve of a fullness that escapes. The mystery of intentionality lies in the divergence from . . . or in the modification of the temporal flux."[55] Here we might further delineate the "temporal flux" in Levinas's early thought as his rejection of the ego that is self-contained via the absorption of past, present, and future into temporal unity. Time is not dependent upon the perceiving subject; rather, it is woven into the *il y a* and anticipates (and thereby directs) consciousness.

By the 1950s, Levinas had dedicated some two decades to formally articulating the advances and pitfalls inherent in the theories of Husserl and Heidegger, and he had arrived at the decisive conclusion that Western philosophy desperately needed another option, especially in light of the global catastrophes of the first half of the twentieth century, to its systematic suppression of the Other in favor of the constant illumination of the all-encompassing and, indeed, violent Subject. Thereafter, his entire philosophical corpus would be dedicated to two interrelated projects. First, he would attack the philosophical reification of the Subject as the toxically fundamental notion that undergirds all of Western philosophy. And second, he would elucidate, in its many diverse forms, the temporal process of alterity. His formal work on these and closely related topics spanned more than six decades, from his doctoral dissertation on Husserl, written in French and published in 1930, through *A l'heure des nations*, published in French in 1988 and translated into English by Michael B. Smith in 1994.[56]

As he grew ever more dissatisfied with the ways in which Husserl and Heidegger's philosophies continued to elevate and empower the human subject at the expense of any ethical engagement with otherness, Levinas's own philosophical career gained momentum, culminating in the publication of his two major treatises, *Totalité et infini: Essai sur l'exteriorité* (1961), published in English as *Totality and Infinity: An Essay on Exteriority* (1969),[57] and *Autrement qu'être ou au delà de l'essence* (1974), published in English as *Otherwise Than Being, or Beyond Essence* (1981). In the two monographs, together with a multitude of shorter texts that encompass essays, interviews, and public lectures, he would amplify and refine the claim that his philosophical predecessors had reified the sameness and temporal stasis of subjectivity, or being oneself and identifying oneself from within in any given instant, at the expense of alterity and diachrony, and he would continue to describe the various forms that the inescapably temporal encounter between the self and the Other might take.[58]

To continue with his developing comprehension of the salient role of time in alterity, in his 1961 monograph *Totality and Infinity*, Levinas mounts a defense of subjectivity not as the traditional centerpiece of humanism or a response to the anguish of the Heideggerian *Dasein* but "as founded in the idea of infinity"[59] and thus as irrevocably linked to time. As scholars have noted, his conception of infinity derives from Descartes's Third Meditation, which Levinas adapts to his own purposes as that which both transcends knowledge and resists the solipsistic ego. In essence, Levinas translates Descartes's infinite God into his own conception of the Other: "[Infinity] is produced in the improbable feat whereby a separated being fixed in its identity, the same, the I, nonetheless contains in itself what it can neither contain nor receive solely by virtue of its own identity."[60] He then deploys the terms of Same and Other, together with their corollaries of same and other, in order to assess the foundations of Western philosophy as an extension of "ontological imperialism." This tyranny, to use Levinas's term, manifests most explicitly in the forceful incorporation of alterity into sameness via totality and synchrony, or the "egoist spontaneity of the same."[61] His first volume will persistently attack—and ultimately dismantle—sameness, totality, and synchrony in favor of alterity, infinity, and diachrony.

Totality and Infinity is marked, as scores of scholars have observed, by Levinas's struggle to move beyond the language of ontology in his ongoing conceptualization of alterity.[62] Seán Hand puts the case succinctly: "The work's difficulties arise above all from its fundamental paradox, which is that it tries to present the Other as such, in a philosophical discourse that, by its very inherited nature, enshrines the language of the Same."[63] *Otherwise Than Being, or Beyond Essence*, Levinas's second major monograph, strives to address and perhaps partially remediate the linguistic and discursive tensions that infuse *Totality and Infinity*.[64] The second treatise covers much of the philosophical terrain expounded in *Totality and Infinity*, but Levinas radically amends his discourse and his discursive strategies in order to explicitly illuminate the rhetorical strategies of "avoidance, indirection, and unsaying."[65] Although the language and the philosophical argument in his first volume frequently border on obtuseness and opacity, *Totality and Infinity* nonetheless evinces an evident structure, employs discernable concepts and terms, and coherently situates itself within the discipline of Western philosophy. In *Otherwise Than Being*, by contrast, Levinas utilizes more ambivalent language and an argument that constantly circles back on itself, incorporating enigma, evocation, and equivocation; he introduces a new vocabulary of interrelated terms and tropes; and he reduces the roles and frequency of the previously key terms of *l'autre* [other] and *Autrui* [Other], progressively replacing them with *le prochain* [the neighbor].

The backbone of the second treatise consists of the distinction that Levinas draws between saying [*le Dire*] and the said [*le Dit*], which he articulates thus: "Saying states and thematizes the said, but signifies it to the other, a neighbor, with a signification that has to be distinguished from that borne by words in the said."[66] Whereas in the previous volume he maintained that philosophy had traditionally privileged sameness and subjectivity, here he argues that philosophers have, in the main, concerned themselves only with the said, or the language that promotes sameness and consciousness. The said lends itself to analysis because it contains the themes, ideas, and observations that comprise intentional communication between and among human subjects, whereas saying resists comprehension and legibility because its meaning cannot be encapsulated in the said. More significant to my project, Levinas returns to the issue of time: "It is only in the said, in the epos of saying, that the diachrony of time is synchronized into a time that is recallable, and becomes a theme. . . . But the signification of saying goes beyond the said. It is not ontology that raises up the speaking subject; it is the signifyingness of saying going beyond essence that can justify the exposedness of being, ontology."[67] Whereas in *Totality and Infinity* language plays a central role in ethical relations because the encounter with the Other always involves speaking and responding, Levinas argues in *Otherwise Than Being* that the exposure to the Other effected in saying lies at the very core of ethical relations and, as such, catapults us all into an a priori responsibility for, and responsiveness to, the Other.

He further postulates that prior to consciousness, choice, and a commitment to activity or passivity, the subject is exposed to the Other and rendered capable of speaking and responding to the discourse of others by virtue of alterity. The ethical nature of this exposure is brought out by the verbal link between the ability to respond and responsibility: "To maintain that the relationship with a neighbor, incontestably set up in saying, is a responsibility for the neighbor, that saying is to respond to another, is to find no longer any limit or measure for this responsibility."[68] That is, before I am or can be myself (before I can speak), I am always already responsible for, and therefore called to respond to, the other. My responsibility for the other, enacted in saying, precedes and necessitates my response to the other, which is translated into sociality, justice, and communication through thematization and the said. All of which has enormous implications for temporality.

Levinas describes the "drama of subjectivity" in *Otherwise Than Being* through the metaphor of the hostage, which has replaced the central trope of the host in *Totality and Infinity*: the "I" is no longer host to the Other but rather held hostage by the Other, thus anticipating a temporal relation. In a resonant play on words, Levinas suggests that *par l'autre* [from-the-other] is also *pour l'autre* [for-the-other]: "To undergo from the other is an absolute patience only if by this from-the-other is already for-the-other. This transfer, other than interested, 'otherwise than essence,' is subjectivity itself."[69] He will further develop the substitutional nature of alterity via the intertwined concepts of expiation and persecution. In ethical terms, the responsibility that I assume for the actions of the persecutor forms the basis of my goodness, and this goodness, together with all moral qualities, articulates an obligation arising from the fact that in my condition as subject, I am given over to the Other.[70]

To recap, then, Levinas proposes throughout his career that ethics, or what he conceptualizes as the primordial responsibility of the self to and for the other, bears irrevocably and temporally on the construction of human subjectivity. When asked, some seven years before his death, about his major philosophical concerns, he declared, "The essential theme of my research is the deformalization of the notion of time."[71] At the core of his philosophical argument, sustained and refined over decades, lies a thorough appraisal of the Western ethical tradition and the ways in which that tradition, while permitting a separation between self and Other, has consistently upheld that such separation is always necessarily superseded by consciousness, rationality, or knowledge, all of which are expressions of totality and that privilege the self at the expense of the other. This "horror of the Other" has translated into the widely accepted concept that human beings can theorize and understand ourselves only by absorbing all that is beyond or other than ourselves. By contrast, Levinas maintains that ethics *precedes* all other claims on human subjectivity; before we can conceive of what there is in the world or how we know we must formulate ourselves, and in order to accomplish that, we must acknowledge our relationship to the Other and to others. We do not exist without *first* existing for the Other, an event that thrusts responsibility

upon us. And when we exist, as we must, for the Other, we inescapably evoke the temporal terrain of the ethical. Before I can
analyze the multifaceted practice of temporal alterity as it plays
out through Spain's Gen X novels, I must address and examine
the country's contested history during the twentieth century and the
critical discourse that has formulated, and continues to foment,
the notion, and the practices, of the Generación X in contemporary Spain.

2

Spain's Generación X

The judgment of history is set forth in the visible. Historical
events are the visible par excellence; their truth is produced in
evidence. The visible forms, or tends to form, a totality.
—Emmanuel Levinas, *Totality and Infinity*

It is perhaps a measure of the success of Francoist political indoctrination
that "others" still tend to be seen as existing without rather than within.
—Helen Graham and Jo Labanyi, *Spanish Cultural Studies*

Writers, like all human beings, are affected by and interact with economic, ideological, social, and geographical forces that shape their environments, their intentions and actions, their language, and their fictional narratives. Like their contemporaries, Spain's Gen X novelists were born into specific historical, cultural, and political configurations. They attended an array of educational institutions, they have participated in domestic and international economies, and they have interpreted local and global events through the ever-changing prisms of the media and technology. They have engaged in myriad relationships with partners, friends, parents, neighbors, and strangers. During the 1990s, they began to write narrative fiction as more and less conscious members of religious, linguistic, racial, ethnic, gendered, and biological communities; with words, they strove to intervene in and decipher the promises and failures of human groups that were more and less familiar to them during a certain historical period.

Might we identify a singular factor or a cluster of characteristics from the aforementioned compendium that characterizes Gen X novelists? In the present chapter, I formulate some of the ways in which the writers of this generation have been informed by the discrete historical circumstances of twentieth-century Spain and how critics, scholars, and reviewers have understood and contextualized their narratives from the 1990s onward. I contend throughout the chapter, however, that historical, biographical, and aesthetic similarities are insufficient to define this collective. More particularly, I shall argue in the subsequent three chapters that Spain's Gen X writers insistently mapped onto their narrative explorations an abiding concern with responsibility, justice, and suffering—in a word, ethics—and that they did so through the prism of time and, more precisely, via interrogations of temporal alterity.

The massive social and political changes during the second half of the twentieth century—from an avowedly authoritarian regime in Spain to the progressive (and progressively conflictive) incorporation of heterogeneity into all facets of Spanish society—have unquestionably impacted Gen X writers. In order to effectively elucidate the ways in which Gen X novelists offered up meaningful discourses about otherness during the 1990s, it is beneficial to briefly review the country's political, social, and economic histories since the beginning of the twentieth century. In the pages that follow, I have relied on several superb studies: *España fin de siglo,* by Carlos Alonso Zaldívar and Manuel Castells (1992), published in English by the same publishing company as *Spain beyond Myths* in the same year; Francisco J. Romero Salvadó's *Twentieth-Century Spain: Politics and Society in Spain, 1898–1998* (1999); and, chiefly, *Historia de España en el siglo XX,* by Julián Casanova and Carlos Gil Andrés (2009), published in English as *Twentieth-Century Spain: A History* (2014).[1]

These historians, as well as many of their colleagues, mark 1898 and the loss of Spain's final colonies (Cuba, Guam, the Philippines, and Puerto Rico) as a watershed moment in the political and financial crises that informed the first decades of the twentieth century. The century included at least six discernable sociopolitical periods: the crisis in, and eventual dissolution of, a constitutional monarchy (1900–1923); General Miguel Primo de Rivera's military dictatorship (1923–1930); the dramatically liberalizing Second Republic (1930–1936); a brutal civil war (1936–1939); General Francisco Franco's military dictatorship (1939–1975); and the decisive installation of a functional democracy in 1975 that has survived well into the twenty-first century. These discrete periods were accompanied by several of the same cultural transformations that transpired throughout the rest of Europe and, in the global arena, by "the most accelerated social changes in the history of mankind."[2]

Nevertheless, Spain is unique among its peers on multiple counts; among these, Franco's dictatorship emerged as the consequence of a civil war, waged exclusively on Spanish soil, between the elected Republican government (and its far-flung liberal allies) and the rebel military forces (and their fascist allies). The victory of the latter resulted in the imposition of an authoritarian regime, which both survived the fascist ideology that initially bolstered its claim to legitimacy and reinforced its ideological control over the course of thirty-six years, until the death of its charismatic leader on November 20, 1975. The duration, international reception, and internal dynamics of Franco's dictatorship, together with the vibrant democracies that preceded and succeeded his reign, may well be the distinctive features of Spain's historical profile during the twentieth century. While these traits might, on the surface, seem supplementary to the writers under discussion, they in fact serve to underscore and exemplify some of the paradoxes that infuse and necessitate Levinas's philosophy of alterity within the context of Spanish culture during the 1990s.

In spite of the ease with which century markers can organize historical data, the beginning of the twentieth century did not signal a clean slate in Spanish history. An earlier political phase, known as the Restoration, had begun in 1874, when the Bourbon monarchy, in the person of King Alfonso XII, facilitated the approval of the 1876 Constitution, a document that remained essentially unchanged until 1923, when Primo de Rivera staged a successful military coup and installed himself as the uncontested ruler of Spain. The son of Alfonso XII had reached the age of majority in 1902, and during the ensuing twenty years, Alfonso XIII attempted (and failed) to meld an inflexible dynastic political structure with an increasingly industrialized and popularized state. In other words, and as will be evident throughout my rehearsal of Spain's recent history, hegemony proved intractable, exclusive, and polarizing.

Among Spain's difficult legacies in the twentieth century, historians cite the following: "The insufficient nationalisation of the state, the limits of political representation, the weight of institutions such as the army or the [Catholic] Church, and the lack of legal channels to incorporate the demands of the populace."[3] The first and second characteristics of Spain's system of governance were, at the outset of the twentieth century, inextricably linked to the prevalence of *caciquismo*, or "local favoritism," a complex practice of parochial interference, nepotism, and bribery that emerged with the liberal state in Spain during the 1830s.[4] In addition, the concluding years of the nineteenth century saw the politicization and expansion of the nationalist movements in Cataluña and the País Vasco, which resulted in part from escalating industrialization and some measure of economic growth in both of these regions.[5] And, to further complicate the country's ungainly process of modernization, both the Catholic Church and the national army—long accustomed to wielding considerable influence, power, and financial resources—systematically opposed any curtailment of their own social and economic privileges, associating the potential reduction of their authority with the encroachment of modernity and a democratic political system. Difference thus manifested on myriad fronts as an intensifying threat.

The historically resonant cultural and linguistic heterogeneity in Spain, the slow progress (relative to other European countries) of economic and social development, and the political disenfranchisement of most of Spain's population of 18.5 million laid the groundwork in 1900 for the striking political changes that would careen through the first four decades of the twentieth century. The life expectancy of the average Spaniard in 1900 was less than 35 years of age; the mortality rate (29 people per 1,000) figured among the highest in Europe, as did the infant mortality rate (186 babies out of 1,000 births died before the age of 1); 56 out of every 100 Spanish adults were illiterate; 80 percent of the population lived in locations with fewer than 10,000 inhabitants; and agriculture employed 68 percent of the population to produce 40 percent of the country's wealth.[6]

Taken together, these factors illustrate only some of the challenges facing Alfonso XIII, who, upon ascending to the Spanish throne in 1902, augured a "reform from above" by means of a parliamentary monarchy. Unfortunately, he proved obstinate when it came to dismantling the conditions of, and concessions to, the monarchy.[7] Furthermore, the dominant political parties, which had traditionally alternated power via the artificial mechanism of the *turno pacífico*, or "peaceful turn," were incapable of promoting a unified direction or organizational coherence. Moreover, the Spanish government had to contend, in the first decades of the twentieth century, with a war in Morocco, the ever more contentious nationalist movements in the País Vasco and Cataluña, radical republicanism, and the growth of workers' movements inside and outside of Spain. All these foregrounded the multipronged drive, on the part of Spain's citizenry, toward heterogeneity in the social fabric of the country.

The notable rise, at the beginning of the century, in anticlericalism, antimilitarism, the politicization of workers, and labor conflicts, together with the violence that transpired during the Semana Trágica [Tragic Week] (July 23–30, 1909)[8] and during the army operations outside of Melilla, contributed to the repeated resignations of Antonio Maura, the first prime minister of Spain in the twentieth century, in favor of a slew of ambitious but ultimately ineffective replacements.[9] Thereafter, and until Primo de Rivera's military coup in 1923, all changes in parliamentary leadership were disputed among the political parties and protested by divergent segments of the Spanish populace, the Cortes were regularly suspended, and Spain's neutrality during World War I led to high inflation and contributed to escalating riots, strikes, and demonstrations among the populace. The forced imposition of compliance and uniformity provoked continual civil resistance and overt violence in virtually all social arenas during this period.

By 1917, the legitimacy of the Restoration monarchy and the political organism that it had created were in crisis and under siege from multiple internal and external sources. Any real attempts at reform had been abandoned in favor of tepid responses to whatever threat seemed to qualify as the most immediate. Casanova and Gil Andrés rightfully conclude that the government consistently failed to realize any of the reformist projects because of "the economic and social impact of the Great War . . . the corporativism of the army, the authoritarianism of the Crown, escalation of the Moroccan conflict, the intensity of trade union mobilisation and public protests . . . nationalist demands and the defection of conservative sectors, Catholic associations and employers' groups."[10] The aforementioned catalog of antagonists is indeed impressive in its multiplicity, its long- and short-range impacts, and its shared commitment to enforced homogeneity.

In light of this fatal political cocktail, then, Primo de Rivera encountered scant opposition from any source to his military takeover. He appropriated the familiar nineteenth-century Spanish tradition of nonviolent public intervention when he declared a state of emergency in Spain on September 13, 1923, but he deviated from the previous practice in order to establish a military directorate under his command. The sweeping change in government was supported by the king, the army, and the organizations associated with most employers and the Catholic Church; meanwhile, the vast majority of the general population viewed the military rebellion with indifference. Exceptional measures, such as abolishing the constitution, were rapidly and seamlessly institutionalized. It required a mere five years, however, before the rush of national sentiment turned away from Primo de Rivera, who began losing support and gaining formidable enemies in equal measure.

Seven years after assuming power, Spain's first military dictator was forced to resign amid disharmony within the armed forces, mounting student protests, diminishing support from Alfonso XIII, the rising tide of republicanism, and his own illness.[11] Primo de Rivera's dictatorship nonetheless effected a number of profound transformations that would resonate for decades to come. Among them, María Teresa González Calbet identifies three as noteworthy: the crisis and definitive destruction of the dynastic political parties, the absorption of large swaths of the human and financial resources associated with the internal reform of the monarchy, and the creation of a political vacuum regarding an alternative other than the monarchy and republicanism.[12] As political experiments went, Primo de Rivera's regime was successful in the short term, and it also facilitated both the ensuing national enthusiasm for democracy and the redefinition of an authoritarian alternative. This paradox deeply resonates with Levinas's critique of the totalizing impulses of human subjectivity and his defense of ethical intersubjectivity.

At the same time, modernization and economic growth, linked in part to European trends, prompted acute demographic and structural transformations within the country.[13] Spain's population increased from 18.5 million in 1900 to 23.5 million by 1930. Life expectancy surged, from thirty-five years to fifty years, as did the literacy rate (from 40 percent in 1900 to 65 percent in 1930). Most of the major cities in Spain doubled in size, and some 10 million Spaniards immigrated from smaller towns into cities of at least 10,000 inhabitants. The agricultural sector increased productivity, and the industrial sector added a million workers to its ranks. And finally, national income doubled, such that Spain narrowed the income gap relative to its peers in Europe.[14]

The political and economic pendulums swung spectacularly toward the left with the formation of the Second Republic, legitimized in the 1931 elections, which coincided with an international economic recession. The forward-thinking Republicans dominated the municipal elections of April 12, 1931, and during the five heady years of the Second Republic, the left-leaning, coalition-based government promoted a series of comprehensive reforms that encompassed virtually every institution and all social sectors. In the process, the government also laid bare, and often intensified, the deep-seated antagonism between church and state, employers and workers, and the military and the civilian government—in sum, between those who sought to protect traditional values and those who sought to uphold and promote the republic's modernizing agenda. And the cultural and social schisms between conformity and change only intensified as the century advanced.

Assaults against public order—in the form of demonstrations, revolts, strikes, anarchist insurrections, assassination attempts, and failed military coups—commenced almost immediately after the 1931 elections, as did the formation of a representative government, a lawful electoral system, and the first Republican constitution in Spain's history. The landmark constitution of December 9, 1931, included provisions for a separation between church and state, civil marriage and divorce, suffrage for women, and compatibility between the republic and the autonomy of its municipalities and regions. Certain manifestations of social difference were thus celebrated and legitimized. Whereas the initial Republican government, over which Prime Minister Manuel Azaña presided, thrived for a remarkable two years, the next three years saw twelve revolving governments, with five different prime ministers and fifty-eight ministers.

Between 1933 and early 1936, roiling hostilities emerged among and within the various political parties and alliances that contributed to the ever-changing Republican government and between the church and the Republican government. Moreover, the rise of extreme right and fascist organizations within Spain, the sometimes violent mobilizations by leftist groups and workers, harsh government reprisals, and the gradual defection and alienation of select military officers all contributed to the second successful military coup of the century in Spain, one that would launch the Spanish Civil War (1936–1939). Seventy-two percent of the female and male adults voted during February 1936 in favor of the Frente Popular [Popular Front], a moderate party whose stated agenda included political amnesty and social reforms. Amid popular protests and bellicose aggression, including the incarcerations and assassinations of high-profile leaders at both ends of the political spectrum, the president of the republic, Niceto Alcalá Zamora, was dismissed by the Spanish parliament, and Manuel Azaña was elected in his place.

Meanwhile, the ultraconservative Catholic press was actively agitating against the legally chosen government, and when the Republican Civil Guard murdered José Calvo Sotelo, a prominent conservative leader, on July 12, 1936, Franco and his military allies declared a state of war. Although the Republican government managed to initially thwart the victory of the military rebellion, the fragmentation and polarization of Spanish society—in conjunction with the long-simmering antagonism of the Catholic Church, landowners, and influential sectors of the military toward the Second Republic—unleashed a catastrophic three-year armed confrontation. Paul Preston has referred to this period, together with the "ideological cleansing" that characterized its aftermath, as the Spanish Holocaust.[15] The Spanish Civil War concluded with the installation of a repressive military dictatorship, headed by Franco, who then enacted several decades of harsh retaliation against those who had fought in defense of, or were in any way associated with, the Second Republic. Philosophical, political, and cultural differences were not tolerated, and any overt sign of alterity was viciously suppressed through torture, incarceration, and death.

In addition to harnessing the ideological conflict between political solutions and military solutions, the Spanish Civil War accentuated the entrenched divisions between social classes and between Catholicism and anticlericalism. Casanova and Gil Andrés also signal the fundamental role in Spain's domestic struggles of "an international context that had been thrown out of balance by crises of democracies and the onslaught of communism and fascism."[16] On the one hand, the Republican government saw the dizzying succession of three prime ministers between 1936 and 1939, whereas the Nationalist rebels were quickly and efficiently organized under a sole military and political leader throughout the conflict; military unity thus quickly trumped political diversity. On the other hand, the Catholic Church, from pulpits throughout the country, sought to consolidate its own authority and influence by fomenting the Nationalist rebellion and openly opposing the elected government, which it considered both immoral and heretical.[17]

Outside of Spain, tacit and formal support from countries was unevenly divided between the two warring factions. Hitler, Mussolini, and Portugal's António de Oliveira Salazar supplied Franco's Nationalist forces with arms and some 100,000 soldiers, most of whom were paid and/or had enlisted in the militaries of their home countries. The Nationalists also drew from the military forces of the Moroccan protectorate and the Carlist militia (known as the Requetés, or "Red Berets"). On the Republican side, France, England, and the United States proclaimed a policy of nonintervention as early as the summer of 1936. The Republicans eventually succeeded in buying munitions from the Soviet Union and incorporating some 37,000 volunteer fighters from the International Brigades into their army, but the economic cost of these black-market arms was enormous, the number of fighters was far fewer, and the so-called neutrality was a death blow to the Republicans in the face of continuously robust financial support for the Nationalists.

Casanova and Gil Andrés, among others, categorize the Spanish Civil War and the sustained retaliation, systematic subjugation, and decidedly "uncivil peace" that followed as "the beginning of a period of violence without precedent in the history of Spain."[18] As one major consequence of the three-year siege, the Spanish populace of approximately 24 million was decimated. According to numerous sources, some 160,000 combatants died during the war (100,000 in the Nationalist zone and 60,000 in the Republican zone), and another 200,000 men and women were executed during the conflict.[19] Upon the conclusion of the war, Franco and his government energetically pursued the domination and extermination of the vanquished through imprisonment, torture, legalized persecution, government-sanctioned censorship, surveillance, and forced "reeducation." More than 270,000 Republican sympathizers were jailed as of 1940, and at least 50,000 people were executed during the ensuing decade.[20] Some historians estimate that another 150,000 civilians died in Spain from hunger and disease between 1940 and 1942. In addition, according to the regime's own statistics, approximately 500,000 Spaniards fled into exile as a result of the Spanish Civil War, many of them never to return.

The first decade of Franco's dictatorship was not without severe domestic challenges, however. Both Spain's economy and its military had been ravaged during the course of the civil war. Shortages in food, raw materials, and human labor defined the early postwar years, known colloquially as *los años de hambre* [the hunger years], and the Spanish army, in practical and conceptual terms, was incapable of participating in World War II.[21] As a result, Hitler and Mussolini retracted their support from Spain in 1941, and Franco was thereby obliged to formally withdraw from the international economy and from global politics, opting instead for the illusion of financial self-sufficiency through state-enacted autarchy. During this interval of enforced economic nationalism, the country was denied entry into the United Nations, the vast majority of countries withdrew their ambassadors from Spain, and France closed its borders with its southern neighbor.

For the duration of the 1940s, salaries in Spain hovered below the prewar mark; periodic inflation drove prices up a yearly average of 13 percent until 1945 and toward the 23 percent that marked 1950–1951. Poverty, rampant hunger, rationing, a high mortality rate, and a thriving black market constituted the norm during this decade. Overt protest was punishable by death, and religious education and attendance were compulsory, as the Catholic Church strove for the re-Catholization of Spain. Fascist ideology, which had served as a bulwark for the Nationalists during the war, expanded into the social and political sectors after 1939; membership in the single political party, the Falange Española Tradicionalista y de las

JONS, as well as in its corollary organizations for youth (Frente de Juventudes [Youth Front]) and women (Sección Femenina [Feminine Section]), boomed and thrived throughout the 1940s.

When the international political climate swerved in the 1950s as a result of both the defeat of Germany and Italy in World War II and the emergence of the Soviet Union as the antagonist of the day, Spain's fortunes, and its usefulness to the allied governments of Europe and the United States, dramatically improved. Franco exploited the burgeoning animosity between the United States and the USSR in order to reap desperately needed monetary and military aid in exchange for the installation of four American military bases in Spain at Torrejón de Ardoz (Madrid), Morón (Seville), Rota (Cádiz), and Zaragoza. Between 1953 and 1963, Spain received some $1,688 million in economic aid and more than $500 million in military aid. Predictably, on November 4, 1950, the United Nations reversed its earlier resolution excluding Spain, and the country officially joined the U.N. in 1955.

In additional signs of liberalization, after 1950, Spaniards once again migrated from the countryside to the cities in ever-increasing numbers, and urban industrialization encouraged the resurgence of the newly empowered working classes—with the consequent labor unions and strike activity, particularly during the 1960s. Additional sectors of the Spanish population, foremost among them university students, began to openly dissent at approximately the same time as Luis Carrero Blanco, longtime advisor to Franco and new minister of the undersecretariat of presidential affairs as of 1951, sought to divest the Falange, Spain's fascist political party, of its authority and encourage new legislation that would guarantee the tenets of Francoism after Franco's death. The early 1960s also saw the opening of Spain's economy to foreign investment and tourism, both of which contributed to the notable influx of capital, the brisk expansion of industrialization, the decline of agriculture, and the continued depopulation of rural areas as workers moved within Spain from rural areas to the cities, and from Spain to other countries, in search of better living conditions and higher-paying jobs.

Economic development in Spain, as in other developed and developing countries, manifested contrapuntally during the 1960s in heightened consumerism and cultural apathy; more Spaniards bought more goods, traveled farther and more often, and generally experienced a heretofore unmatched level of economic well-being. The government-controlled media consistently attributed national prosperity to Francoist ideology, setting up a polemical contrast between the current situation and the purported financial, political, and social anarchy that had preceded the Spanish Civil War. The entry of foreign capital, people, and influence, together with the upsurge in mobility of a large sector of the Spanish population, occasioned the propagandistic slogan, employed with remarkable success by the country's tourism industry during the 1960s, that Spain was indeed different. These claims of difference were, however, rarely viewed at the time in positive terms when it came to the country's political structure or the civil rights of its citizens. And into this intensifying cultural maelstrom were born the writers who would later be associated with the Gen X.

During the same decade, Franco and his supporters continued to foster cosmetic liberalization while ever larger swaths of the populace continued to demand structural changes. In 1966, Manuel Fraga Iribarne, the minister of information, spearheaded the Press Act, which officially deregulated the regime's control of the media. In practice, however, the new law replaced official censorship with self-imposed and self-administered censorship, but it also allowed for the creation of several mildly critical journals and the possibility of public debate. The following year, the parliament passed La Ley Orgánica del Estado [The Organic Law of the State], which permitted a degree of religious freedom and parliamentary elections, both of which allowed the authoritarian government to claim that it had liberalized Spanish culture—when in reality, Catholicism continued to be deeply entrenched, and only approved candidates were elected to the parliament. In addition, the government made explicit provisions for the return of the Spanish monarchy in the person of the grandson of Alfonso XIII,

Juan Carlos de Borbón, who was to function as the head of state but not the head of government. On July 22, 1969, the Spanish parliament, with Franco's blessing, voted resoundingly in favor of Juan Carlos to lead a "Monarchy of the Movimiento Nacional [National Movement] which would permanently maintain its principles and institutions."[22]

By 1970, the seventy-eight-year-old Franco and his followers were engaged in a concerted effort to assure his political legacy, whereas his opponents were agitating to steer the country toward sweeping social changes and a full-fledged democracy. Throughout the 1960s and early 1970s, the dictator's plans encountered serious obstacles. The mounting regional strife in the País Vasco during the early 1970s spawned increasingly hostile demonstrations among workers and separatists; after a brief recovery in 1971–1972, the Spanish economy again failed; Catholic clergy in Spain gradually distanced themselves from the dictatorship and overtly pursued social justice and human rights; and in December 1973, Basque terrorists—members of the Euskadi Ta Askatasuna (ETA)—assassinated Carrero Blanco, Franco's political heir apparent, some six months after Blanco's appointment as prime minister. In the face of blatant public disorder, industrial unrest, persistent economic instability, and the decline of the aging dictator's health, the most reactionary elements of Franco's government summarily grabbed the political reins in order to minimize any infiltration of liberalizing influences during the ensuing transition. Franco immediately named Carlos Arias Navarro as Carrero Blanco's replacement. The new prime minister staffed his government with old-school Falangists, resolutely excluded all politicians with any potential ties to the king, and sponsored new antiterrorist legislation in August 1975, which was then enforced retroactively. It would seem that the pendulum had again swung definitively toward enforced homogeneity.

When Franco died on November 20, 1975, a return to predevelopment politics loomed large even in the face of widespread social agitation, regional factionalism, opposition from the Catholic Church, and yet another economic recession. The entrenched right-wing faction, with overt support from Spain's considerable army, initially assumed control of the government, as Franco himself had planned. Simultaneously, Juan Carlos was crowned king in accordance with the Act of Succession of the Head of State, and he swiftly articulated a desire for democratization, which would bring Spain in line with other European countries, foster its attractiveness to the emerging European Union, and include all Spaniards regardless of their gender, regional affiliation, and religion. Although the king incorporated into his cabinet outspoken liberalizers, archconservative politicians continued to control key institutions in Spain, which included the parliament, central and local administration, the judiciary branch, and the armed forces. Confronted with escalating prices, high unemployment, the return of Spanish workers from foreign job markets, the effects of the first oil shock of 1973, and an uneasy domestic business community, Arias Navarro tried to squelch some of the opposition's demands by announcing the removal of restrictions on the press and unofficially allowing most political parties to participate in the national electoral process.

These measures were nonetheless insufficient to secure Arias Navarro's political future. When he resigned from the post of prime minister in July 1976, after the Spanish parliament rejected his proposals to legalize political parties under strict conditions, the king immediately appointed senior Francoist bureaucrat Adolfo Suárez.[23] Historians often identify Suárez as one of the true bellwethers in Spain's rapid transition to a functional and internationally recognized democracy. Suárez proved an ingenious choice; because of his sterling track record with the country's conservative politicians, he was allowed substantial freedom to reform the government from within. Moreover, because he had managed the state-run television service, Suárez was intimately acquainted with the power of the media and knew how to manipulate his image as a young and nonthreatening alternative to those government officials whose age and political affiliation reminded the Spanish citizenry of the civil war and its aftermath. It could even be argued that his brisk rise to political prominence anticipated the country's collective fascination with, and investment in, youth as a condition of contemporary national identity.

After positioning allies in some strategic cabinet posts and filling other ministry positions with a mix of liberals and conservatives, Suárez realized a set of broad reforms within a month of taking office: he and his government extended the basic personal liberties of freedom of association and assembly, granted amnesty for political prisoners, and announced plans for political liberalization.[24] In September 1976, he unveiled his strategy to legalize political reform, which included the election of a two-chamber parliament and the legalization of all political parties, save for the Spanish Communist Party (which would be legalized some seven months later on April 9, 1977). Two months later, and after protracted political maneuvering, Suárez's proposal gained official support, by means of a majority vote, in the Spanish parliament. He then scheduled a national referendum for December 1976, in which 75 percent of the electorate voted, and 94 percent of those voters were in favor of the proposed referendum.

The first unequivocally democratic general election in nearly four decades was then programmed for June 1977, an election in which more than 18 million Spaniards, or 78.7 percent of the population, voted. In a stunning reversal of Franco's declared intention, and within a single year, Suárez had succeeded in drastically revising the political landscape of Spain and in laying the groundwork for the country's ensuing entry, both literally and metaphorically, into the European Community and the global political arena. As a crucial component of these profound changes, Spain required a new constitution, one that would reflect a legal and structural commitment to pluralism and facilitate future development. In 1978, Suárez and leftist political leaders—including Felipe González, head of the Partido Socialista Obrero Español [Spanish Socialist Workers' Party] (PSOE)—drafted a viable constitution that settled, among other long-standing points of national tension, the roles of the monarchy, the church, and the regional autonomies. This constitution was approved by referendum at the conclusion of that same year.

In the first election held under the new constitution in March 1979, Suárez's party, the Unión de Centro Democrático [Union of the Democratic Center] (UCD), again prevailed, but this time it fell significantly short of an overall majority. Although ideological compromise had imbued Suárez's political tenure, with the implementation of a liberal constitution, national attention turned to the faltering economy, worsened by the second oil shock of 1979, and the possibility of legalizing divorce—one among many symptoms of the profound social changes occurring in Spain. The moderately conservative UCD proved unable to achieve consensus concerning the scope of these changes, and Suárez unexpectedly resigned in early 1981.

During the temporary vacuum in national leadership, military reactionaries, many of whom had harbored resentments over the direction of the government since Franco's death, finally attempted to assume leadership of the government by force on February 23, 1981. Their failure only confirmed that the political pendulum had swung solidly toward democracy and modernization. Juan Carlos played a crucial role in tempering the actions and responses of the military, and the newly installed prime minister Leopoldo Calvo Sotelo, backed by the UCD, renewed a public commitment to the spirit of compromise.[25] Because he subsequently achieved membership in the North Atlantic Treaty Organization (NATO) against strong opposition from the socialists, however, Calvo Sotelo unwittingly paved the way for the consolidation of the leftist elements of parliament, and particularly the PSOE among them, to acquire power in order to avoid another coup attempt.

Campaigning on an anti-NATO platform and a moderated ideological stance, Felipe González and the PSOE swept the October 1982 election, winning the overall majority that the UCD had previously lacked and uncovering perhaps the most glaring limitation of the 1978 constitution—namely, that a single political party could win an overall majority, install its head as prime minister, and dominate parliament. It would appear that hegemony could take many forms, even in a country as resolutely committed to democratic ideals at that historical moment as Spain. In the minds of the Spanish electorate, nevertheless, with the victory of the socialists, the formal transition from an authoritarian dictatorship to a modern functional democracy was now complete.

Like Adolfo Suárez, Felipe González understood the importance of manipulating his public image in order to maximize his charisma and political authority. As a result, he and the PSOE held the reins of national power for an astounding period of fourteen years (1982–1996) until internal scandals involving allegations of influence peddling, money laundering, bribery, financial improprieties, covert "terror" squads, and general corruption swung the political pendulum back toward the right in the shape of the newly constituted Partido Popular [Popular Party] (PP) and its equally young and charismatic leader, José María Aznar. During his tenure, González's government shouldered a slate of daunting tasks: stabilizing the economy, deterring domestic terrorism, ushering Spain into the European Economic Community (EEC), achieving the integration of the autonomous communities into national politics and the national market, and clarifying and diminishing the scope and role of the military. The PSOE-led government made notable strides toward all these goals, with ongoing economic recovery and Spain's entry into the EEC on January 1, 1986, supplying the most visible and enduring signs of González's success.

Much like 1975, 1992 denotes a benchmark year in the domestic and global public imaginations because of the visibility associated with several international events held in Spain: the Olympic Games in Barcelona, the World's Fair in Seville, the designation of Madrid as the European Capital of Culture, and the intensely fraught "celebration" of the quincentenary anniversary of Cristobal Colón's transatlantic voyages. On the one hand, the country indisputably emerged on the world radar in 1992 thanks to the confluence and success of these spectacles. On the other hand, the bill for lavish national spending quickly came due, and in 1993, the country recorded its worst economic figures since 1942. Inflation spiraled, the foreign deficit skyrocketed, and unemployment rose to 24 percent, disproportionately affecting Spain's young workers.[26] As one among scores of consequences, on May 13, 1993, the

Spanish government was forced to devalue the peseta more than the European Monetary System rules allowed.

Spain had fully transitioned to a successful democracy by 1996, as evinced by its membership in the European Community; the creation of a stable welfare state; the relegation of the monarchy, the military, and the Catholic Church to subordinate social roles; the emergence of the autonomous communities; and the reduction of terrorism. The country achieved another milestone in consigning Francoism to the past when conservatives managed to assign the new face of Aznar and the new name of Partido Popular to the old conservative political party of Alianza Popular [People's Alliance]. Aznar's party rode the wave of the disintegration of the PSOE to political prominence and an electoral victory in 1996. Thanks to an international economic boom and the resultant growth of the domestic economy, by 2000, Spain could boast of the highest per-capita income its citizens had ever seen (83 percent of the EU average) and the reduction of the national unemployment rate to 11 percent.[27] These measures, together with the cultivated image of moderated spending, social dialogue, and successful anti-terrorism actions on the part of the legal institutions of the state, all but guaranteed the victory, and subsequent absolute majority, of the PP in the 2000 elections.[28]

Throughout my book, I contend that one acutely profound way of understanding Spain's political and social turn from authoritarianism to democracy, from overt political and social control to increased personal liberties, and from mandated obedience to accountability consists of connecting these turns to the broader cultural move from an enforced emphasis on static sameness to the nuanced valuation of temporalized difference. In complementary fashion, most scholars attribute the singularity of Spain's Gen X, in part or in the main, to political, economic, and technological factors that informed Spain after 1975. As Carmen de Urioste has observed, these writers "han crecido con la democracia y . . . no han conocido ni la guerra, ni la posguerra, ni la dictadura" [have grown up with democracy and . . . have known neither the war, nor the postwar, nor the dictatorship].[29] As a group, Gen X authors have unequivocally enjoyed more individual and collective freedoms than their predecessors; more possibilities existed in the Spain of the 1990s than at any prior moment for writers to publish their work in constantly proliferating venues. Due in part to intense competition within the expanding publishing industry and to an equally intense focus on marketing as the key to claiming a larger share of consumer spending, the concept of and practices associated with "youth" constituted notable components in "branding" the Gen X phenomenon.[30] As Tara Brabazon maintains in her study of popular memory and the transnational phenomenon of the Generation X, "Youth is far more than a description of an age group, or a stage in a rite of passage. . . . The making of youth culture was not an amorphous result of ill-defined social changes, but determined by an economic system that required niche markets to continue and increase the rate and role of consumption."[31] And upon fully embracing both democracy and capitalism during the transition, Spaniards were more than ready to engage in consumerism and eagerly respond to marketing campaigns of all stripes.

Although a consideration of historical chronology is insufficient, in and of itself, to define Spain's Gen X, only the truly naive would argue that literature, as with any cultural product or event, arises in a historical void. To this end, and throughout the twentieth century, literary critics and historians have persistently arranged Peninsular literature chronologically and according to generational criteria. In his 2001 discussion of Gen X writers, whom he describes as the "narradores españoles novísimos de los años noventa" [the brand-new Spanish narrators of the 1990s], José María Izquierdo cleaves to Pedro Salinas's six requirements for a generation of writers, crafted in 1935 in relation to Spain's Generation of 1898: "a) coincidencia en nacimiento en años poco distantes; b) homogeneidad de educación recibida; c) relaciones personales entre los miembros del grupo; d) experiencia generacional; e) lenguaje generacional; y f) actitud crítica pasiva o activa hacia los grupos literarios y artísticos anteriores" [(a) the coincidence of birthdates within a few years; (b) homogeneity in education; (c) personal relationships among the members of the group;

(d) generational experience; (e) generational language; and (f) passively or actively critical attitude toward the previous literary and artistic groups].[32] Toni Dorca and Urioste, in early assessments of the Gen X, identify two and three additional literary generations coexisting with the Gen X, respectively.[33] They align the first generation with consecrated authors active from the 1940s onward, who include Camilo José Cela, Miguel Delibes, and Gonzalo Torrente Ballester, among others. For his part, Dorca recognizes one posttransition generation that encompasses Marina Mayoral, Juan José Millás, Javier Marías, and Antonio Muñoz Molina (among others), whereas Urioste distinguishes between the "midcentury generation" (Juan Marsé, José María Caballero Bonald) and the "new narrators from the transition" (Marías, Lourdes Ortiz, José María Guelbenzu, and others). By contrast, Izquierdo finds five coexisting generations of writers in Spain as of 2000: the generation of 1936 (Cela, Delibes, Torrente Ballester), the midcentury generation (Carmen Martín Gaite, Ana María Matute, Marsé, Juan Goytisolo, etc.), the generation of '68 (Esther Tusquets, Manuel Vázquez Montalbán, Eduardo Mendoza, and their contemporaries), the "writers of the years" (Marías, Rosa Montero, Muñoz Molina, and others), and finally, the Gen X.[34]

Alternatively, in 2003, Santos Alonso identified seven distinct generations of writers working simultaneously in Spain: the postwar generation, who began writing in the 1940s; the generation of writers exiled from Spain during, and as a result of, the Spanish Civil War; the midcentury generation previously noted; the generation of "innovators" from the 1960s; the generation of 1975; the generation of the 1980s; and most germane to my study, "los novelistas que empiezan a publicar en la década de 1990 [y] pertenecen por edad a la generación de españoles nacidos a partir de 1960" [the novelists who begin to publish in the decade of the 1990s (and) belong by virtue of their age to the generation of Spaniards born after 1960].[35] The extent to which the predominant strategy of chronology via generation limits or clarifies, or limits *and* clarifies, literary texts and their historical, sociocultural, and ideological webs of significance continues to spark lively debate,[36] but it remains a fact that many, if not most, critics, educators, reporters, reviewers, and publishers continue to describe the genres related to twentieth-century Peninsular literature in light of biographically distinct human groups, usually in combination with additional rubrics.

In consonance with this practice, then, in the 1990s, editors, journalists, and academicians in Spain and in the United States fastened on an emerging cluster of Peninsular authors who, they argued, pertained to a "new" (and thus alternative) literary generation. At the risk of exclusivity, I provisionally include within Spain's Gen X some seventy-nine authors, all of whom published novels in Spain during the 1990s.[37] Because of the heterogeneity of the authors in question, not to mention their disparate literary production and evolution since the 1990s, critics did not (and do not) easily concur on the broad significance, the shared characteristics, the relevance, or even the specific members of this particular group of writers, but they did seem to initially agree that Gen X authors were distinct from their antecedents in Spain and from their contemporaries in other national literary traditions. Their early novels reflected a set of common, albeit fluctuating, elements, and they and the literary texts that they authored were closely related to the discrete historical circumstances of contemporary Spain. In dialogue with previous and current commentators on Spain's Gen X writers, then, I maintain that these writers also evinced an abiding commitment, in their early novels, to narrative explorations of alterity and time and that this commitment is, in fact, the fundamental convergence among all these novelists.

Born in Spain between 1960 and 1974,[38] Gen X writers personally and professionally came of age in a country radically dissimilar from but nonetheless related to the Spain of their parents and grandparents. They have contributed to a markedly globalized and globalizing culture; they have benefitted from the social, political, and economic advantages of a stable democracy; and they have created fictional narratives during an epoch characterized by widespread—and always expanding—technological literacy. They also matured as artists during a series of historical moments characterized in Spain and elsewhere by the omnipresence of a commodity culture, which underscored the power of marketing factors and charged terms like *youth* and *newness* with extreme value.[39] And, like writers of narrative fiction past, present, and future, these writers chronicled sociality, or the ways in which people interact with one another within a plethora of communities.

In sum, this constellation of writers coincided with a crucial shift in contemporary Peninsular society and narrative. They also endeavored to address familiar questions about an unfamiliar decade: What did it mean to have been born and experienced childhood in the closing decades of Francoism, to have crossed the threshold into adulthood during the initial decades after Franco's death, and to imagine and write novels during the 1990s? The year 1996 marks the official recognition in Spain of the emerging Gen X, with special issues of *Ínsula*, *Leer*, *Quimera*, and *El Urogallo* devoted to mapping some of the parameters and characteristics of the newest literary generation, together with the critical responses that their novels had provoked thus far.[40] It bears noting, especially given the sustained cultural emphasis on the uniform "youth" of the authors and their public, that the authors themselves stridently proclaimed their uniqueness and independence. As Ramón Acín trumpeted from the pages of *Ínsula* in 1996, "Frente a la uniformidad de antaño hoy triunfa la pluralidad" [In the face of yesterday's uniformity, today plurality triumphs].[41] More than two decades later, such claims for plurality have been complemented by a stress—among commentators, at least—on the bonds of cohesion. I will suggest that a commitment to alterity in fact lies at the core of the Gen X narrative, that this commitment manifests in several ways, and that it is primarily attributable not to any one sociocultural event or feature of Spanish society but to the temporality of ethical intersubjectivity as articulated by Levinas.

By the turn of the new millennium, two anthologies of short fiction, *Páginas amarillas*, edited by Sabas Martín (1997), and *After Hours: Una muestra de cult fiction*, edited by Javier Calvo (1999), together with a volume of interviews conducted by Noemí Montetes Mairal and published in 1999, had further disseminated the notion of a Gen X unique to Spain, and the three texts had also initiated the process of determining the relevant participants.[42] On the other side of the Atlantic, the Modern Language Association hosted a double session during December 1996 on Spain's Gen X, from which articles by Dorca and José María Naharro-Calderón emerged in 1997 and 1999, respectively, with Urioste's seminal "La narrativa española de los noventa: ¿Existe una 'Generación X'?" also appearing in 1997. In the opening decade of the twenty-first century, a plethora of scholarly articles refined and expanded the characteristics and the members of the Gen X, and by 2010, several compelling book-length monographs and edited volumes had emerged.[43]

The early disagreement about many of the issues related to the new group of novelists began with what to call them. Germán Gullón, one of the generation's most ardent initial defenders, provisionally distinguished the texts by these writers as "la narrativa del Grupo X de la última generación de narradores" [the narrative of the X Group from the most recent generation of narrators] in the 1996 issue of *Ínsula*, devoted auspiciously to "Spanish Narrative on the Edge of the Millennium," but he hastened to specify that his denomination referred more specifically to the subgroup of hard realists.[44] In that same forum, Santos Sanz Villanueva alluded to "estos novísimos narradores" [these brand-new narrators].[45] Echoing Gullón, Urioste and Dorca in 1997 combined a generational marker with a diachronic referent in referring in the titles of their essays to the same group of writers as "la generación X" and "la narrativa española de los noventa" [generation X, Spanish narrative of the nineties] (Urioste) and "joven narrativa en la España de los noventa" [young narrative in Spain from the nineties] (Dorca).[46] Elsewhere in her 1997 essay, Urioste added to the list of possibilities "[la] primera generación de escritores de la democracia española" [the first generation of writers from the Spanish democracy] and the "generación de los veintitantos" [generation of the twentysomethings].[47] On another front, Andrés Carabantes, paying tribute to José Ángel Mañas's landmark first novel, titled *Historias del Kronen* (1996), coined the term "la tribu de Kronen" [the Kronen tribe] to describe the writers in question.[48]

In a related fashion, Izquierdo, writing in 2001, assigned to the group the term "narradores españoles novísimos de los años noventa" [brand-new Spanish narrators from the nineties] while also referencing the labels of "Generación JASP," "Cofradía del cuero," and "Jóvenes caníbales."[49] Christine Henseler helpfully includes the phrases "Generation Blank," "Generation Biberón," and "Generation Sesame Street" in her seminal 2004 essay on Mañas, Loriga, and Etxebarria.[50] Recent monographs that focus on this set of writers have tended to favor the *Gen X* descriptor,[51] although Luis Mancha San Esteban continues to echo Mañas's novel (and Carabantes's designation) in his 2006 monograph, aptly titled *Generación Kronen.* I have opted for the term *Gen X* throughout my discussion because it has predominated among critics and because it bears witness to the global dimension of both the production and the reception of these writers.

As for the characteristics that define Gen X writers in Spain, most critics converge on multiple issues. First, they highlight the mass marketing of "youth" as key to the advent and the success of the new narrative generation.[52] As an extreme example, one might point to the initial success of Violeta Hernando's novel *Muertos o algo mejor*, published in 1996, when the author was a mere fourteen years old. Critics have responded in diverse ways to the "youth" factor associated with Gen X writers. At one end of the spectrum, they describe the social and/or marketing phenomenon while noting that the writers themselves exploit this characteristic in order to interrogate the perils of consumerism: "Existe, por consiguiente, un recelo hacia los jóvenes creadores que pretenden explotar bajo un disfraz de rebeldía las ansias de consumo de la sociedad. Paradójicamente, los propios escritores tienen conciencia de esta problemática y la trasladan a las páginas de su ficción" [There exists, as a result, mistrust toward the young creators who try to exploit, under the disguise of rebelliousness, the society's anxieties regarding consumerism].[53] At the other end of the spectrum, they have assigned a series of derogatory terms to the marketing of youth, which, they argue, facilitates the publication of inferior literature. Some of these include the "Lolita effect" (Guelbenzu), "juvenialization" (Ignacio Echevarría), and "cultural peterpanism" and "trendiness" (Vázquez Montalbán).[54]

Second, the confluence between Spain's consumerist tendencies, the editorial opportunism of Spain's editorial industry and the media, and the spotlight on novelty and youth as intertwined marketing ploys resulted in a kind of explosion in the publication of narrative texts by young writers. Dorothy Odartey-Wellington, citing Javier Memba, claims that "the 1990s saw the largest output of publications by 'young' writers than any other period in Spanish literary history."[55] During this same decade, established publishers in Spain—such as Anagrama, Planeta, and Plaza & Janés—created series that were dedicated to new writers with the goal of vigorously promoting first-time novelists from the Gen X such Belén Gopegui, Ismael Grasa, Ray Loriga, and Eloy Tizón, to name only a few. And as a secondary component in the construction of a formidable "reception complex" by Spain's publishing houses, the most lucrative literary prizes were often awarded to writers from this same demographic. As only some examples, Anagrama's Herralde Prize went to thirty-four-year-old Luisa Castro's *El somier* [*The Somier*] in 1990 and thirty-one-year-old Marcos Giralt Torrente's *París* [*Paris*] in 1999, with three other Gen X novelists recognized as finalists in 1994, 1995, and 1996; Pedro Maestre's *Matando dinosaurios con tirachinas* [*Killing Dinosaurs with Slingshots*] won Destino's Nadal Prize in 1996, when the author was twenty-nine years old, with thirty-four-year-old Juana Salabert's *Arde lo que será* as the runner-up; Lucía Etxebarria's *Beatriz y los cuerpos celestes* [*Beatriz and the Heavenly Bodies*] received the same prize two years later, when the author was thirty-two, with thirty-year-old Ignacio García-Valiño's *La caricia del escorpión* [*The Scorpion's Caress*] as the runner-up; and finally, Juan Manuel de Prada, at twenty-seven, received Planeta's Premio Planeta in 1997 for *La tempestad* [*The Tempest*], and in 1999, twenty-five-year-old Espido Freire became the youngest winner of the Planeta with her novel *Melocotones helados* [*Frozen Peaches*]. Additionally, selected new publishing houses, foremost among them Lengua de Trapo, were formed with the stated goal of publishing narrative by the new generation of writers in Spain: "Lengua de Trapo es una editorial que nace con la intención de dar cabida a las nuevas generaciones de escritores. Más que la edad o el sexo, los responsables de la editorial aseguran que buscan una nueva mirada narrativa" [Lengua de Trapo is a publishing house that is born with the intention of having space for the new generations of writers. More than age or gender, the responsible parties in the publishing company guarantee that they are searching for a new narrative perspective].[56]

Third, critics often note the transnational, postnational, and globalizing cultural dynamics that imbue both the contexts and the texts associated with Spain's Gen X. As one among many examples, Urioste discusses the generation in light of the dual axes of "la internacionalización—es decir, la globalización—de la política y de la economía española durante los años ochenta y noventa" and "la privatización o individualización—es decir, localización—experimentada por la sociedad durante ese mismo período de tiempo" [the internationalization—in other words, the globalization—of Spanish politics and economy during the eighties and nineties; the privatization or individualization—in other words, localization—experienced by the society during that same period of time].[57] She further refines her analysis of globalization, or what she calls transnationalization, in terms of the appearance of an innovative form of knowledge, or identity politics, that favors connection and connectivity among individuals beyond specific time-space coordinates—all of which configures new forms of identity.[58]

Fourth, and as the early scholarship on the Gen X amply demonstrated, the fortunes of the entire group were initially intertwined with those of a highly visible subgroup known as the "hard realists" or "dirty realists."[59] Some Peninsular Gen X writers were inclined, especially during the 1990s, to employ technical strategies that emulated those of hard realism or dirty realism in order to underscore the preoccupations, habits, and cultural references of a certain so-called youthful demographic of the Spanish population.[60] Either critics intentionally or unintentionally conflated the hard realists with the entire generation—thereby eliding the substantive differences between the subgroup, who constituted the minority within Spain's Gen X, and the entire generation—or focused exclusively on the hard realists as *the* most significant subgroup within the larger generation. It is not coincidental that the very term *Gen X* underscored the stylistic and ideological similarities between the subgroup in Spain and the United States' cultural phenomenon first identified in 1991 by Douglas Coupland in his now classic novel *Generation X: Tales for an Accelerated Culture*.[61] Juan Bonilla, Lucía Etxebarria, Ismael Grasa, Ray Loriga, Pedro Maestre, José Ángel Mañas, Daniel Múgica, and Benjamín Prado were the writers from this subgroup most often cited during the 1990s, and Gabriela Bustelo, Francisco Casavella, Félix Romeo, David Trueba, and Roger Wolfe sometimes appeared on the roster of names as well.

As a fifth characteristic, critics have unanimously recognized gender as a factor in publication and reception for the Peninsular Gen X writers and as an indication of the larger social changes that surged through the country during the 1990s.[62] While women have always, I would maintain, played some part in defining the literary imagination of Spain, they became increasingly visible in the public eye during the 1990s; more women writers published literary texts and participated in mainstream and alternative literary culture by writing columns, articles, and reviews in Spanish popular and intellectual forums. As Izquierdo has written, the prevalence of women writers in the Gen X constituted a "reflejo del cambio social en la España democrática propiciado por la integración de la mujer en la sociedad durante los años ochenta" [reflection of social change in democratic Spain fostered by the integration of women into society during the eighties].[63] In 2001, Urioste and Izquierdo both identified more than a dozen women writers from among Spain's Gen X whose novels appeared in the 1990s and who were born between 1960 and 1974.[64] The women writers from this generation are frequently minimized (or overlooked altogether) in most discussions, and this same critical elision occurs routinely to Gen X authors who write in Peninsular languages other than Castilian, such as María Jaén and Sergi Pàmies. Although I cannot help but contribute to the marginalization that stems from any attempt at categorization, I attempt to partially remedy those errors by not limiting my study to work by the hard realists, by highlighting novels by women authors in each chapter (Bustelo, Sanz, Riestra, Gopegui, Salabert, and Castro), and by including Peninsular writers who publish in Catalan (Pàmies) and Galician (Riestra and Castro). Nevertheless, much more work, especially in regards to Basque, Catalan, Galician, and Valencian members of the Gen X, remains to be done.

What sets Spain's Gen X writers apart from other writers and other literary generations within Spain and beyond? Critics have thus far generated a plethora of explanations. Dorca, among others, attributes the distinctiveness of the Gen X to a crisis in values at the end of the century.[65] Colmeiro suggests in 2001 that the first "authentically post-Franco" generation "sufre la desaparición de la memoria histórica y la ética del 'compromiso' que movía en buena parte a sus mayores" [suffers from the disappearance of historical memory and the ethic of "compromise" that largely informed their elders],[66] and Izquierdo applies the same "historical amnesia" in equal measure to the reading public.[67] For their parts, Yaw Agawu-Kakraba views the generation in light of postmodernism, whereas Urioste, Henseler, José María Naharro-Calderón, Eva Navarro Martínez, and Jorge Pérez have emphasized the deep and wide influences of mass media, popular culture, and technology. In the present chapter, I have rehearsed chronology, biography, aesthetics, and critical reception as additional factors in the singularity of the generation. As I will argue in the succeeding three chapters, however, the uniqueness of these writers, and their generation, lies in their unswerving interrogation of Levinas's philosophy of ethical alterity, particularly as it manifests in temporality.

3

Repeating the Same Violence, or The Failure of Synchrony

Veo veo, El frío, and *Mensaka*

I'll be your mirror.
Reflect what you are in case you don't know
—Lou Reed, "I'll Be Your Mirror"

The ground of suffering consists of the impossibility of
interrupting it, and of an acute feeling of being held fast.
—Emmanuel Levinas, *On Escape*

Emmanuel Levinas offers to students and scholars of all literary traditions, as well as to those who attempt to account for perception and subjectivity, a philosophical model of ethics as both grounding and exceeding metaphysics and epistemology. And temporality occupies a crucial place in his conception of alterity as a means to adduce the relationship between Being and Otherness that anticipates and transcends the imposition of ontological symmetry. Because in Levinas's work the structure of time animates the structure of ethics, I intend in the present chapter to track alterity as the sustained critique of the competing and ethically divergent story of synchrony through Gabriela Bustelo's *Veo*

veo (1996), Marta Sanz's *El frío* (1995), and José Ángel Mañas's *Mensaka* (1995).[1] This first group of novels by Spain's Gen X writers suggests one way in which ethics gestures toward alterity by extending a nuanced and multivalent critique of ontological sameness and temporal unity.

Any consideration of Levinas and narrative fiction must acknowledge his difficult position on art and, more specifically, on literature. As Alain P. Toumayan concisely summarizes, art for Levinas "is not the founding but the foundering of the world."[2] Although he systematically dismantles several of the precepts of Platonism, Levinas shares with Plato a deep-seated suspicion of art, partly on the basis of its inherent illusion and capacity for mimicry (i.e., the image) and partly because art supposedly congeals time into some sort of eternal valuation. The first encourages disengagement, and discourages responsibility, in the perceiver, whereas the second consolidates, and indeed mandates, the primacy of subjectivity and reason. As Levinas states in the opening lines to one of his earliest commentaries on aesthetics, "The function of art is expression, and . . . artistic expression rests on cognition. An artist—even a painter, even a musician—tells. He tells of the ineffable. An artwork prolongs, and goes beyond, common perception."[3] Here telling unavoidably comprises and displays time as sequence and extension, not to mention evolution toward a transcendent end. And for Levinas, the time of art illusorily dislodges alterity by universalizing, and therefore homogenizing, human subjects and human perception together with the artistic objects that they generate.

Given Levinas's fluctuating antipathy toward aesthetic products, whereby "the Infinity of the idea is idolized in the finite, but sufficient, image,"[4] one might well be tempted to discard narrative fiction, arguably the prototypical expression of telling, as all too emblematic of the perilous distractions of literature. To make matters potentially worse, the genre of narrative and the scholarly apparatus that promotes it have long been pulled toward the pleasures of mimeticism, resolution, and the supposed consolidation of individual and social identities, to name only some of the totalizing impulses gathered together under the broadly conceived label of realism. Nevertheless, and in spite of his protestations to the contrary, the majority of Levinas's philosophical expositions are rife with literary examples, many of them narrative, even to the point that he has astonishingly proposed that "it sometimes seems to me that the whole of philosophy is only a meditation of Shakespeare."[5] Metaphors and metaphorical thinking are in fact spectacularly evident throughout his writing. Jill Robbins has lucidly analyzed "the literary dimensions" in Levinas's own texts, which, she concludes, "have everything to do with the force of his ethical discourse."[6] In the specific milieu of narrative fiction, one might well counter that all narratives, fictional and otherwise, are always more or less about selves and others in relation, and, as Levinas himself postulates, "every social relation leads back to the presentation of the other to the same without the intermediary of any image or sign, solely by the expression of the face."[7]

Perhaps the lingering ethicality of narrative fiction can be approached exegetically by means of temporality; one might in fact assert that the story of ethical alterity is the story of time (and vice versa). To that end, Levinas opposes to the seductive rhythms of poetic activity "the language that at each instant dispels the charm of rhythm and prevents the initiative from becoming a role," and he further proposes that language "is *rupture and commencement*, breaking of rhythm which enraptures and transports the interlocutors—*prose*."[8] The discourse of prose, he appears to here imply, pushes against the idolatry of the (poetic) image precisely by pursuing ethicality into time, by interrupting the duration of human perception, and by imagining the break of alterity as fundamentally temporal. I hope to show, in chapters 3, 4, and 5, just this movement in three distinct approaches to temporal alterity.

In its most simplistic formulation, for Levinas, the entrance of alterity into being, our always already present ethical answerability to and for the Other and others, reveals diachrony, or what Sam B. Girgus has referred to as "a time of disruption,"[9] because of the impossibility of temporal coincidence between Self and Other; the perceiving self can never share the same time as the Other. Although

Levinas develops and refines his theory of the temporalization of ontological asymmetry throughout the six decades of his scholarly career, he explicitly hinges time to alterity almost from the outset, and he does so overtly in *Time and the Other*, published originally in French as *Le temps et l'autre* in 1947. There he critiques Martin Heidegger's conception of the encounter between Being and itself, which is confirmed and prolonged through "ecstatic temporality": "In Heidegger there is a distinction [between *Sein* and *Seindes*, between *existing* and *existent*], not a separation. Existing is always grasped in the existent, and for the existent that is a human being the Heideggerian term *Jemeinigkeit* [Mineness] precisely expresses the fact that existing is always possessed by someone."[10] Levinas posits that time is instead the necessary precondition for the encounter between Being and Other, an encounter that forestalls the autonomy of the transcendental Ego that has underwritten, in one form or another, all of Western philosophy. He assigns the term *diachrony* to his understanding of time as "this *always* of noncoincidence, but also the *always* of the *relationship*, an aspiration and an awaiting, a thread finer than an ideal line that diachrony does not cut,"[11] and he devotes a considerable part of his subsequent work to the elaboration of diachrony as the temporal manifestation of alterity.[12]

In order to better understand the time of diachrony, Levinas proceeds, in *Time and the Other*, to unpack the reified temporal notion of synchrony. He contends that Western philosophy has, at least since the exposition of Kant's cogito, privileged time as synchrony, whereby the Ego confirms coherence and continuity through its unproblematic and unmediated consciousness. This willed illusion of temporal omniscience, what Levinas calls "the egology of presence affirmed from Descartes to Husserl,"[13] celebrates the dominion of individual self-awareness and the metaphysical ideal of rational autonomy in which "'I think' comes down to 'I can'—to an appropriation of what is, to an exploitation of reality."[14] As part and parcel of such an ideal, all temporal separation, rupture, discontinuity, unknowability, and to use Levinas's preferred term, mystery is reduced to "the egology of synthesis, the gathering of all alterity into presence, and the synchrony of repre-sentation."[15] As the next logical step in the so-called presentism of Western metaphysics, the single and solitary subject successfully claims time for itself: "The subject is alone because it is one. . . . Solitude is thus not only a despair and an abandonment, but also a virility, a pride and a sovereignty."[16] In synchrony, so Heidegger's story goes, solitude is affirmed through temporal duration, through which the perceiving self remembers the past and antic-ipates the future as harmonious and supremely legible extensions of the present: one present signifies all presents, "my now" flows unchecked into "our now," and the unified present gathers into itself all (other) time. The systematic reductiveness of synchrony forecloses all additional temporal possibilities and, with them, the very notion of otherness. It is this reductiveness—manifested as the primacy of egology, the violent logic of repetition, and the syn-chrony of representation—that the three novels discussed in the present chapter will interrogate by multiple means and to vari-ous extents. Critique will not, however, inspire any further move toward ethical alterity until the novels considered in the succeed-ing chapters.

While the precise contours and longevity of Spain's Gen X con-tinue to inspire debate and disagreement, in the 1990s, critics on both sides of the Atlantic were quick to seize upon a specific subset of the much larger generational cohort as a reflection of Peninsular youth culture during Spain's rapid move from postdictatorship into democracy. Novels by Bustelo, Lucía Etxebarria, Ismael Grasa, Ray Loriga, Pedro Maestre, José Ángel Mañas, and Benjamín Prado, to name some of the most prominent authors, paved the way for the critical identification of the work of this entire generation with dirty or hard realism, an imitation of a narrative style made famous in the English-speaking world by writers such as Bret Easton Ellis and Charles Bukowski.[17] The Peninsular writers, and among them Etxebarria, Loriga, and Mañas, gained fame and recognition as the proxies for a discrete socioeconomic group in Spain—namely, the disenfranchised, middle-class, Euro-Caucasian consumer. Their novels, and especially those published during the 1990s, evinced a set of shared characteristics: often narrated and focalized in the first person, the texts shadowed the actions of an adult protagonist who moved through one or multiple urban environments; the authors tended to favor a coded linguistic register that derived from a certain age-specific demographic and spotlighted urban slang and references from contemporary consumer culture; and the novels foregrounded the conspicuous intake of drugs and alcohol, often to the point of excess. All of the novelists linked to the Gen X were initially (and erroneously) thrown together by critics and placed under the umbrella of "neorealists," or the synonymous terms *hard realism* and *dirty realism*.[18] Moreover, well into the twenty-first century, most scholarly discussions of these writers have focused on Mañas's tetralogy (and primarily *Historias del Kronen*), a trio of novels by Ray Loriga, and other fictional volumes that clearly conform to the distinctive aesthetics and themes of neorealism. Of the nine novels considered in my project, *Veo veo* and *Mensaka* exemplify this brand of realism, though all three novels analyzed in the current chapter stress the perils of youth culture.

It bears noting that the two women to regularly be considered as charter members of the Gen X, in part because they have favored neorealism in selected novels, are Etxebarria and Bustelo. Both novelists have long insisted upon a feminine and feminizing vision of contemporary Spain.[19] Commentators of Etxebarria's novels tend to underscore her interrogation of capitalist culture, her unpacking of gender differences, and her celebration of contemporary metropolitan life in Spain. Less well known and certainly less prolific, Bustelo has thus far published three novels.[20] *Veo veo* (1996), her first, proffers a parodic account of the violent reduction of intersubjectivity to egology by way of repetition, addiction, and nostalgia, all of which will also figure in *El frío* and *Mensaka*. The female narrator-protagonist proves incapable of—and in the main, disinterested in—imagining either exteriority or futurity; instead, she succumbs to the endlessly repeating loop of the "reality effect" as modeled by visual and verbal media.[21]

Like other Peninsular Gen X novelists, Bustelo populates *Veo veo* with twentysomething urban consumers who look to sex, drugs, and popular media for signposts and stimulation.[22] The action of the novel is organized around the glitzy nightclub scene in Madrid during the late 1980s, and in these and other novels that typify the neorealism subgroup, a first-person narrator-protagonist shifts from place to place, usually within the cityscape of Madrid or Barcelona, in search of the next high, which never quite captures or replaces the previous high. Neorealist novels insist, by definition, upon referentiality, but *Veo veo* teeters toward extravagance in its encyclopedic list of 1980s films, actors, directors, TV shows, celebrities, Madrid landmarks, marketing icons, song lyrics and titles, fashion designers, and high-end clothing and accessories.[23] Additionally, while Bustelo's inaugural novel shares with most other Gen X novels an exacting commitment to the exhibition and circulation of popular culture, Spanish and otherwise, in contrast to her peers, the author embeds the peripatetic journey of a female protagonist within an elaborately articulated external threat that propels the plot, the characters, and time itself forward and backward in equal measure while also managing to disturb narrative closure.[24] Any relational reciprocity is eventually and irrevocably subsumed into a single unified and solitary human subject who is caught up (and by) the twin illusions that, according to Levinas, underpin egology: temporal omnipotence and unproblematic consciousness. These, in turn, underwrite ethical irresponsibility, stagnation, and metaphorical and literal violence. Bustelo thus deploys an unwavering attack on the sameness that is fomented by self-absorption, but as is the case with the trio of novels examined in the current chapter, *Veo veo* does not put forward any alternative road map toward alterity.

The novel does, however, reiterate the temporal violence of sameness as the narrator-protagonist, Vania Barcia, recounts her physical and verbal odyssey in the first person. Her journey begins when she consults with an unidentified male psychiatrist in order to dispel the encroaching fear that she is being pursued by an unwelcome and unknown stalker. The psychiatrist, to whom she jokingly assigns the moniker Mickey Rourke, prescribes a vacation

to the distraught woman, but Vania continues to sense the menac-
ing presence of a stranger. She swiftly hires Peláez, a private investigator, who uncovers hidden microphones and two-way mirrors in
her apartment, video-recording equipment in the neighboring residence, and a slew of videotapes that document Vania's most intimate moments in her bathroom and bedroom. The visuality that
threatens to engulf the protagonist also situates her within a far-
flung game, possibly of her own making, that includes an anonymous caller in search of someone named Soledad, well-informed
fortune hunters, and the reenactment of Vania's "wild-child" past.

In response to conclusive proof that she is in fact being actively
monitored by someone, the narrator casts aside her monastic habits of moderation and instead sets off on a two-week spree (which
corresponds to the duration of the narrative) through Madrid's
fashionable and not-so-fashionable nightclubs, restaurants, and
bars. In the process, she revisits previous haunts, rekindles previous
friendships and pseudoromances, and renews her previous reliance
on artificial stimulants of all stripes. She also makes the acquaintance of Ben Ganza, an enigmatic Brazilian who unaccountably
knows everyone she knows and shows up wherever she happens
to be. Predictably, the pair embarks on an extended and ultimately
effective seduction—but only after several aborted encounters.

Much less predictably, in the final twenty pages of the novel,
the protagonist mistakes her new lover for an intruder and fatally
shoots him with Peláez's revolver. Shortly thereafter, she receives
an anonymous letter in which the writer, who is likely Ben himself, reveals that the deceased was in fact a vengeful ex-boyfriend
whom Vania had rejected several years earlier during her misspent
youth. The missive further recounts that after their traumatic
breakup, he had retreated to Brazil, where he had made his fortune and had undergone extensive plastic surgery after a motor-
cycle accident. He had then returned to Spain bent on revenge,
proceeding to infiltrate Vania's world and then stripping her of
any illusion of liberty. The letter, intercalated into the protagonist's
interior monologue, breaks off without identifying the author or

enumerating the events that occurred once Ben gained access to his intended target.

After she unintentionally eradicates Ben, and once she discovers the extent and depth of the conspiracy against her, Vania comes undone, purchases her own gun, and goes back to her apartment to commit suicide. At the last minute, she instead aims at one of the mirrors in her apartment and shoots Peláez, who had been watching her from the adjacent apartment with a video camera located on the other side of the mirror. Upon realizing that she has murdered yet another man, she flees to the office of the psychiatrist in order to confess everything and delegate control of her life over to an authority figure. He convinces her to check into a "sanatorium" and even drives her home to pack a suitcase. When they arrive at her apartment, however, they find no dead body, no broken mirror, no gun, and no evidence whatsoever to corroborate any of the incidents from the previous two weeks. After voluntarily admitting herself to an unspecified mental institution on the outskirts of Madrid, spending several days under heavy sedation, and meeting a male patient whose history eerily resembles her own, Vania elects to go back home. She opens the door of her apartment to the sound of the ringing telephone, and when she answers it, a male voice—the same male caller who has been calling throughout the two weeks—again asks for Soledad. The last four lines simulate the fading sound of an otherwise occupied telephone line: "Bip-bip-bip-bip. / Bip-bip-bip. / Bip-bip. / Bip."[25] Vania has come full circle back to herself, time has doubled back on itself, and in Levinasian terms, synchrony complements egology.

It bears noting that, like many characters in the Gen X narrative, the protagonist is first and foremost a consumer; as Candice L. Bosse perceptively asserts, Vania "experience[s] her life as if it were a quasi-performance; that is, she channels her energy into consumerism, one of high end goods, and thus, actively manufactures the type of self that she wants to be peeped on, both inside and outside the home."[26] Furthermore, the narrator routinely inflects her consumption with a hefty dose of nostalgia, an attitude that, in the context of my current argument about ethics, aptly complements a perceiving subject who attempts to exert control over her circumstances through the fusion of subjectivity to temporality; the always absent past assumes priority over the present through the unity afforded by memory. Nonetheless, Bustelo decisively places the remembering narrator at the brink of physical, emotional, and even ethical chaos by drawing a clear boundary between Vania's restrained patterns of consumption prior to the narrative present and her increasingly frenetic behavior during the two weeks that mark her recommitment to sex, drugs, and rock and roll. All returns, either temporal or spatial, conclusively eschew alterity, any awareness or consideration of the Other and others, and indeed, relationality in every sense.

Thanks to her conscious articulation of, and engagement with, a panoply of recognizable cultural referents from a particular historical moment in Spain and beyond its national borders, the protagonist explicitly drives a (re)connection to her own history while also projecting a strangely anachronistic sense of herself; as Henseler perceptively states, "*Veo veo* sets the scene through temporal oppositions."[27] In one sense, Vania adheres to the youth cult in Spain of carpe diem, provocatively analyzed by Mark Allinson,[28] that permeates many neorealist instances of the Gen X narrative, but in another sense, her self-described reclamation of hedonism and indulgence is spectacularly signaled as a homecoming, implicating both a prior departure and a subsequent arrival. Vania's narrative traces the paradoxical path of a perceiving and speaking subject who attempts to fully inhabit a present moment that is literally and figuratively shot through and through with her past. By the end of the novel, and after the protagonist has killed off the participants in her two most significant relationships, the only available future that remains to her, as I will subsequently argue, is yet another return to the same—the same self and the same time.

The novel strategically commences with Vania's description of an ordinary door, which serves as the gateway to the psychiatrist's office; it is noteworthy that she reports (in the allusive "now" of narration) that she arrived, arguably in spite of her best efforts, at the threshold and at the appointed hour. As a result, she has minutes to spare or change her mind: "Y yo aún estaba a tiempo. Podía dar media vuelta y largarme" [I was still on time. I could turn around and leave].[29] The temporal resistance encompassed in *still* is here laid bare and will pervade the unfolding history. Her earliest meeting with someone else, a male representative of medicalized power, registers as a game of multiplying mirrors, echoing the lyrics from Lou Reed's song, which serve as the epigraph to Bustelo's novel ("I'll be your mirror. / Reflect what you are in case you don't know"[30]), and anticipating, in one ironically harmonious swirl, an inconclusive ending to the ensuing narrative descent into the past of a supposedly singular self who folds all time into her present.

The protagonist subsequently imagines that the doctor watches her; she projects onto his actions her own desperation and then tags the entire scene as "hazily familiar": "El muy capullo me miró inquisitivamente, como si yo fuera a solucionarle alguna duda a él, en vez de solucionarme él la vida a mí" [The moron looked at me inquisitively, as if I were going to resolve some doubt for him, instead of him resolving my life for *me*].[31] Her words will prove prophetic in that all perception by others boomerangs back to the controlling perceiver as one more justification for her paranoia, one more explication of her deteriorating mental state, and one more "mirror" that displays back to her (and to the reader) the unified image of herself and her iron-clad dominion over time. Everything and everyone in the plotline bolsters Vania's ego and diverts her from even acknowledging, much less facing toward, any difference, be it ontological, temporal, or ethical. Others and otherness express as derivative copies of the narrator-protagonist's dizzyingly oppressive egology.

As a prime verification of the protagonist's all-encompassing self-absorption, one need look no further than Vania's (lack of) relationships with others.[32] As the narrative progresses, she rapidly cycles through a parade of past friends, lovers, acquaintances, and colleagues, all of whom are diminished and eventually discarded because of their familiarity to and with her. As only one among the seemingly endless examples, during the first installment of her return to Madrid's nightlife, she and a "loyal intermittent lover" commence the evening at a trendy restaurant named Archy's, with the acknowledged goal of seeing the other diners in attendance and, more importantly, of being seen by them.[33] In the midst of banal conversational repartee with her bored (and boring) male companion, Vania realizes that her previous patterns and diversions no longer guarantee any relief because she cannot see or understand anything or anyone that does not reflect her; perhaps predictably, the narrator attributes the source of this sameness to the stagnation in the world around her:

> Qué sensación tan inquietante. Se podía estar meses, años sin salir de copas por Madrid, podían pasar cosas, se podía uno casar, tener hijos, podían morir parientes, podía haber guerras, podía hundirse el sistema comunista al otro lado de nuestro continente, podían describirse las supernovas, los agujeros negros, y los noctámbuleros seguían ensayando una y mil veces las mismas escenas insulsas.

> [What a weird sensation. One could go months, even years without going out on the town in Madrid, things could happen, one could get married, have kids, relatives could die, wars could be fought, the Communist system on the other side of the continent could fall, supernovas could be discovered, black holes, and the nightwalkers would continue to perform the same stupid scenes one thousand and one times.][34]

It bears remarking that the narrator contributes, here and throughout the time span of the novel, to the relational—and thus the ethical—homogeneity that she so vociferously disparages. And her imagination stretches only to familiar social interactions that she controls by attaching them to her past; she thereby affirms herself as a perceiving subject who comprehends time as an unproblematic extension of herself and knits it into a seamless whole with no beginning and no ending. The exercise and imposition of repetition are fundamental to the exposition of time here and elsewhere because it formally forestalls difference, ethical alterity, and Levinas's diachrony.

That said, the drama and conflict of and in *Veo veo* emerge with the interruption of new elements into Vania's quotidian existence. Although she can grasp alterity only as a threat to her own personal security, Vania is compelled to seek outside herself for corroboration that she is indeed the target of escalating vigilance by mysterious observers whom she can neither glimpse nor discourage. She turns to two (male) authority figures, a psychiatrist and a private investigator, to corroborate her suspicions. The first, a scientist, dismisses her fears as the product of an overwrought mind, whereas the second finds evidence of her stalker and thereby becomes embedded in the protagonist's ongoing crisis. With the gradual intercession of a third party, Ben Ganza, into her inner circle, the conflict gathers momentum and hurtles toward a climax. Vania falsely believes that she has authored an original narrative, based in the romance formula, and that she and the man of her dreams will be propelled into a different future. Unfortunately, the past literally catches up to her and overwhelms both her present and any potential tomorrow.

Veo veo confirms, by means of resolutely literary and narrative strategies, Levinas's intertwined premises that murder is impossible and that violence is exerted on the other via time. These double maxims manifest literally in *Veo veo* insofar as three executions take place during the narrative present: Vania hears of the murder of El Cejas, her purported stalker, from Peláez, and she fatally shoots both Ganza and Peláez himself. In the latter two cases, she strikes out at an imagined target and in response to her mounting paranoia, after which each corpse disappears and Vania is left to narrate her own future as unstable, malleable, and solitary. Because Vania establishes herself as a dangerously inept reader, her narration of the moments preceding Ben's murder merits extended exegesis: "Como aún estaba con media alma en el planeta de los sueños, al principio no me di cuenta, pero a los pocos segundos me percaté de que había alguien metido en mi habitación. Una figura negra, a la que no se le veía la cara" [Because half of me was still in the land of dreams, at the beginning I didn't realize it, but within a few seconds I sensed that someone was in my bedroom. A dark figure, whose face I couldn't see].[35] Her initial rationalization for the murder leans on an inability to distinguish reality from fantasy because she is caught between sleep and wakefulness; once she gains consciousness, she can only interpret the presence and actions of the "faceless" intruder as someone so threatening to her survival that the extreme solution of annihilation (and just this solution) occurs to her. She has apparently forgotten about her hours-old sexual encounter with Ben, and it never occurs to her to ask that the so-called stranger identify himself. The one emotion that she recollects is her own fear, which then jolts her into retaliatory violence.

Tellingly, Vania receives the letter concerning Ben's checkered past only after she kills him and after he has been forcibly removed from any future with the protagonist. The epistle anticipates resolution by detailing the motives, chronology, and ineluctability of Ben's scheme to unravel the protagonist's assumed sanity and safety. The puzzle pieces of the narrative, focalized from the vantage point of Vania's realization, fit together harmoniously and give credence to Vania's paranoia and her aggression: she manages to successfully cast herself (at least in the context of her own conscience) as the unwitting victim of an unhinged predator.

Peláez's murder bears some resemblance to Ben's death, at least as they are reported by the perpetrating narrator. Once again, Vania fatally shoots someone known to her, whom she mistakes for a stranger in a moment of crisis. This time, however, before she aims at the mirror, she rehearses the notion of turning the gun on herself: "El final. El final lo iban a ver ahora mismo, hombre" [The end. They were going to see the end right now, yes indeed]. In consonance with the protagonist's starring role in the drama of her life, she elects to perform a one-woman peep show for her phantom audience: "Ahora lo ves, ahora no lo ves. Cómo lo ves" [Now you see it, now you don't. Now you really see it].[36] Only in the last second does she opt to forego victimization, and when she aims her gun at the mirror, she miraculously manages to hit the invisible Peláez with a single shot. The temporal oppositions that Henseler has identified are here made manifest for both the protagonist and the reader: *first* we see, *then* we do not see, and finally we *truly* see. Reason, cause and effect, and a certain spatial determinism overwhelm any possibility for alterity or futurity.

The narrator's response is, as it has been throughout her narrative, to energetically pursue numbness, evade responsibility, and cast about for a stimulant that will allow her to figuratively and literally disappear. Immediately after she kills Peláez, Vania snorts heroin, downs an entire bottle of whiskey, and runs to a medical authority who peddles the curative properties of drugs. With little prompting, he convinces her to admit herself to a lockdown treatment facility and abdicate all responsibility, a course of action that receives additional corroboration when doctor and patient return to the scene of the crime and find absolutely nothing. Once ensconced in the facility, Vania allows herself to become so medicated that she floats in and out of consciousness for days. Time has collapsed into itself and has been efficiently absorbed into the perceiving subject. The reader is left to conclude that Vania is delusional, that she has invented everything—perhaps as the result of too many narcotics but more likely as the result of her infatuation with her own past and her own subjectivity. What better way to foreclose the need for any kind of relationship, temporal or otherwise, than to be incapable of transcending the endless loop of one's own mind?

Even while she is heavily drugged and under constant medical observation, Vania cannot avoid the repetition of her own story, which she hears from a male patient. Toni Dorca analyzes this scene as "la reduplicación [que] alcanza proporciones metafísicas" [the reduplication that achieves metaphysical proportions].[37] Instead of looking beyond the surface and possibly glimpsing someone other than herself, she halfheartedly listens to the stranger's words, which then reflect back to her the previous two

weeks as an extended adventure in solipsism. Somewhat predictably, the resident psychiatrist, whom she nicknames Froid (a combination of Freud and the French word for "cold"), diagnoses the
Godiva complex as the root of all of Vania's problems: "Yo sólo digo
que las relaciones entre dos personas siempre se articulan en forma
de juego, y ustedes dos [Vania y Ben] están jugando a Godiva y
Peeping Tom, aunque según la interpretación metasicológica de
la leyenda, es necesario que exista un tercer personaje en la som-
bra" [I am just saying that relations between two people are always
articulated as a game, and you two are pretending to be Godiva
and Peeping Tom, although according to the metapsychological
interpretation of the legend, a third person has to exist in the shad-
ows].[38] The third person alluded to in the above quotation is not,
in contrast to Levinas's formulation, the distant and future other
but the authoritative husband whose love for his beautiful wife has
created the scenario whereby the proverbially naked woman roams
freely and the transgressive "other man" is suitably punished for
his extramarital desire. Apparently, all men who desire the unmarried Vania are definitively castigated, but none registers as sufficiently "other" to interrupt the protagonist's self-absorption.

From her time in the sanatorium, Vania—ever the recalcitrant
student—takes as her lesson that all events thus far correlate with
a feigned performance and that she has not really killed anyone.
Logically, it follows (in her mind, at least) that if she did not murder
anyone, then all potential actors are still alive and plotting against
her in ways both subtler and more perverse than anything that
she has yet experienced. And from this awareness, she deduces
that her life is in fact not hers but theirs. As conclusive proof, the
final words of the novel return Vania-as-listener (and the voyeuris-
tic readers) to earlier calls, earlier callers, earlier vigilance, or to the
same caller seeking the same "Soledad" in a later moment. But
nothing and no one are really different. Time has not moved forward (or backward) because the human subject in *Veo veo* cannot
move beyond the totality of egology without recourse, which she
refuses, to the other and otherness. In answer to the fundamental

question about whether "Soledad" [loneliness] resides at the other end of the telephone line, the answer would seem to be a resounding yes, yes, and still yes.

The spectacle of failed eros also occupies center stage in Marta Sanz's *El frío*,[39] but in the second novel, this failure gives way to a split narrative of the frustrated integration of the Other into the Same and others into traumatized subjects; alterity does not successfully assert itself, nor is a partial or effective encounter with the other realized. Sanz's novel probes the edges of subjectivity in its display of human agents who perform irresponsibility and unresponsiveness as the breakdown that precedes ethical alterity. However, while the erotic encounters do not result in intimacy with any Other, neither do they generate knowledgeable, coherent subjects who prevail over division. Instead, *El frío*, like *Veo veo*, limns the gaps between the egoism that Levinas critiques and the future extended by and to alterity through the promise of eros and fecundity.

From the outset of Sanz's text, the reader is confronted with two narratively temporalized versions of the same event. Composed of thirty-five sequentially numbered chapters, *El frío* conjoins three shifting viewpoints: an unnamed woman recounts a bus trip to visit her lover, Miguel, who is interned in a sanatorium for an undisclosed psychiatric disorder; Blanca Egar, a nurse at the same hospital, sadistically infantilizes her patient Miguel until he conclusively rebels; and a man named Miguel dismisses his visiting lover and punishes his aberrant nurse. In the odd-numbered chapters, the woman recollects, mostly in the first person and in the present tense, her journey by bus to and from the medical facility and her emotional history with Miguel. The even-numbered chapters seesaw between the conflicting visions of Blanca and Miguel as each invades and retreats from the other. Braided together, the chapters calculate the ways in which human subjects encounter and attempt to recover from the temporal trauma of otherness.

The distinct plotlines are bridged—on the surface, at least—by two desiring female subjects who direct their amorous attentions to the same male object. In the first instance, the narrator and her lover exchange places across time and space; in their past relationship, according to her account, he was the intelligible subject and she the unintelligible other, whereas in the present moment, she asserts subjectivity and assigns to him the place of ontological and sexual difference, an arrangement that is replicated in the second story line. In this line, Blanca initially directs and stars in the drama of her interaction with Miguel; she dresses him, moves him, speaks for him, and interprets his actions to other residents and employees. In a word, she *possesses* him—to the point that he gives the impression of existing solely as an extension of her will. From the interstices of the clinically detached narrative perspective, however, it becomes clear that Miguel stealthily exercises agency, and imposes synchrony, from the margins. He silently encroaches on the intimacies of other patients and staff members, converting private solitudes into public exhibitions. As a final sign of his triumph, after he orchestrates Blanca's terrified submission, she retreats to communal institutional spaces (the kitchen, the art room, the halls) and forced sociality with her coworker, whereas he retires, alone and content, to his room.

Sanz's novel is not antirelational. On the contrary, it reads as extravagantly relational, as so many examples of selves and others and the trauma that undoes complementarity. For the first-person narrator, her desire and her subjectivity crumple when her lover rebuffs her, but her narrative also launches from this same point. Although her demands for recognition intensify throughout the text, she receives recognition only from herself because her lover is conspicuously absent and because she mentally rebuffs the other passengers on the bus while folding them into her emotional chronicle. As part of that process, she reminds herself (and the reader) of previous and current suffering, both of which are exacerbated by the activities of her fellow travelers. Her pain also manifests in the frequency with which she shuttles, in the present tense, between the first-, second-, and third-person perspectives, as exemplified in the succeeding passage: "Yo adivino, aprehendo sus oscilaciones bajo el agua. La veo. La radio puede explotar; está conectada a la red eléctrica y en este cuarto la humedad arde. Ten cuidado. No quiero ver tus espasmos, que me dejes sin irte, sin que la estructura blanda de mi propia voluntad decida, por fin, alejarse. A la búsqueda de un nuevo cristalino, uno distinto, otro" [I guess at and I apprehend her movements under the water. I see her. The radio could explode, it's connected to the electric outlet and in this room the humidity burns. Be careful. I don't want to see your spasms, leave me alone without going anywhere, without the bland structure of my self-will deciding to finally go away. In response to the search for a new crystalline lens, another one, different].[40] The *I*, *you*, and *she* all refer to the same person, who attempts to fill the void left by her obligations to the Other. Levinas has written that "the relationship established between lovers in voluptuosity, fundamentally refractory to universalization, is the very contrary of the social relation. It excludes the third party, it remains intimacy, dual solitude, closed society, the supremely non-public."[41] In the absence of the (gendered) hospitality that Levinas attributes to alterity, the erotic encounter has diminished the female subject, provoking a chain of echoes designed to restore her to herself. In the narrative of her past, alterity was precluded by the disappearance of the female object into the male subject. In the present story, the narrator envisions excessive disorder where there once was excessive order. Her lover owes her, but because she clings so desperately to her need to see herself reflected in and by him, she cordons off her access to otherness and her own future status as an other.[42]

In the parallel narrative, the reverse occurs. At first glance, an ethical interpretation of the relationship between Miguel and Blanca is more straightforward because the two participants seem to defy ethicality. The plot of sexual domination, so at odds with the Levinasian ideal of erotic intimacy, spells an exceedingly intricate dance of subjection and liberation. When Blanca tries to erase Miguel's agency, she assumes that she is converting him into a wholly visible being—the antithesis of the feminine welcome. He reacts by retreating, like the "other" narrator, into himself, but unlike her, he violently projects that self onto others. In each case, the result is the same: Miguel and the unnamed woman are alone and adrift. But he seeks solitude, interiority, and separation, whereas she perhaps still imagines some kind of connection as she walks literally and figuratively toward an exit, forestalling the future and subjugating the past to her will.

El frío novelizes the exhibition of failed proximity, the temporalized inside-out of erotic love, and the pathologization of selves who try to reclaim consciousness by dictating (to) the other. In order to lay claim to themselves, the woman, Miguel, and Blanca attempt to re-member one another, such that the novel elucidates synchrony as salvation. The first lines of the text, which are not, to be certain, the originary lines, read as follows: "Tú lo sabes ya de sobra, pero yo voy a repetírtelo. No me has dejado decir ni una palabra. Me has apartado suavemente; te has dado la vuelta" [You already know it only too well, but I'll tell you again. You haven't let me say a single word. You have gently removed me; you have turned your back on me].[43] The unidentified addressee to whom the narrating woman speaks already knows her story disproportionately prior to the time of their shared story, and she, in turn, has already fitted the *I* to itself. She discursively predicts and remarks her lover's dismissal and distance, thus reinforcing the desirable solitude that she hopes to experience as an antidote to her current suffering. Synchrony names this aloneness as deeply temporal; as Levinas has declared, "Existing is mastered by the existent that is identical to itself—that is to say, alone. But identity is not only a departure from self; it is also a return to self. The present consists of an inevitable return to itself."[44] It is this synchronous "return to self" that spreads into and throughout the temporal aspects of *El frío*.

In the early installments of her narrative, and as she metaphorically and literally travels toward Miguel, the woman simultaneously recalls and recoils from the illusion of their common time, which is completed and therefore past. She accomplishes this by lacing the times of before, during, and after into a causality; at the same time, she dons and then discards, like so many ill-fitting coats, the identities of those around her. Whether it be the homeless woman, the disapproving businessman, or the loquacious bus driver, all of those external to her immediate perceptual boundaries jeopardize her renewed control, which is based in the distinction between inside and outside. Insofar as she insists on lucidity by impressing her uncontested self-awareness into the events before and after her present, she affirms and sustains sequence and agency. Insofar as past and future disrupt and destabilize her present presence, and insofar as others aggressively (re)insert themselves into her consciousness, alterity constrains any possible knowledge of self and other in the fictional world created in and by Sanz's novel. But coherence and continuity, as expressions of Levinas's Said, win out as they must according to the logic of affliction that girds *El frío*.

The opposite perceptual play molds the alternating plotline, filtered through an omniscient narrative voice, which teeters precariously between the perspectives of Blanca and Miguel. As befits the rising tension that suffuses these intervals, specific details about their communal physical environment are grounded in the present moment and encroach upon any ethical interaction. Tellingly, Miguel appears, prior to Blanca, on the scene in the second chapter, and after finalizing a series of mundane activities, he contemplates his inverted reflection in the floor tiles beneath him. Blanca intrudes into the moment and initiates the chain of occurrences that will typify their relationship: "Blanca llega y le coge por el codo; cada día, en ese preciso instante, Miguel levanta la cabeza y sonríe" [Blanca arrives and takes him by the elbow; each day, at that precise instant, Miguel raises his head and smiles].[45] With painstaking precision, the all-seeing narrator describes the spatial arrangement of the rooms, doors, and walls in the same present tense that s/he uses to locate the unfolding subjugation between patient and nurse. The past, which can only be a perfect duplication of the current moment, does not interrupt, and the only sign of a future incident consists of Blanca's announcement to Miguel that a visitor will arrive at three o'clock, effectively positioning the "other" woman's story inside of their joint futures, where it will languish as the narrative advances.

El frío concerns the ethics of relationality turned upside down. The proximity of the other person—which, for Levinas, commands ethical responsibility—has always already distressed the perceiving subject, who attempts to transform memory into causality and expectations into inevitability. The three participants drag themselves through time—that is, they justify their anguish by establishing and inserting themselves and each other into a chronology. As the original and final voice, the first-person woman upholds her victimization at the hands of Miguel, a role that she has repeated prior to her narration and is repeating in the process of telling her story. She transposes her now terminated entanglement with Miguel onto the bus passengers around her and rehearses the phases of the pair's history by constantly reading herself against and into the actions that surround her. As only one among copious instances, after silently promising that she will ignore the kissing couple behind her on the bus, she mentally spews forth a litany of insults, only to recall that those very same insults were, at some other point in time, directed toward her and her lover.

The structure of the novel also twists time toward the additional characters who, to a certain extent, imitate the relational dynamics that emanate from the first-person narrator's recovery of her lover and their shared past. In the sections involving Miguel and Blanca, one perception pervades the omniscient voice, one character speaks and thinks, and one clearly dominates. Their mutual story, which never ventures beyond the physical space of the psychiatric institution, could be described as the tale of Miguel's revenge and yet another chronicle of causality. The chapters devoted to the sadomasochistic duo are replete with horrific imagery and graphic language. In contrast to the intensely interiorized tone and direction of the unnamed woman's narrative, the omniscient narrator externalizes the incidents in the sanitarium by concentrating on the sensorial presentation of bodies, food, textures, surfaces, landscapes.

The pivotal moment in their history of reciprocal bondage transpires when Miguel grabs Blanca by the neck and terrorizes her with a stolen crochet hook, at which point he speaks for the first and only time: "Voy a sacarte la yugular y cuando esté fuera de la piel voy a pincharla y te desangrarás de esa sangre rosa chicle que te hincha los pies y las varices de los muslos y la carne de la lengua" [I'm going to rip out your jugular and when it's outside of your skin, I'm going to puncture it and you'll bleed to death with that bubblegum-pink blood that swells your feet and the varicose veins in your thighs and the flesh of your tongue].[46] The antithetical "thrust" of the quoted passage attests to a bloody circularity insofar as the present concentrates on the blood that literally flows through and bloats Blanca's body and the future merely intensifies or "bloats" that time. It is difficult to imagine a more challenging vision of sameness or a more chillingly violent fusion of Same and Other.

The return to the present extends through Blanca's shocked retreat and Miguel's understated bedtime ritual. In the first instance, the nurse dissimulates to her coworker, and the two women agree to actively ignore Miguel and all other patients from that moment onward. In the second instance, the victorious Miguel carefully discards his used pajamas in favor of a brand-new pair, after which "se acuesta, se arropa, lee un rato. Cierra los ojos" [he lies down, tucks himself in, reads for a little while. He closes his eyes].[47] There is no interiority here. Each person has relegated the other to the past, and each advances seamlessly into continuity and reflection by sealing off both temporality and otherness.

Meanwhile, in the closing episode of her story, the remade singular woman arrives "home" both alone and in the company of strangers with whom she has refused to interact, preferring instead to cast them as foreign visitors. No one waits for her at the bus terminal, and she has no luggage to claim and no baggage handlers to tip because her return is outside of time; she can conceive of no future, no time other than the present moment, no place other than the bus terminal. Levinas has commented in "Reality and Its Shadow" that "the characters of a novel are beings that are shut up, prisoners. Their history is never finished, it still goes on, but makes no headway."[48] For Levinas, history stalls when Being resembles and doubles itself, which is precisely the case with the fictional characters of *El frío*.

The last scene of the novel encodes precisely this directional blankness: "Camino hacia la salida con la mente en blanco" [I walk toward the exit with my mind blank].[49] In contrast to an affirmative ending, the concluding words of *El frío* accentuate a loss of consciousness. After all of her memories, all of her self-motivated and self-directed coherence, the woman can think of nothing and no one. She has attempted (and failed) to make sense of her past, framed exclusively within the limits and substitutions of her relationship with Miguel. *El frío* temporalizes the unethicality of synchrony as one expression of the art of time. If, as Levinas theorizes, "identity is not only a departure from self; it is also a return to self,"[50] then the triple presents of and in the novel interrogate this illusory "freedom of beginning." In the three timelines, the characters come back to themselves by abandoning the time(s) of others, mastering the possible and firmly grasping the present. In the absence of cultural, political, and even sociological histories that might reference contemporary Spain, Sanz's text exaggerates the solipsistic temporality of trauma in subjectivity. Accordingly, the novel interlaces not one but three versions of solitude and calls each out of time and to a nonexistent future.

If *Veo veo* underwrites the traumatic interiority and insularity of the perceiving subject and *El frío* interrogates the dialogic damage that selves direct toward "their" others, then *Mensaka* relocates the same suspended relationality within a veritable chorus of perceiving subjects, all of whom are tragically self-enclosed. José Ángel Mañas's Kronen tetralogy is composed of the aforementioned *Historias del Kronen*, *Mensaka* (1995), *Soy un escritor frustrado* (1996), and *Ciudad rayada* (1998).[51] Like the other novels in the tetralogy, *Mensaka* supplies a cross section of the activities of Spain's contemporary "youth culture"; it foregrounds an oral style of narrative and is liberally laced with slang, it includes copious references to contemporary music and film, and drugs and sex figure prominently. *Mensaka* also exhibits a series of narrators and narrative points of view, all of whom are linked to a loosely defined relational community. The narrative style of the separately focalized chapters incorporates stream of consciousness, dialogue, and a version of first-person reporting. The plotline is stitched together from these competing interests and experiences and directs the novel toward predictably frustrated outcomes, all of which register (again) as versions of the failure of alterity and diachrony to displace egology and synchrony.

In *Mensaka*, Mañas encourages a seemingly objective vantage point; characters report sentiments, fears, and fantasies, but they do so in ways that emphasize distance from their own experiences. As if to underscore this distance, the sixteen individually focalized segments are framed by two objective segments, the first a written version of an interview that appears at the beginning of the literary text and the second an epilogue that re-presents the events from the point of view of a detached observer. It is also important to note that the novel unspools almost entirely in the present tense, a stylistic choice that reiterates the seductive promise of immediacy and realism. The characters themselves occasionally remember events, but they narrate and "see" in the same time frame and thus contribute to the fantasy of simultaneity.

Mañas's second novel begins with an *"Extracto de la entrevista aparecida en un fanzine musical el 3 de octubre de 1994"* [*Excerpt from an interview that appeared in a music fanzine on October 3, 1994*].[52] Notably, the reader is informed neither of the title of the fanzine nor of the name of the interviewer; the three interviewees, on the other hand, are referenced both by the first initials (F., D., and J.) and by the corresponding names (Fran, David, and Javi) that the interviewees use to refer to one another. From the first lines, the author locates the novel in the synchrony of real time and creates tension between the interviewer and his "subjects" as well as among the interviewees themselves. From the outset, the speech act is characterized as suspicious in that the unnamed interviewer has added to the written text a parenthetical commentary that explicitly mocks the interviewees, a commentary that presumably does not appear in the oral interview, although it is referenced in some of the statements of the interviewer. For example, to Fran's observation *"Es un buen momento para música como ésta"* [*It's a good time for music like this*], the interviewer responds, "*O sea que sois unos oportunistas*" [*In other words you guys are just opportunists*] and then, we are led to assume, writes but does not share with his subjects, "*Risas tensas. (Nosotros pensamos que SON unos putos oportunistas)*" [*Tense laughter. (We think that they ARE opportunistic bastards)*].[53] Some of the other parenthetical comments lean toward more irony, but the hostile tone is also evident in the verbal sparring of the three musicians, as when Javi responds to David's comment that "*por una vez has sido conciso. Estoy alucinado*" [*for once in your life you've been concise. I'm freaking out*].[54] Finally, the available language falls well short of efficacy when David resorts to onomatopoeic sounds in order to describe their so-called hardcore style of music; when asked by the interviewer, "*Qué es el Hardcore para vosotros?*" [*What is Hardcore for you guys?*], he answers, "*Pues yo qué sé, chunta chunta*" [*Man, I don't know, bang, bang*].[55] While on the one hand, the narrative projects the image of unmediated access to the thoughts, intentions, and feelings of the characters, in fact these same perceiving subjects are duped and degraded by one another. Their discursive environment registers first and foremost as manipulatively hostile and isolationist, setting the standard for the narrative events to come.

The succeeding sixteen chapters are divided and labeled with the first initial of one of eight characters whose perspective controls each chapter. These eight narrators are loosely linked to each other by affinity or family ties. David, Javi, and Fran are identifiable from the fanzine interview, and each musician has a female love interest, respectively Bea, Cristina, and Natalia. In addition, Javi's younger sister, Laura, narrates two chapters, as does Ricardo, an acquaintance of the three musicians who detonates one of the primary lines of action. This strategy of multiple narrators, each of whom narrates two sections, again emphasizes the illusion of referential access to a particular character when in fact the novel, taken as a whole, settles firmly on the side of illusion by pitting the various sections (and the characters to whom those sections pertain) against one another. While the subsequent chapters detail an almost frenetic level of activity, in most cases, this activity is repetitive and does not satisfy the characters in any substantial way beyond the opportunity to emote and to attempt to meet their physical needs such as food, drugs, and sex.

The first chapter sets the stage for all of the chapters to come. David—the messenger, or *mensaka*, to whom the title of the novel alludes—reports, with a kind of camera-like vision, his comings and goings on his Vespa as he collects and delivers packages from various locations in Madrid. Into the factual report he inserts his own internal discourse—and the discourse of others, although sometimes the characters speak aloud only to themselves or to the faceless masses—and his semi-stream-of-consciousness thoughts: "Y por el camino todavía le estoy dando vueltas a muchas cosas y pienso que como el tema este salga bien Bea tú dejas tu curro inmediatamente y yo le meto al jefe la moto por el culo aquí lo que pasa es que el que tiene pelas es el rey y los demás tontos" [And on the road I'm still turning over everything and I think that if this goes well, Bea, you can leave your job immediately and I'll tell my boss where to put the bike here what happens is that whoever makes money is king and everybody else are idiots].[56] While the author has clearly chosen to approximate a more disjointed narrative style, the lack of punctuation only serves to highlight the fact that the characters, when they break into this alternative mode, are only skimming the discursive surfaces. They tend to reveal little (if any) conscious self-awareness or engage in any intimate interactions with others, be they strangers or familiars.

As one example, in the first chapter, David encounters numerous people in the course of his movement across the thoroughfares of Madrid. For the most part, he alienates these strangers by failing to observe the social rituals required by differences in social class, occupation, gender, and/or age; likewise, he constantly articulates his own sense of isolation and difference and acts out his resulting hostility, anger, and possible paranoia. When a group of children laugh at him, he responds, "Miro al pepino, mosqueado, y luego les miro a ellos y meneo la cabeza. Paranoias tuyas, David. Me pongo los guantes, estornudo un momento y le doy a los pedales.

Mi cara debe de estar toda roja, a causa del frío, y encima estoy de mala hostia. Tratar con gentuza siempre me pone de mala hostia" [I look at the dickhead, irritated, and then I look at the others and shake my head. You are paranoid, David. I put on my gloves, I sneeze for a minute, and I start up the bike. My face is probably all red because of the cold and on top of that I'm in a bad mood. Dealing with jerks always puts me in a bad mood].[57] This is only one of many such incidents in the initial chapter, but it aptly characterizes David as solipsistic and "out of time," in multiple senses of the phrase. Like Vania, he is stuck in an endlessly repeating loop of self-perpetuating subjectivity, and like her, his drive toward synchrony costs him dearly.

On the one hand, he seeks out and engages in social interaction, but on the other hand, he repeatedly experiences and gives voice to the absence of intimacy. Although there is no clear central character, David's (mis)fortunes would seem to ground the novel. His perspective initiates the narrative action; he is the sacrificial victim who is eventually assigned responsibility for his friend Ricardo's transgression—namely, his refusal to compensate drug dealers (one of whom, not coincidentally, happens to be Javi's sister, Laura) for goods purchased, sold, and consumed. The dissatisfied merchants take out their frustrations on David, who has allowed Ricardo to live in his house and who has also verbally defended his so-called friend, by beating the former to the point that he spends five months in the hospital recuperating from the physical trauma and is replaced in the band, which was on the cusp of signing the ever-elusive record deal.

Other plotlines include Javi's brief relationship with Cristina, a heroin addict, who trades him sex for drugs and is then framed, while in Javi's bedroom in the house he shares with his parents and his sister, for the theft of the mother's jewelry (stolen in reality by Laura); the frustrated interactions between David's girlfriend, Bea, and Ricardo and between her and Ramón, the band's manager, with whom she has a one-night stand; the discussions and conflicts between Fran and Natalia. All of these plotlines diverge and converge in seemingly arbitrary permutations, but they in fact serve to cement temporal and relational stagnation and violence.

The final epilogue both reiterates and departs from the rest of the novel. Like the opening interview, the narrative situation of the epilogue is decidedly more objective in that it features an observing narrator who focuses on, but does not focalize, the actions and reactions of David, who has spent the five months between the last segment of the main text and the epilogue recovering from the beating that occurred at the hands of Laura and friends at the conclusion of the sixteenth segment. The epilogue also returns to the first chapter, narrated and focalized by David, in which he traverses the streets of Madrid on his motorbike delivering and picking up packages. This time, however, he meets up with Fran and Natalia, who deliver the news that he has been replaced in the band by a new drummer. The "brillo feroz en los ojos" [ferocious shine in his eyes] that accompanied his arrival has faded to something much less optimistic: "Sus ojos han perdido el brillo animal que traían al entrar en el bar. Ahora tienen un brillo mortecino, mate" [His eyes have lost the animal shine that they had when he entered the bar. Now they have the dull look of someone who's dying].[58] When faced with the loss of his dreams and illusions, David does not opt for a confrontational response; rather, he feigns an optimistic rejoinder:

> "Lo comprendes, ¿verdad?"
> David gira la cabeza a medias.
> "Sí, claro. No pasa nada. Por mí no te preocupes. Saldré adelante" fuerza la sonrisa. "Os veré en el próximo concierto."
> David abre la puerta del bar.

> ["You understand, right?"
> David turns his head halfway around.
> "Yeah, sure. No big deal. Don't worry about me. I'll be OK." He forces a smile. "I'll see you at the next concert."
> David opens the door to the bar.][59]

Like *Veo veo* and other novels in the subgroup of neorealism, *Mensaka* chronicles the trials, tribulations, and subculture of a discrete demographic of Spain's disaffected youth. And like these novels, it makes abundant use of the linguistic and cultural codes that identify this group. At the heart of this and other novels, however, lies an all-encompassing interest in, commitment to, and excavation of the dynamics of intersubjectivity and alterity. The novel is deeply social, even if the relationships do not appear to afford many positive or affirmative effects. These characters face each other, but they do not look at each other. They frantically search for the same—to see themselves reflected in and projected back to themselves. Theirs is a closed world, an environment that produces empty rituals, repetitive action, meaningless dialogue, and a closed synchrony. Perception is emphasized, but it is not productive. Language succeeds only at the most obvious level; the characters communicate basic needs and information but do not speak or listen to one another.

On the surface, *Mensaka* would seem to privilege face-to-face (in both senses of the term) interaction. Characters speak and think aloud, and the two are often synonymous. Self-expression is viewed and presented as pivotal to self-awareness, construction of subjectivity, and social coherence. However, the novel reveals that sociality is merely a cover for intense egotism. In Mañas's novel, the violence of the same is reinforced and repeated almost to the point of parody. The reader is faced with an intensely social novel; as the protagonist thinks to and about himself, "David es diferente. Ese es el problema: es demasiado diferente" [David is different. That's the problem: he's too different].[60]

Veo veo, *El frío*, and *Mensaka* collectively explore the tragedy of solitude as an illusory antidote to present trauma. The time of the other must be subsumed again and again through the fiction of synchrony. Suffering forges coherence and forswears futurity. The internal causality of the individual displaces and fractures all possible futures and, therefore, any notion of alterity. By the same token, the novels conclusively critique egology in terms of the collective frustration and frigidity of human desire. If we read the texts allegorically, we can discern the inevitable traces of Spain's painful exclusionary history in the nuanced conflicts between the individual and the collective, past and present, universalism and pluralism, Same and Other. Taken together, the novels by Bustelo, Sanz, and Mañas exhort us to consider again and always the price of temporal mastery and the promise of ethical responsibility.

4

The Betrayal of Diachrony

El secreto de Sara, Anatol y dos más, and *Tocarnos la cara*

No sabiendo cuándo llegará el amanecer,
abro todas las puertas
—Emily Dickinson, "LXXXIX"

To be conscious is to have time—not to overflow the present
by anticipating and hastening the future, but to have a distance
with regard to the present; to relate oneself to being as to a
being to come, to maintain a distance with regard to being even
while already coming under its grip. To be free is to have time to
forestall one's own abdication under the threat of violence.
—Emmanuel Levinas, *Totality and Infinity*

Like the novels discussed in the earlier chapter, Tino Pertierra's
El secreto de Sara (1996), Blanca Riestra's *Anatol y dos más* (1996),
and Belén Gopegui's *Tocarnos la cara* (1995) are quintessentially
relational, and the relations are oriented toward claiming ethical responsibility for, and responsiveness to, the Other through
time. Moreover, in all of the novels considered in chapters 3 and 4,
the subjects succumb to sameness because they commit to a

chronology, and they thus doubly impose *their* time onto the other or alterity; each fictional text eclipses otherness by accentuating the causality of the past, the preservation of the present, and the foreclosure of the future. Whereas *Veo veo*, *El frío*, and *Mensaka* offer up narrative perspectives that purposefully (and immediately) acquire coherence through the violent imposition of self onto Other, in the novels by Pertierra, Riestra, and Gopegui, the temporally bound subjects boldly *attempt*—albeit fleetingly—to make time for the face-to-face relationship even as they eventually return to themselves and co-opt the other into their own histories.

If the novels analyzed in chapter 3 unevenly reinforce the power of synchrony, then the trio of novels discussed here exposes a second approach to the art of time. I propose that this approach paradoxically exhorts, but ultimately postpones, ethical responsibility. In other words, the novels by Pertierra, Riestra, and Gopegui temporarily point toward diachrony, or the lapse of time that does not return, before giving way to totality by means of deferral. If, as Emmanuel Levinas tells us, "consciousness is resistance to violence, because it leaves the time necessary to forestall it,"[1] then the three novels considered in the present chapter summon and then evade alterity, eventually disrupting the urgency of ethical responsibility for and to the other. Although fictional narrative now begins to exceed the violence of synchrony and the limits of Levinas's own inherited prejudices regarding art, it ultimately falls prey to the totalizing impulses of egology over time.

In chapter 3, I invoked Levinas's early consideration of temporality vis-à-vis alterity in *Time and the Other* in order to sketch the contours of synchrony. I now turn to his first major book-length treatise, *Totality and Infinity* (1961), for an extended meditation on the summoning and delay of alterity. Here he resumes his elaboration of the temporal dimension of alterity even as he initially favors spatial images to provide the scaffolding for his evolving theory.[2] This means that Levinas's own prose unwittingly animates that which he critiques on at least two fronts. First, he prioritizes space, and particularly the space that the self understands and inhabits, over time, which has the potential in Levinas's own thought to anticipate being. And second, his continuous reliance on images, and more particularly on metaphors, belies a (perhaps unconscious) debt to literary language and to narrative more broadly conceived, as I will discuss further in chapter 5.

One may discern in *Totality and Infinity* at least three goals: to critique the foundations of Western philosophy as constructed upon the notion of *totality*, to articulate and dismantle the basic premises of Heideggerian phenomenology, and to hypothesize the Other, or the personal you, as otherness more generally with the aid of metaphors that encompass exteriority, habitation, love, and fecundity. As was evident in his previous work, a primary and insurmountable separation between self and other resides at the heart of the philosophical argument that comprises *Totality and Infinity*, and alterity both constitutes the metaphysical grounds that make such a separation possible and displays the separation within an increasingly temporal dimension; the self exists because, and not in spite of the fact that, the Other is irreconcilable with *and prior to* it.

Levinas also begins to hinge this exchange to language in declarations such as the following: "Every language as an exchange of verbal signs refers already to this primordial word of honor. The verbal sign is placed where someone signifies something to someone else. It therefore already presupposes an authentification of the signifier."[3] Here and throughout the volume, he prioritizes language as an intrinsically verbal event that occurs in the context of the Said, or the signifier. He will explicitly revise this formulation in his second book-length treatise, *Otherwise Than Being, or Beyond Essence* (1974), first published in English in 1981,[4] which I will examine in chapter 5.

Throughout much of *Totality and Infinity*, Levinas aligns alterity with infinity, theorized as "characteristic of a transcendent being as transcendent; the infinite is the absolutely other."[5] He postulates infinity, modeled partially on Cartesian infinitude, at this juncture in his argument in resolutely spatial terms as beyond, exterior, and distant: as Severson summarizes Levinas's thought here, "The other disturbs the [Hegelian] system primarily by introducing a *distance* or *transcendence* too exterior for assimilation into the system."[6] Within the Levinasian paradigm, as explained in *Totality and Infinity*, time registers either as economic, historical, constitutive—and therefore as the consolidation of sameness or synchrony and as an impediment to alterity—or as happiness, dwelling, and the instant, all of which create a primordial *space* for the encounter between self and other.[7] Exhortation and postponement are thus far hypothesized in spatial terms.

By the last part of section 2, however, Levinas has mitigated his reliance on spatial tropes in order to begin to trace the temporally expansive plurality of alterity. Shifting away from the ideas of Descartes regarding time, he claims, "For relationship between separated beings to be possible, the multiple terms would have to be partially independent and partially in relation."[8] He then develops the solution to this paradox by formally acknowledging time as *the* decisive factor for alterity in the third part of section 3, significantly subtitled "The Ethical Relation and Time":

> A being independent of and yet at the same time exposed to the other is a temporal being: to the inevitable violence of death it opposes its time, which is postponement itself. It is not finite freedom that makes the notion of time intelligible; it is time that gives a meaning to the notion of finite freedom. Time is precisely the fact that the whole existence of the mortal being—exposed to violence—is not being for death, but the "not yet" which is a way of being against death, a retreat before death in the very midst of its inexorable approach.[9]

Levinas fills his philosophical deliberations with paradoxes: the temporality of being is both independent of and exposed to alterity, exposure to the other postpones violence and death and the violence of death, and human freedom is both finite and open-ended, and it derives from our temporal position vis-à-vis the other. Levinas here understands literal and metaphorical violence as the supreme act of totality, the rejection of the face, and the exclusion of exteriority.[10] In the previously cited passage, and throughout the ensuing eighty pages of *Totality and Infinity*, he contests

Heidegger's supposition that being is essentially temporal by arguing that prior to temporal essence or synchrony, there stretches "the other who, as infinity, opens time, transcends and dominates the subjectivity (the I not being transcendent with regard to the other in the same sense that the other is transcendent with regard to me)."[11]

Levinas thus theorizes ontology anew—as asymmetrically relational and therefore inescapably temporal: because my indebtedness to the Other, who owes nothing to me, precedes my being, there can be no origin, no first cause, and neither can there "be" a future. Rather, as he had already indicated (but not fully elucidated) in *Time and the Other*, "the future is what is not grasped, what befalls us and lays hold of us. The other is the future. The very relationship with the other is the relationship with the future."[12] If ethical responsibility anticipates being, and if the self can only approach, but never arrive at, the Other, then alterity can only be conceived, perceived, and received temporally; the present and presence of the self are graspable solely through the unknowable future, or the noncoincidence of the other and the Other.

Throughout *Totality and Infinity*, Levinas deploys, among other images, the intertwined metaphors of hospitality and the face because, in combination, they signal the unbounded and anterior responsibility for the other with which the self enters into both consciousness and time: I do not acquire this responsibility—this debt to the Other and to others—as I move through, and forward into, time; rather, my entry into subjectivity and into being is always already framed by, and emerges from, an earlier, and therefore *temporal*, structure of welcome, or the face-to-face relationship. Levinas had, in the initial section of *Totality and Infinity*, conceptualized the "face-to-face welcome" as beyond cognition: "The conjuncture of the same and the other, in which even their verbal proximity is maintained, is the *direct* and *full face* welcome of the other by me. This conjuncture is irreducible to totality; the 'face to face' position is not a modification of the 'along side of.' . . . Even when I shall have linked the Other to myself with the conjunction 'and' the Other continues to face me, to reveal himself in his face."[13] Ethical responsibility inheres in the subject who must welcome, by facing toward, the other, who transcends both being and chronology; the other's *face*, which substantiates the "and" of relationality, provokes reflection on the part of the perceiving self, but that reflection is dedicated to "a calling into question oneself, a critical attitude which is itself produced in face of the other and under his authority."[14] Levinas here complicates the vector of spatiality in his argument, but he does not incorporate temporality as an alternative, or temporality as linked to the authority of alterity, until some 150 pages later.

The concept of relational time as alterity rests on postponement—the postponement of violence, war, and death so that the infinite other, as the site of ethical epiphany, can "open time" to asymmetricality. Delay discovers anticipation and clears chronology such that the face-to-face welcome, manifested through language, precedes the subject's will and freedom. As Levinas writes, "Meaning is the face of the Other, and all recourse to words takes place already within the primordial face to face of language. Every recourse to words presupposes the comprehension of the primary signification, but this comprehension, before being interpreted as a 'consciousness of,' is society and obligation."[15] Society, understood in the most expansive sense as relationship, and ethical obligation thus pave the way (and the time) for individual consciousness, and Levinas moves, by the final pages of *Totality and Infinity*, to embrace the metaphysical impact of his claim regarding temporality. He will fully engage the correlation among language, temporality, and alterity in *Otherwise Than Being*. In the meantime, however, the three novels that I will now analyze exemplify the challenges of retroaction, postponement, and temporal discontinuity. The subjects in and of *El secreto de Sara*, *Anatol y dos más*, and *Tocarnos la cara* all endeavor to welcome alterity, to face toward the diachrony of the other, but the pressures and trauma of chronology throw them backward into synchrony, and there they will remain for the foreseeable future.

I begin with Pertierra's short novel *El secreto de Sara* (1996),[16] in which diachrony interrupts only briefly the consolidation of totality and synchrony. The text details the aborted attempt of the protagonist-narrator, Teresa Flores, to approach (and intervene in) the time of the Other through a divisive reunion with her mother, Sara, who lies on the cusp of death. Teresa relentlessly pursues her objective by delving into the divergent and convergent histories of daughter and mother and then stitching into them, in the present tense, an imaginary familial bond. In the process, she reconstructs her mother's revelatory biography—thanks in part to a chorus of supporting characters—and she also recuperates her own memories and then imprints them onto her evaluation of Sara's difference. The daughter also eventually settles on a present-past dialectic in the guise of an illusory "happily ever after" instead of any other-wise future.

Although the narrative action bounces forward and backward toward diachrony, shuttling between secrets and disclosures and between ethical obligation and independence, the novel ultimately celebrates synchrony by subsuming the a priori responsibility of the self for the other into the subject's demand for temporal continuity. In advancing her distinct and, according to the narrative logic presented in the novel, superior consciousness via time, Teresa successfully avoids futural alterity in favor of a "whole" (and uninterrupted) past, and she thereby turns away from, and not toward, the welcoming face of the other, eschewing ethical responsibility altogether.

The narrative action and the first-person perspective solder "then" and "now" to one another in spite of the strong initial pull of otherness proffered by *El secreto de Sara*. Teresa, a successful journalist, is summoned by relatives to Sara's hospital bed in Noega[17] some weeks after the older woman has suffered a cerebral edema, has lost her memory, and hovers in medical limbo. On the heels of a seventeen-year absence, the rebellious daughter now strives to understand, and thus make peace with, her overbearing and emotionally distant mother as well as her familial past. Sara's attending physician recommends that, as a parting gift, Teresa recover the story of her mother's life and retell it to Sara, who currently can recall nothing and no one: "Podrías hacer un reportaje sobre tu madre. Creo que ella agradecería saber lo que fue su vida antes de dejarla" [You could do an article on your mother. I think she would be grateful to know her life before leaving it].[18] To this end, Teresa interviews several key people who knew Sara in her youth, she unearths and sorts out multiple mysteries regarding her own fraught paternity, she strings together a basic outline of her mother's biography, and she invents a false history that she recounts to her mother days before the latter's death. In so doing, the prodigal daughter appears to have effectively amended the gaps in her own personal chronology and, as a prospective reward, pursues a promising romance with her mother's doctor, which is then projected onward into the presumably felicitous future of the couple.

Composed of twenty-four discrete segments, Pertierra's novel oscillates between nine chapters in the narrative present, delineated sequentially according to the days of the week, and thirteen consecutively numbered chapters that roll out the narrative past.[19] When considered together, the two temporal strands summon up the discordant genealogy (and successive dissipation) of the mother and daughter's estrangement from one another, but the braided time zones display unequally because the daughter's self-justification, judgment, and push to know prevail over all other interlocutory interventions. Furthermore, the time-specific chapters are enclosed by a prologue and an epilogue, both of which Teresa configures.[20]

The narrative also incorporates a chain of microtexts by secondary characters who speak or write about the history that they once shared with the now silent Sara; they thus recover the past and insert it into the present, and Teresa effects a similar operation by "representing" all of the stories about Sara and then subsuming all discourse authored by others into her own. Although the adult daughter corroborates the unknowability of Sara's time in the present, when confronted with the ethical claims of her mother's unfamiliar history, the narrator subsumes the other into herself and her time, thus shunning the responsibility, and the time, of alterity. Revision begets synchrony, and any potential for diachrony fades as the novel (and Teresa's quest for the temporal control) progresses.

The chapters allotted to the chronology and chronologies of Teresa and Sara Flores assume two guises throughout *El secreto de Sara*: Teresa revisits and stokes the resentments toward her mother that permeated her youth and adolescence, and a parade of acquaintances offers direct insight into Sara's heretofore opaque past. In the first series of encounters, many of which involve her own memories, the protagonist methodically gathers evidence to vindicate once more her sudden flight from home at the age of eighteen, and in the second, she hears and reads testimonies to Sara's enduring struggles and sacrifices. These testimonies feature oral responses from her mother's sister, Eva, and Sara's best friend, Laura; a fragment of the written memoir by her mother's first lover, Dr. Víctor Márques; a letter from Teresa's father, Roberto, to Sara on the eve of the couple's honeymoon; and several conversations with "Tío Vari," Teresa's uncle and Eva's husband. Ever the consummate commentator, Teresa attempts to shadow her mother into diachrony by "conversing" with those who knew Sara best, but the protagonist in fact only exports their replies into her own narrative, effectively subsuming her mother into herself and her mother's history into her own.

As one from among many instances of the daughter's overwhelming presence in the present, Sara's sister responds orally to questions—put forth by Teresa but not included in Teresa's narrative—about their parents, their childhood, and the young Sara's affinity for poetry and music. Eva's answers temporarily elide the disjunctions between mother and daughter, but Teresa's invisible authority envelops her aunt's recollections and already directs Sara's future, as corroborated by Eva's final declaration to Teresa, which she utters at the conclusion of both the interview and the chapter in which said interview occurs: "De todos modos, eso es algo que decides tú, ya ves que yo he hablado con toda sinceridad y no te he ocultado nada. ¿No es eso lo que querías?" [In any case, that is something that you will decide, you see that I've talked with complete sincerity and I haven't hidden anything. Isn't that what you wanted?].[21] Immediately prior to this moment, Eva has intimated that she and Teresa will likely continue to collaborate in their recovery of Sara's story and that the interviewer would do well to soften and blur certain details, presumably to protect the presently vulnerable Sara from having to relive painful experiences from her past. Although Teresa ultimately heeds her aunt's advice by creating an alternative history for her mother, she does so by erasing the other and terminating her investigation into Sara's chronology once she has uncovered the secrets most relevant to her own personal history.

This temporal seesaw reaches an apotheosis with Roberto's suicide note, placed climactically at the close of the penultimate "day" chapter. The brief letter reaches Teresa (and the reader) "out of time" because the narrator reads the document covertly in the present of the narrative action and only after deceiving her uncle into believing that she will dispose of the unopened letter. In his confession to Sara, made some thirty-seven years earlier, Roberto gestured toward an unknown future, which resulted from a cryptic past. He accounted for his impending death in sacrificial terms: "No quiero que pases toda tu vida desgraciada sólo por poder dar un apellido a tu hijo. Si algún día ves a su verdadero padre, dile que yo nunca he llegado a ser rival en tu corazón. Eso le llenará de orgullo. Adiós" [I don't want you to live an unfortunate life only in order to give your child a last name. If someday you see the child's true father, tell him that I never became a rival in your heart. That will fill him with pride. Good-bye].[22] It is highly doubtful that the proposed meeting between her mother and Víctor Márques, Teresa's biological father, ever took place because, according to Víctor's memoir, Sara abandoned her first employer's house without ever informing him or his parents that she was pregnant with his child. Furthermore, Víctor has maintained his ignorance for more than three decades. Teresa, by contrast, has, as of this moment in her story, already met with him (although neither seemingly knew of their blood tie), and she now stands in for the intended recipient of the letter.

The revelatory impetus of *El secreto de Sara* pervades every aspect of Pertierra's novel, conflating Sara's secret(s) and Sara-as-secret. In both formulations, personal chronicles explain and make legible the present, and Sara's chronology supplements Teresa's current angst. The disclosure of secrets, and especially the riddle of Teresa's paternity, presses the future into service as the "natural" consequence of knowledge concerning the past. For her part, Sara discovers nothing in the course of Teresa's investigation because she remembers nothing, she cannot speak for herself, and she exists primarily as a temporary physical addendum and permanent emotional complement to her daughter—a suffering other far removed from the perceiving subject. Teresa, on the other hand, efficaciously employs her mother's history to rationalize and resolve her own present emotional difficulties and to press (herself) on into the future, a future that includes no ethical responsibility and no others.

Once Sara's enigmas (which pivot on the enigmas of others) are solved, her value to Teresa's narrative, and to Teresa's present, wanes, and the mother's time is absorbed into her daughter's predictable, and predictably contiguous, future. But Teresa's present-tense narration initially resists the temporal weight of synchrony and solipsistic absorption. In a curious echo of Levinas's preface to *Totality and Infinity*, the prologue to *El secreto de Sara* refers to both the termination of Sara's life and the end of the narrative present, but it also breaks with chronology. After doggedly insisting, in the initial paragraphs, on the primacy of her "self" (and *only* her "self") as the compass for the subsequent story, Teresa articulates her debt to her mother, stating, "Gran parte de lo que soy se lo debo a mi madre" [I owe a large part of who I am to my mother].[23]

Although the reference to debt jibes with Levinas's understanding of alterity, two lines later, the narrator ostensibly jettisons all that she has learned about her mother's time in favor of the significance of such knowledge for her own time: "Estos dos últimos meses transcurridos desde su accidente hasta su muerte, ocurrida esta mañana, han convertido el rencor en algo parecido a la comprensión. Y en lástima, por ella y también por mí, dos desconocidas que sólo se miraron a los ojos cuando ya era demasiado tarde" [These past two months, from her accident to her death this morning, have transformed rancor into something like understanding. And into pity, for her and also for me, two strangers who only looked one another in the eye when it was too late].[24] The protagonist's early statement temporarily abjures the equivalence, exhibited throughout her narrative, between any meaningful return to the past and to past suffering. Now she claims compassion and pity as solid bridges between her time and Sara's time, even though she acknowledges in the present tense of her story that it "was" already too late.

In the previous quote, the narrator also minces few words in the first (and paradoxically, the last) of many such descriptions of the physical and emotional chasms between the two women. Although she belatedly recognizes temporality as a crucial facet of her mother's lingering alterity, Teresa simultaneously assigns to herself the role of the stranger and thus "forgets" her debt of ethical responsibility to her mother and, by extension, to all others—be they Sara's others or her own.[25] Her mother's death, the finality of not-being, could have, later in the narrative, triggered the daughter's awareness and admission of her ethical debt and postponed, perhaps indefinitely, the narrator's return to sameness and totality, but it does not. Instead, the phantasm of alterity recedes into a distant and unremarkable past, absorbed into the self's need to know and her triumphant restoration of temporal continuity.

At no time is this more palpable than in the moment before Teresa relays to Sara her fictitiously happy past: "Uno mi mirada a la suya y compartimos enigmas y secretos, malentendidos y temores, dudas y sinsabores, fracasos y deslices, tristeza e incomprensión. De nada te sirve ya la verdad. Sólo sería útil una conversación entre la niña que fui y la madre que fuiste, en la que yo pudiera hacerte las preguntas que sólo ahora conozco y tú pudieras darme las respuestas que ya no conoces" [I join my gaze with hers and we share enigmas and secrets, misunderstandings and fears, doubts and heartaches, failures and indiscretions, sadness and incomprehension. Truth doesn't help you anymore. It would only be useful to have a conversation between the girl that I was and the mother that you were, in which I could ask you the questions that I know only now and you could give me the answers that you no longer know].[26] Although she speaks directly to, and also about, Sara, the protagonist's words provoke precious little response—in part because her interlocutor is, in a very real sense, beyond language and beyond Teresa's time and in part because Teresa has already determined Sara's response, which, not surprisingly, resembles her own. According to the protagonist's account of their "encounter," they now share the same vision of the present, and the narrator overdetermines the future by refashioning it to accommodate their manufactured common past, about which they could supposedly converse only if each woman could recuperate her own self.

Interestingly, Teresa has gathered knowledge into her hypothetical "now," whereas Sara has lost meaning and access to any time, be it past, present, or future. In the present moment of the narrative, the mother can only see through the eyes of the daughter. In confirmation, after Teresa regales her mother with a fabricated tale of propitious endings, Sara finally speaks; she haltingly queries her daughter "¿He . . . sido . . . feliz?" [Have I . . . been . . . happy?],[27] to which her only child responds in the affirmative. The narrator has successfully remade her mother's history in accordance with her own desire, and Sara expires shortly thereafter. Fairytale endings in the present clearly trump previous suffering and future possibility.

What does Pertierra's novel imply about the nexus between futurity and alterity? The role of memory in the approach to alterity bears mentioning at this juncture. As Levinas himself declares, "Memory is founded on this incorruptibility of the past, on the return of the I to itself,"[28] and the function of memory, in *El secreto de Sara* and in the subsequent novels analyzed in this chapter, is certainly to facilitate the subject's recognition of herself. Jeffrey Dudiak helpfully explains Levinas's understanding of memory: "Being, disengaged from its being in the dispersal of sensations that is the temporalization of time, is re-collected by the memory, gathered . . . into an identity, wherein the temporality of time, modification without change, is gathered into a present, that is, brought into correlation with a consciousness that identifies it as the same."[29] In the particular instance of *El secreto de Sara*, Teresa narrates in both past and present, as if she is able to transcend any and all discontinuities thanks to the power of her words and her memories.

Pertierra's novel also suggests that the protagonist's future will be an extension of the harmony that she has fashioned between past and present, in which all enduring conflicts between her and her mother have evaporated. Sara's timely death has removed any obstacles or resistance—any fissures that would interrupt the smooth temporal surface of Teresa's consciousness. But the narrator is also strangely "out of time" because her mother's history continues to encroach, literally and figuratively, upon Teresa's present. To that end, and in the last line of the epilogue, Teresa opens her deceased mother's wallet to find a carefully folded newspaper article. The reader vicariously inhabits Teresa's time as she narrates her reaction, presumably for the first time, to the document: "Lo saco. Está amarillento y doblado varias veces. Lo despliego. Es una página entera. Reconozco la cabecera, reconozco el estilo de la maquetación, reconozco el contenido y un escalofrío me atraviesa el cuerpo de arriba abajo: 23-F: *LA NOCHE MÁS LARGA* / por Teresa Flores" [I take it out. It is yellowing and folded several times. I unfold it. It is one complete page. I recognize the heading, I recognize the style of the layout, I recognize the content and I shiver shoots through my body from head to foot: 23-F: *THE LONGEST NIGHT* / by Teresa Flores].[30] Sara had carried tangible evidence of her daughter's professional success through the years, even as that document now reduces the dead woman to a mere addendum in the narrator's voracious campaign for self-confirmation and synchrony. However, instead of transitioning into future relationships, Teresa now recognizes that the past has fully eclipsed the present, and in this moment, it has also fully overtaken the future. The narrating subject(s) will also temporarily recuperate the time of the other(s) in the next novel to be considered.

Blanca Riestra's debut novel, *Anatol y dos más* (1996),[31] might not immediately seem to be pertinent to an exploration of aborted diachrony as thus far elaborated in the present chapter. Associated explicitly, and for the duration of the narrative action, with the iconic city of Santiago de Compostela, the text would appear to prioritize spatial dynamics, as the three principal characters alternately cling to their shared residence or wander through cafés, bars, and streets.[32] The narrative also alludes repeatedly to the rainy and chilly climate of Galicia as an allegory for the emotional states, perceptions, and consciousness of the protagonists. Human experience is measured by Levinas's "clock time": the days accumulate into months, which pour forth into a year; the time of interiority (with its illusion of freedom) is ubiquitous, and the novel pointedly eulogizes sensations and sensorial experience. *Anatol y dos más* cannot, however, be reduced to or contained by thematizable chronology or temporal essence because the ethical demands of alterity jeopardize the synchrony of both the narrator and the narration.

In the "here and now," the principle perceiving subject, in the present and in the past, attempts to make time for the face-to-face encounter with the other by postponing—albeit momentarily—his awareness of any future. He tries to approach alterity by delaying self-sufficiency and self-awareness in the recollected present instead of responding to the anticipation of diachrony. It could well be argued that the narrator-protagonist cannot reverse the force of his own time making, but the protagonist of Riestra's novel nonetheless finally grasps that the future of the other will continue to elude him because his ethical debts remain unpaid in the present. In other words, because he is compelled to document his history and to imprint it on others, he cannot sustain the face-to-face welcome (or time) of the other.

Anatol y dos más surveys the creation, evolution, and dissolution of a triangular friendship, nurtured during a single year, among three university students: Pepe, Gustavo, and Paula. From their home base of a damp three-bedroom apartment in the heart of Santiago, the threesome embarks on a string of encounters with the city's residents and with one another. These interactions are narrated consecutively, as they must be, but they retain an aura of coincidence, randomness, and singularity. The first-person narrator,

Pepe, studies economics at the nearby university and aspires, like Teresa in *El secreto de Sara* and Sandra in Belén Gopegui's *Tocarnos la cara*, to be a writer. By all accounts, his efforts on both fronts are lackluster, and when he reads his prose to his friends, they respond less than enthusiastically.

Riestra's novel incorporates, perhaps more so than the other two novels studied in this chapter, disjunctive time lines and narrative positions. In the main, Pepe chronicles in the first person the forward movement of economic time, or Levinas's understanding of essence as interest,[33] in the present. He does so by recording and interlacing the thoughts, words, sensations, and actions of the three friends. Within their time, however, an omniscient narrator (also Pepe) intersperses a series of nine italicized sections, some of which are linked together and all of which are also dedicated to the interior lives of the three companions. In this second narrative strand, Pepe has metamorphosed into Anatol, a name and persona bestowed upon him by Paula, and he effectively recedes in these loosely linked episodes into the role of the author. In both strands, Pepe-as-narrator surveys and articulates his vacillating attraction to both Gustavo and to Paula, who are, he discovers, drawn to one another.[34] When, in the final pages of the novel, he interrupts Gustavo and Paula in the middle of a sexual encounter, the narrator realizes too late that he has been exiled—perhaps permanently—from any future with his friends and beyond himself. In this moment, and from the vantage point of five years after their shared time, the narrator determines his future to be one of stalled interruption: "Y supe que la vida era eso. Supe que la vida era eso" [And I learned that life was just that. I learned that life was just that].[35] The relationship between and among the various times in the novel, together with the precise meaning of *that*, constitute some of the delayed signs of alterity of the novel.

Riestra's text is partitioned into fifty-nine segments, grouped into five "chapters," the titles of which disclose escalating temporal gaps in the chronology of the three friends: First, Second, Ninth, Fifteenth, and Zillionth. What starts out as a strict progression transmutes into the impossible repetition of synchrony framed by the narrator's return to subjectivity. Each delineated section is further subdivided into an irregular number of quasi-independent narrative fragments (six, sixteen, ten, fourteen, and thirteen, respectively), which vary in length from two sentences to five pages. These episodic fragments juxtapose the saga of the trio's year-long relationship, in regular typeface, and the italicized extracts from Pepe's novel in progress. Whereas the first-person narrator sews together past and present in the first chronology, Pepe absents himself from the second line, narrated exclusively in the present tense. The link between these two versions of the same events will rehearse the recognition and eschewal of diachrony.

Like Gabriela Bustelo in *Veo veo* and José Ángel Mañas in *Mensaka*, Riestra leans on epigraphs to anticipate the narrative to come; she juxtaposes unattributed Spanish-language translations of quotations from French poet René Char (1907–1988) and German poet Friedrich Hölderlin (1770–1843).[36] The two writers summon the past into the present while also hinting at an ambiguous future. With Char's "El cielo ya no es tan amarillo ni el sol tan azul. Se anuncia la estrella furtiva de la lluvia" [The sky is no longer so yellow nor the sun so blue. The furtive star of the rain is announced],[37] Riestra switches the colors of the sun and the sky in order to track the migration of time from "then" to "now," and the depiction of the future via an image of rain promises to eclipse the earlier time zones.

Hölderlin's question, "¿Qué es lo que hace que un hombre desee con tanta fuerza?" [What is it that makes a man desire with so much force?],[38] posits an additional cipher, this time about the mystery of human desire. The second epigraph likewise gestures forward and backward in time as the speaker intertwines origin ("¿Qué es . . .") and objectless passion ("desear con tanta fuerza"). And, if the two epigraphs are insufficient indicators of the violence of nostalgia that will inform what is to come, before the formal narrative commences, the author highlights a single line of text on an otherwise blank page, save for the page number: "De cómo el mundo era frágil" [On how fragile the world was].[39] Even though the unattributed sentence anchors history and the human recollection of that history, it intimates that time is neither stable nor solid. And into the potential gaps, Riestra inserts a different story about the exhortation and postponement of alterity.

The text commences *en media res* with the as-yet-unidentified narrator's present-tense rehearsal of Paula's slow ascension to the third-floor apartment that she shares with Gustavo. Notably unkempt and unaccompanied, the young woman labors to climb the stairs: "Cuando llega al descansillo, después de bregar por tramos orinosos y mal iluminados, la escena se repite. Nadie responde a las embestidas. Paula contempla furiosa el Sagrado Corazón sobre la puerta y se decide a empuñar otra vez llavero y paciencia" [When she arrives at the landing by way of urine-filled and badly lighted flights of stairs, the scene is repeated. No one responds to her banging. Paula furiously contemplates the Sacred Heart above the door and decides to once again take hold of her set of keys and her patience].[40] Pepe here erases himself from the scene in order to depict Paula as alone, excluded, and weighed down. He observes and describes her as if from a vast distance, a distance that she will never manage to overcome because she is stuck in a present that is not hers. For the duration of that present, as Pepe recalls it to himself five years later, he and, to a lesser extent, Gustavo will try to face toward her and make time for her, but they will fail because they have already arrived too late to their ethical responsibility for another. In addition, they keep getting in each other's way; although Pepe occasionally remarks on his attraction to (and desire for) his other friend, the two men are sufficiently absorbed with Paula, and they vie for her attention and for the opportunity to rescue her from her constant difficulties.

When Pepe confronts Gustavo, in the narrative present, about the latter's emerging desire for Paula, his times and words collide with one another; after Gustavo himself euphorically repeats Paula's words (which are themselves a repetition of Rimbaud's poem) to Pepe in Pepe's own story, "hubo un silencio. . . . Fue como si hubiese vivido ya otra vez el mismo instante. Un regusto de ceniza y como un vuelco de sensaciones" [there was silence. . . . It was as if I had already lived once again the same instant. An aftertaste of ash and something like a one-hundred-and-eighty-degree switch in sensations].[41] Pepe experiences a time lapse—but one that already [*ya*] returns him to the same instant instead of moving him closer to the diachrony that awaits Gustavo and Paula. The negative effect of delay is corroborated through the images of aftertaste, ash, and the reversal of physical sensation.

The initial scene proves prescient: after the heavily laden Paula finally manages to open the door to their apartment, and as Pepe either observes—or perhaps only imagines that he observes—his housemates, Gustavo engages in idle conversation with Paula as he cleans their shared kitchen. Once he has accomplished his task, he turns off the light and the heater and then summarily closes the door after himself, abandoning the nonreactive Paula to the dark. He returns to the kitchen at some unspecified future moment to find her in the same position, "tan ausente como antes" [as absent as before].[42] Unlike the extroverted Gustavo, the unidentified narrator shadows the vacant woman in "her" time and place, but like his friend, Pepe does not intervene in any meaningful way. Neither he nor Gustavo can gauge or assuage the depth or duration of their friend's suffering, now or later, and Paula's anguish only increases as the year progresses. This same temporal pattern, established in the first pages of the novel, will determine the subsequent narration.

The narrator stakes his claim to the unfolding drama in the following section with "Yo vivo en la habitación que hay al fondo" [I live in the bedroom that there is in the back].[43] In his first overt interaction with another person within the chronology, he does not speak directly to anyone. Instead, he listens to (and reproduces) Paula's judgment on his unspecified errors, which link the histories of others to their shared present. Instead of accepting (or even seeking) any responsibility, however, the narrator swiftly transfers his failings to humankind: "Podría, incluso, jurar que casi todos erramos, que es humano errar, que somos muchos los que erramos y que soy uno más, y no el primero, que ha errado en este mundo cruel. *Pero no tengo tiempo* para alzar la cabeza y hacer acto de contrición" [I could even swear that almost all of us err, that to err is human, that those of us who err are many and that

I am only one more among them, and not the first, to err in this cruel world. *But I don't have time* to raise my head and engage in an act of penance].[44] He has time now for Paula because he has already imposed his consciousness upon her. Both the narrator and Gustavo will return, again and again, to the incomprehensibility of Paula's suffering, but they will not seek its source in their own synchrony. Pepe is especially guilty of eschewing any responsibility for his friend—in part because the character of Gustavo functions as a handy scapegoat and in part because of temporal distance.

Not coincidentally, the next section of the novel, titled simply "Segundo" ["Second"], begins in and with the narrator's memory: "Muchas veces recuerdo como éramos antes, cómo éramos cuando nos conocimos" [Many times I remember how we were before, how we were when we met one another].[45] Later Pepe reveals that he is twenty-four years old and that five years have elapsed since he lived with Paula and Gustavo in Santiago. Like both Teresa in *El secreto de Sara* and Sandra in *Tocarnos la cara*, Pepe establishes and relies on a temporal frame within a temporal frame. Though he will revert periodically to the present of his holistic memory, it is his forged history with his friends that holds him, includes him, and summons to him the ethical responsibility for the Other.

In the nine italicized sections from Pepe's untitled novel, the narrator inserts himself as the character Anatol, a name that reminds Paula of a Russian dancer and a novel by P. G. Wodehouse. The corresponding fragments detail Paula's gradual withdrawal from Pepe, even as she gains more agency and interiority through his narration of her. In the first italicized section, strategically placed after one of many segments replete with the collective voice of *nosotros* [we/us], the unnamed omniscient narrator concentrates almost exclusively on Paula, who has decided not to get out of bed. She imperially summons Anatol, but he retreats before she can coerce him further. In response to her demand for attention, sympathy, and a glass of milk, the narrator casts himself into the third person: "*Anatol ya está a salvo al otro lado del pasillo*" [*Anatol is already safely on the other side of the hall*].[46] In later sections,

Pepe/Anatol will withdraw even further into his future knowledge of her eventual betrayal.

By the last italicized section, positioned in the "Zillionth" chapter, Anatol is entirely absent from Pepe's double narrative and has become merely a topic of conversation for his friends. These friends have stretched to include another writer, Mara, and the two women finalize Pepe's third-person narrative about them by dissecting the limitations of verbal language. Paula is particularly virulent in her assessment: "*Las palabras son como tornillos, tuercas o papeles de envolver. No hay nada detrás. Yo nunca quise volver a escribir. Nunca, fíjate. Desde que supe que las palabras no servían más que para hacer cadenas y collares y chucherías, lo mandé todo a paseo. No me arrepiento*" [*Words are like nuts, bolts, or wrapping paper. There's nothing behind them. I never wanted to return to writing. Never, really. Ever since I learned that words didn't serve any purpose beyond making bracelets and necklaces and cheap stuff, I stopped it all. I'm not sorry*].[47] Given to whom she is speaking, and who is speaking about her in a narrative that is not her own, it would seem that Pepe-the-writer is falling further and further behind the time of his friends and becoming more and more committed to the solipsism of his future and the illusion of authorial freedom.

In addition to serving as the nexus of desire between Pepe and Gustavo, Paula registers as other vis-à-vis the narrator because of her visible and verbal suffering, which distances and separates her. She also attributes her enduring pain to her relationship with the two men: "*Ellos me modelaron, decidieron mi ideología. Amputaron mis historias. Me quitaron la caída y la bondad y la entrega y el tremendismo*" [*They modeled me, they decided my ideology. They amputated my stories. They took away my descent, my kindness, my surrender, my drama*].[48] The fact that she communicates this to Mara, a "new" friend who has replaced Paula in Pepe's daily life, only underscores Paula's encroaching dependence. As if these losses were not enough, she then compares Gustavo and Pepe to parts of her body: "*Uno no se puede independizar de su propio cuerpo. Sólo puede quemarlo. Ellos son parte de mi cuerpo. No puedo prescindir de un riñón o de un brazo"* [*You can't separate yourself from your own body. You can only burn it. They are a part of my body. I can't do without a kidney or an arm*].[49] Her transition from other to an extension of the same is almost complete.

As the novel swings between the narrator's present memory, the novel that he was writing, and the "now" of the past that he shared, at least temporarily, with Gustavo and Paula, anxieties and tension deepen. In Pepe's double narration, Paula grows more self-absorbed and manic, and the two men respond to her and to one another with more distance and desperation. Where Gustavo sees separation, however, Pepe perceives union; as the narrator comments toward the end of the novel, "Gustavo, ella es nosotros. MIERDA. Ella no es otra cosa que nosotros" [Gustavo, she is us. SHIT. She is nothing but us].[50] With these words, he would seem to confirm Paula's own assessment of their relationship.

Desire and memory crash into one another by the end of the novel. Pepe admits, years after the fact, that he had suspected something brewing between his friends but that he was incapable of deciphering its meaning at the time: "Pero sólo adivinando el código secreto de muecas, gestos y estados de ánimos, sólo leyendo en los impermeables pensamientos de mis amigos, hubiese podido adelantar el desenlace" [But only by guessing the secret code of grimaces, gestures, and moods, only by reading into the impenetrable thoughts of my friends, could I have anticipated the outcome].[51] The constant shifting between past and present makes it difficult, if not impossible, to distinguish between then and now—between the year in which the three friends lived together and the future in which Pepe can only relive the past.

Not coincidentally, he recounts the last chapter, and the culminating event in their friendship and their year of discovery, in the past tense. Discovery infuses the final scene with the repletion of *supe* [I learned]. In the midst of his narration, however, he intercedes with yet another present-tense meditation on solitude: "Yo estoy solo pero todos estamos solos. Incluso ellos están solos" [I am alone but we are all alone. Even they are alone].[52] Upon opening the door to Paula's room, Pepe opts for the illusion of objectivity, framed by what he thinks he saw—"Eso fue lo que vi" [That is what I saw][53]—and can later recall to himself. Significantly, he compares the bodies of the lovers to the highly anticipated Galician spring: "Vi dos cuerpos más traspasados que mayo y junio y mucho más húmedos" [I saw two bodies more thoroughly soaked than May and June and much wetter].[54] Pepe "breaks the seesaw" of their mutual desire, and when the two lovers turn toward him, he only has eyes for Paula's nipples, which he describes, in the same passage, as "the jumpy eyes of a lie." The truth of *eso* is revealed to be the prevalence of deceit, and the friendship is now relegated entirely to the deceitful past, where it will be resurrected only through a fictitious and self-repeating memory, which foregrounds loss and stasis. As the novel's title intimates, Pepe has been replaced by Anatol, and the "two others" do not even merit names.

Like the two novels discussed thus far, Belén Gopegui's *Tocarnos la cara* exposes a partial and temporary instance of alterity, which is eventually (re)absorbed into the reigning ontological paradigm of totality by means of synchrony.[55] It might be argued that of the three, Gopegui's text details the most successful instance of sustained diachrony. In her novel, the narrative weaves together, in a tripartite arrangement of consecutive chapters, the activities of an emergent experimental theater group known as El Probador [literally, "The Fitting Room"] and composed of Óscar Azores, Ana Hojeda, Íñigo Martínez, and Sandra, whose last name is never disclosed. El Probador is located in Madrid and directed by Simón Cátero, who convenes the four actors of varying talents. Sandra, the most itinerant of the quartet, records and recalls the creation and dissolution of the collective, transcribes the words and thoughts of the other performers, intercalates some of the documents that influenced Simón's original vision, and takes notes on their training sessions. In a strange melding of temporalities, she claims as her muses both fidelity, which might align with synchrony, and invention, which gestures toward/intimates diachrony. Moreover, as Ignacio Soldevila Durante comments, "Sandra . . . desde la primera frase, manifiesta sus dudas en cuanto a su competencia para contar una historia" [Sandra, from the first sentence, manifests her doubts with respect to her competence to tell a story].[56]

Insofar as she recollects, and thus rereads, the series of events leading toward and away from the foundation and dissolution of El Probador, she organizes historical time, or clock time, and makes the past and the future contingent on a fixed set of texts. Insofar as she purposefully creates the chronology of those events, she incorporates herself and her contemporaries into that time and verifies that her history is their history. While the other actors do have a past, which periodically interrupts the story of El Probador, Sandra repeatedly characterizes herself as a vacant woman, alluding to her lack of employment as well as to her existential isolation. In theory, as she herself proposes, she will be effortlessly shaped, filled, and inserted into time by her relationships with the other members of the theater group. With her peripatetic participation in, and narrative responsibility for, El Probador, she willingly accepts the role of mediator, but to what end? Sandra would seem to be perfectly positioned to face toward, and perpetually await, the future of the other and/or others, but such is not to be the case.[57]

The stated goal of the theater troupe consists of enabling a client's deepest desire, of opening up alterity to the instant, such that the client will emerge from the staged encounter transformed. According to the official program, the selected patron discloses her or his innermost wish to one of the actors, who then projects a human mirror through which the desiring subject may become the optimal image of herself or himself. In contrast to the reduced company of many of the other novels considered throughout the current project, Gopegui's narrative ushers forward an extended community of characters. In addition to the four principal actors, their teacher, and the expanding list of clients, three secondary figures, all of whom are linked to Simón, intervene in the mission and the performances of El Probador. First, Pedro Alexéi works with the actors and arbitrates between them and Simón until he divulges, toward the close of the novel, that he is dying. Second, the journals of José Ángel Espinar lay out the conceptual map for

El Probador, and Sandra reads to us, in the course of the novel, from his written correspondence with Simón. And third, Fátima Uribe, Simón's former wife, founds a competing theater group and persuades some of the actors to join her, thus hastening the demise of her ex-husband's theatrical experiment and, with it, the eclipse of Sandra's narration by Simón.

The members of El Probador believe, at different times, that they will literally touch the face of the Other through their dramatic encounters; as Hayley Rabanal insightfully writes, "Conceived as a face-to-face encounter, the *Probador* can be understood as seeking to establish a foundation for solidarity by trying to make explicit, or render conscious, the dual process of self-determination and recognition of one's responsibility for the other which Levinas argues pre-exists consciousness."[58] In other words, by temporarily effacing their own identities in order to extend to the desiring others an alternative version of themselves, they consider their efforts to be highly ethical. In practice, however, the ideal runs aground from the start because solidarity cannot transcend the violence of sameness. As an early indication, during a preliminary session between Íñigo and a potential client named Pedro, the former charges, "Yo sufro, tú sufres, él sufre. ¿No ves que eso es lo único que pasa? ¿No ves que nadie sabe lo que debe hacer?" [I suffer, you suffer, he suffers. Don't you see that's the only thing going on? Don't you see that no one knows what to do?].[59] Pedro answers by facing Íñigo and substituting in the place of suffering the act of lying. He presumes that otherness is the result of, rather than the precondition for, change. In the exchange cited above, Pedro offers up to Íñigo an uncommon response, one that defines otherness as infinite acceptance and generosity, but he cannot accomplish alterity because he is not obligated to others in the present and because he violently imposes his own unifying past upon them. Similarly, the clients of El Probador studiously avoid presence and the present, their differing presents. In keeping with Levinas's own concerns about art, the actors and their public experience the performances as images, as at least one step removed from the reality of their temporal dissonance from one another.[60]

Against his doubts about literature, however, Gopegui defends the temporality of narrative and the possibility, albeit fleeting, of diachrony, in which the welcoming subject faces toward, and thus takes responsibility for, the other.[61]

The ethical potential of diachrony, the differing of the identical, and the lapse of time that does not return are all marked most directly through the narrative dominance of Sandra. At the outset of Gopegui's novel, Sandra narrates in the present tense about a historical (but not immemorial) past figure, and her narration immediately alludes to the difference and the lapse of time: "Ésta es la historia de un esfuerzo y una desbandada, pero hay algo que no consigo entender. Es como ver un avión parado en el cielo. O como aquel Palacio de los Deportes cuya cubierta de hierro se desplomó" [This is the history of an attempt and an escape, but there is something that I don't understand. How to see an airplane that is stuck in the sky. Or the Sports Pavilion whose iron roof collapsed].[62] When she undertakes to transcribe the story of El Probador, she can only summon up the outline—the temporal shape of the pertinent events rather than the sequence—and she can only secure that shape by means of analogous images; she cannot recall, much less recount, the sound or sight of the destruction that necessarily trails her memory. Like *El secreto de Sara* and *Anatol y dos más*, writing appears to suffer severe limitations in *Tocarnos la cara* because it cannot successfully orient the narrating subject toward alterity; the past eventually overcomes both the present and any possible future.

Sandra attributes to the ensuing chronology that she produces, in the course of her narrative, the heavy promise of forward motion. But instead of knowing, seeing, or relaying continuity, and thereby equating "I think" with "I can,"[63] she situates time in the discontinuities of stories and of human comprehension, both of which eschew Levinas's totality and approach but do not yet arrive at infinity, conceived concisely as the time of the other.[64] As a transcriber of texts and, therefore, as a producer of knowledge, she is assigned the task of converting the current and previous "records" of El Probador into a material discourse and a tangible past. As one of the actors, she is also ethically responsible to her colleagues, to her mentor, and to a greater or lesser degree, to all of the clients who approach the theater group for another future. In an arguably intentional move from epistemology to ethics, she promotes temporal discontinuity by taking on the responsibility of the past as unknowable and ungraspable, but she does not, because she cannot, see into the "future as other."

As only one illustration of her repeatedly doomed efforts to unhinge time from being, early in the overlapping histories of El Probador and Sandra's authorship, she follows Simón to a strip club. He introduces her to a sex worker whom he has renamed Fátima, after his ex-wife, and then proceeds to highlight the potential similarities, known only to him, between the young woman and the original Fátima.[65] In his role as teacher, he instructs Sandra on the particulars of his failed marriage and on his inability to effect change in spite of the surrogate Fátima, who can never return Simón to the site of his definitive happiness. Simon wraps up the scene by reiterating his impotence and by decrying the corporeal return of his ex-wife to Madrid. They will not reunite, but Simón will substitute a series of lovers, including Sandra herself, for Fátima, and Fátima will replace El Probador with her own theater company, staffed by most of Simón's actors. What looks like repetition, however, is in fact temporal noncoincidence, underscored by Sandra's representation of time as discontinuous.

Although Sandra's voice and vision permeate most of the novel, the final section is surprising for its irregularity. She revisits her initial image of the temporally frozen sports pavilion and sees it anew, as if gravity and time have resumed: "Ahora sí: los cables de acero que la sujetaban se han soltado, la cubierta está sola en el aire" [Now yes: the steel cables that used to hold it have been released, the roof is suspended in air].[66] It is but a short step to equate the spectacular disappearance of the supporting roof and the more mundane failures, both temporal and otherwise, of El Probador. Nature is multiple, Sandra contends, thus confirming a translation of pluralism whereby all of the individual elements are equal, whereby responsibility is assumed after individuality, whereby alterity is an effect and not a cause. The actors of El Probador have echoed the fantasies of their peers, which are subsequently their own fantasies, and at the end of the novel, they have all retired to their own stories and to futures that bear a striking resemblance to their desires.

Simón interrupts this homogeneity only after seducing Sandra, and he finalizes the narration with his authoritative account of the past, which confirms his starring role. He integrates Sandra's story into his own, and Sandra's self into his self, and he then determines that she is a reliable witness; he writes that he recognizes himself in her words even though he facetiously maintains that he has become *her* reflection. Unfortunately, he comprehends the relationship between self and other—a relationship that he has been performing, staging, and directing throughout the text—as one of incessant conflict: "Digo también que dos personas cuando se miran se enfrentan. Siempre hay violencia en el hecho de admitir a otro. Hay que violentarse, hay que hacerse fuerte, hay que obligarse a saber que ni toda la comida ni todo el sitio son nuestros" [I say also that when two people look at one another, they confront one another. There is always violence in the fact of admitting the other. One must force oneself, make oneself strong, there is always an obligation to know neither all of the food nor all of the space is ours].[67] The key word in Simón's statement is *admitir* [to admit]. Agency and resolve saturate his description. As the teacher and instigator of the theater group, as well as a self-proclaimed seducer, Simón is anything but receptive, anyone but the Other, despite, or perhaps because of, his pronouncements to the contrary. In this proclamation, Simón enunciates the antithesis of Levinasian alterity, but the difference between *Tocarnos la cara* and *El frío* is that his statement finalizes an otherwise ethical experience. As Levinas himself maintains, "Violence does not consist so much in injuring and annihilating persons as in interrupting their continuity, making them play roles in which they no longer recognize themselves, making them betray not only commitments but their own substance."[68]

By trying to span the distance between sameness and difference, the actors of *Tocarnos la cara* begin where, for example, the lovers of *El frío* left off, at least in theory. Relationality pervades all aspects of Gopegui's novel, and erotic intimacy regularly exceeds the other relationships in a number of ways. First, Simón confesses toward the end of the novel that, unbeknownst to his students, he imagined El Probador as an instrument of revenge. As a prototypical Don Juan figure, Simón also employs El Probador to generate a series of substitutional seductions, first with Ana and later with Sandra. As Sandra herself comments early on, "A diferencia de otros donjuanes, Simón no engañaba para ocultar, sino para exhibir su engaño y que la mujer en cuestión se viera en el deseo de redimirle" [Unlike other Don Juans, Simón didn't deceive in order to hide, but to exhibit his deceit and so that the woman in question would see in herself the desire to redeem him].[69] Significantly, Simón narrates the final twenty pages of Sandra's text in order to intervene in the lofty goals of El Probador. In the place of welcome, generosity, and responsibility, he inserts violence, scarcity, and liability.

Although Sandra opens the novel by claiming that she is relating "la historia de un esfuerzo y una desbandada" [the story of an attempt and a disbanding],[70] her phrase applies equally to several stories displayed throughout the novel. The history of El Probador certainly marks both effort and disbandment, as do all of the erotic histories chronicled in the novel. For Simón, in the constant projection and recuperation of desires and needs, alterity is merely the illusion of permanently postponing his debt to others. But what of the others? The efforts of the theater group, for instance, may finally come undone, but they underscore the call of being for the Other—of exceeding one's own subjectivity in order to put forward hospitality to and assume prior responsibility for the Other. Sandra perhaps comes closest to this welcome by scarcely recalling Simón's seduction of her. Her narrative calls into question his egoism and suggests the prospect of intimacy, even though it is not sustained. She watches and prepares for the signs of otherness, even if those signs have already been co-opted by sameness.

Whereas the novels discussed in the previous chapter all map the damage that comes with the ruin and resurrection of subjectivity, in these novels, the subjects take longer to arrive at synchrony. *El secreto de Sara*, *Anatol y dos más*, and *Tocarnos la cara* all settle on protagonists who, to greater and lesser degrees, face toward the Other by inserting themselves into diachrony and by narrating about the other. But they are not successful because they view alterity from the starting point of their own histories, which presupposes consciousness. In the novels that I consider in the next chapter, the subjects are positioned after alterity and relate to the other by means of diachrony, which expresses through the Saying of language.

5

Diachrony and Saying

Arde lo que será, Sentimental, and *La fiebre amarilla*

Sabem que l'imant atreu la magnetite, però ignorem si la magnetita
també atreu l'imant o hi és arrossegada contra la seva voluntat.
—Sergi Pàmies, *Sentimental*

But to hear a God not contaminated by Being is a human possibility no less
important and no less precarious than to bring Being out of the oblivion
in which it is said to have fallen in metaphysics and in onto-theology.
—Emmanuel Levinas, *Otherwise Than Being, or Beyond Essence*

Instead of defiantly withdrawing into the temporal synthesis
imposed by consciousness and self-sufficiency, as do the subjects
analyzed in chapter 3, or paradoxically pursing others through time
only *after* consolidating subjectivity, like the subjects discussed in
chapter 4, in the novels that I now explore, the subjects face toward
diachrony, answer for the priority of the other, and follow alterity into time through traces of saying. Juana Salabert's *Arde lo que
será* (1996), Sergi Pàmies's *Sentimental* (1995), and Luisa Castro's
La fiebre amarilla (1994) invoke the ethical responsibility for the
other that precedes all genealogical beginning, exceeds the coherence and the chronology of the present, and marks the loss of any
enduring knowledge of the future. To this end, the three novels

respond, in a poignantly literal sense, to Levinas's later thoughts on time, narrative, and ethics as expounded in his second (and final) major treatise, *Otherwise Than Being, or Beyond Essence* (1974/1981).

If time, as theorized previously by Levinas in *Totality and Infinity*, eventually determined the postponement of the ego at the scene and in the narration of ethical alterity, then diachrony, as explicated in *Otherwise Than Being*, stretches before and beyond metaphysical essence to reveal the anarchic priority and anteriority of the other before consciousness and language—indeed, even before relationality. Levinas introduces new concepts and metaphors into his second major treatise in order to conceptualize the next philosophical iteration of alterity. He expands his theoretical base to include not only our ethical debts to the other but our ethical debts to *all* others. In other words, he equates humanity with proximity and proximity with justice, or the inclusion of the third person or the neighbor.

Whereas he concentrated on the face-to-face, exteriority, and love in *Totality and Infinity*, he organizes *Otherwise Than Being* around the metaphysical and, more particularly, the *temporal* disjunctions in and through language, which precede consciousness and thrust us unavoidably into our awareness of ethical debt. And if in the earlier volume he relied on tropes such as fecundity, habitation, and enjoyment to make a compelling case for eschatology as "a relationship with *a surplus always exterior to the totality*,"[1] in his second volume, he elaborates images of the suffering that infuses our relationship to others and to alterity: hostageship, persecution, betrayal, and atonement. In so doing, he effectively takes up where he left off in the last lines of the preface to *Totality and Infinity*: "[The word] belongs to the very essence of language, which consists in continually undoing its phrase by the foreword or the exegesis, in unsaying the said, in attempting to restate without ceremonies what has already been ill understood in the inevitable ceremonial in which the said delights."[2] And in *Otherwise Than Being*, Levinas investigates "unsaying the unsaid" in the context of time.

In both volumes, Levinas continues to inquire after the origins, the expression, and most importantly, the event of the a priori responsibility of ethical alterity. To this end, and in both philosophical venues, he sustains an ongoing dialogue with numerous predecessors who have influenced his thought. These include, most notably, Plato, Descartes, Kant, Hegel, Husserl, Bergson, and Heidegger. While he steadfastly maintains the methodology that he developed during his formative training in phenomenology, in his second treatise, he attempts to exorcise some of the *discursive* obstacles that characterized his previous work. Because of his increased attention to language, and to the pitfalls of invoking language as essence, the differences between the two texts are dramatic and substantive for my argument regarding the art of time. As Diane Perpich cogently observes, *"Totality and Infinity* engaged in an extended narrative that purported to show how a separated and atheist ego could nonetheless come to be commanded by and responsible for an other."[3] In the earlier volume, Levinas started from the fact of subjectivity and attempted to theorize backward in order to arrive at alterity, which then (and only then) could make ethical claims via the face-to-face welcome. Time in this scenario manifested as a turn away from the synchrony wrought by consciousness and toward the diachrony of unknowable (albeit bountiful) origins. In brief, and as many of his commentators have discussed in great detail, in *Totality and Infinity*, Levinas used the philosophical discourse of rationality to postulate an extrarational approach to otherness.

Otherwise Than Being, by contrast, bears witness to Levinas's attempt to counter the language of reason, the language of the ego, in order to hypothesize the priority of the other as radical, enigmatic, and extradiscursive. Rather than the subject returning to an "immemorial past" that is framed by our ethical debt to the other, the other's ethical claims on us precede all subjectivity, all language, all knowledge, and those claims in fact *enable* subjectivity, language, and knowledge. Our ethical responsibility for the other is the anarchic and anachronistic condition of human identity. Moreover, we always arrive too late to take responsibility for the other because our entry into both consciousness and language occurs *after* the fact of alterity; we are constantly too late to assuage the suffering of the other, which is therefore always already our suffering. Because Levinas directly links suffering to alterity, a tone of lament pervades *Otherwise Than Being*.

Against the self-justifying narrative of egoism, from which *Totality and Infinity* could not entirely escape, Levinas now juxtaposes "a lapse of time that does not return, a diachrony refractory to all synchronization, a transcending diachrony."[4] Diachrony, or the temporalization of ethical anteriority, expresses as equivocation and mystery by referencing an irrecoverable and unrepresentable past, prior to consciousness, that thrusts the subject into unavoidable and escalating obligation. Once again, the relational base of Levinasian ethics proffers a measure of coherence: "The relationship with a past that is on the hither side of every present and every re-presentable, for not belonging to the order of presence, is included in the extraordinary and everyday event of my responsibility for the faults or the misfortune of others, in my responsibility that answers for the freedom of another."[5] The freedom of another can never begin in the same present, occupy the same instant, or make itself known to the perceiving subject. Ethical responsibility ensures that an individual consciousness can never subsume the Other by means of duration because the knower is always already located in a chronology that it can never comprehend via consciousness or the language of reason. In short, synchrony continues to constitute the name that Levinas assigns to our illusion of temporal mastery through unity and diachrony—the term by which our experiences of consciousness, the present, and most significant to *Otherwise Than Being*, *language* become graspable *after* we accept the fact of otherness and our ethical answerability to all others.

Levinas tracks his central premise, that as human subjects we arrive too late to the drama of alterity, into the corresponding drama of language by addressing the unresolvable conflict between the said and the saying, which is itself inextricably linked to time.[6] He continually deepens his understanding of the said throughout the volume to encompass essence, the event of being, economic interest, and thematization. The said comprises our conscious access to language as self-expression and communication, which is fraught, incomplete, and prone to the totalizing violence of sameness. He also repeatedly expands and broadens his understanding of saying in *Otherwise Than Being*, commencing with the exposition in the first chapter: "Saying is not a game. Antecedent to the verbal signs it conjugates, to the linguistic systems and the semantic glimmerings, a foreword preceding languages, it is the proximity of one to the other, the commitment of an approach, the one for the other, the very signifyingness of signification."[7] As Levinas's declaration here demonstrates, early in the argument that undergirds *Otherwise Than Being*, he substitutes temporal priority for spatial proximity.

The assignation of anteriority to alterity means that alterity, and our belated arrival to ethical obligation, is fundamentally *temporal*. Because we are late to our responsibility for the other, we enter consciousness already aware of and having substituted ourselves in place of the other's suffering. Alterity is "diachronous," and diachrony is discursive. Levinas thus posits, in line with Husserl, that because consciousness is framed by the temporality of sensation, "temporal modification is not an event, nor an action, nor the effect of a cause. It is the verb to be."[8] The corollary in language of Levinas's "internal time consciousness" lies with the said, or essence, which can be recuperated, remembered, and most dangerously for Levinas, *narrated*. In addition, language displays as a system of nouns while also evincing a surplus: "A word is a nomination, as much as a denomination, a consecrating of the 'this as this' or 'this as that' by a saying which is also *understanding* and *listening*, absorbed in the said."[9] He further aligns saying with obedience to the *already* said, which makes possible language, cognition, and consciousness. Saying corresponds to the anterior movement of alterity: "The signification of saying goes beyond the said. It is not ontology that raises up the speaking subject; it is the signifyingness of saying going beyond essence that can justify the exposedness of being, ontology."[10] Levinas devotes much of the succeeding discussion to proving that *beyond* translates into "before" and that the temporal lapse, or diachrony, enables subjectivity, identity, the "for-oneself." The event of diachrony is perceivable in the disjunction between the said, or content, and the saying by means of "unsaying the said."

One of the problems that arises for Levinas in the temporal disjunction between the saying and the said has to do with the alleged power of narrative (or prose) to structure and capture the Saying in the said as image, coherence, knowledge, and coincidence. Here Levinas maintains his Platonic distrust of art as perilously derivative: "every work of art is in this sense exotic, without a world, essence in dissemination," and nowhere is this more perilous than in narrative *prose* because "the essence properly so-called, is the verb, the logos, that resounds in the *prose* of predicative positions."[11] Prose, in his formulation, manipulates time and bestows on the speaker (or the writer) the illusion of temporal mastery as well as the capacity and propensity for memory. It enables us, as narrating subjects, to *think* that we control time, language, and language *in* time and that we can thus eschew ethical debt by recasting the other into our image through stories.

In spite of his aversion to narrative, Levinas includes in *Otherwise Than Being* a litany of explanations, approximations, and approaches to saying as exposure, witness, and prophecy—all of which can also resonate through narrative. Because he equates saying with approaching a neighbor (or a stranger), saying marks the prior exposure of the self to the other before the corollary events of thematization, objectification, and communication: "The unblocking of communication, irreducible to the circulation of information which presupposes it, is accomplished in the saying."[12] Narrative fiction can model such exposure and, in the process, expose the infinity (and passivity) of saying. If, as Levinas contends, the prerequisite of subjectivity is persecution and martyrdom, then saying also means bearing witness to that which we cannot escape: our unbounded ethical obligation to another and to all others. The discursive event of prose, or language in time, may in fact be readily positioned to rehearse the event of saying as the act of bearing witness to our inescapable anterior commitment to ethical responsibility, as I will subsequently argue in the context of three novels by Gen X writers.

The third notion, prophecy, returns us to the forward in *Totality and Infinity*, in which Levinas aligns the foreword or the exegesis with "unsaying the said." In the brief anticipatory text, titled simply "Note," with which he commences *Otherwise Than Being*, he associates "beyond essence" (the subtitle of the volume) with a final version of prophecy and, simultaneously, as one of the propositions of the volume: "To conceive of this abnegation prior to the will as a merciless exposure to the trauma of transcendence by way of a susception more, and differently, passive than receptivity, passion, and finitude."[13] In simpler terms, Levinas understands prophecy as the negation of the present and of representation through proximity, responsibility, and substitution.

How do Gen X writers respond to the pitfalls posited by Levinas's understanding of art in general and narrative fiction in particular? First, all narrative is constituted by and through language, and according to Levinas, all language gestures toward an unrecoverable saying in that it reveals to language users, be they speakers or writers, via diachrony our anterior ethical responsibility for the other. Ethical priority does not disappear or even diminish in certain occurrences of the said because the said does not, cannot, *control* or erase the saying. One explanation of literary language alights on its potential—some would say its *duty*—to follow and reveal the traces of the saying in the said, that which lies beyond signification and points us toward our always already delayed acknowledgment of the fact of alterity. Throughout his career, Levinas himself relied time and again on the tropes of narrative fiction, and on specific examples of narrative fiction, to communicate, engage, and translate his philosophical concepts. And, in the specific arena of time, I would argue that of all the literary genres, narrative fiction—and here I return to my central premise concerning the narrative fiction of Gen X writers—engages and discloses synchrony and diachrony because it most closely engages time.

In consonance with the novels thus far analyzed, *Arde lo que será, Sentimental*, and *La fiebre amarilla* are all fastened to the recognition and unfurling of alterity, the three texts interrogate the dissonance between same histories and other futures, and they all track alterity through time and into the interstices of the saying. In short, as three more instances of fictional narrative, they press on Levinas's reservations concerning the liabilities of literature in order to gesture toward our a priori ethical responsibility for the suffering of others. The three novels that I here take up in this chapter eloquently adduce some of the ways in which human subjects acknowledge their loss of control over time and over the synchrony of the said. In so doing, they begin to cultivate ethical obligation by anticipating the other's suffering, and our proximity to such suffering, in saying. The narratives evoke multiple moments of slippage in which vestiges of the saying reveal themselves in the said of the narrative text, and diachrony as *the* crucial component of this formulation is exposed.

Arde lo que será (1996), Juana Salabert's second novel,[14] veers from the ethical debts incurred, but never fully acknowledged, in. the previous trio of novels and toward the betrayal and suffering that inhere in alterity by means of diachrony. Like the other novels considered in the current chapter, the said, or theme of totality, is exposed by the saying, or event of alterity. Whereas sexual passion is virtually absent from *Sentimental* and *La fiebre amarilla, Arde lo que será* highlights an erotic yearning that, on the surface, divides the subjects from their individual chronologies and from language and underwrites the ethical obligation to the other through the intertwined acts of suffering and substitution. Although familial damage gradually encroaches on the a priori ethical debt of the self to the other, it cannot, in the end, completely expunge obligation. Childhood, as the historical moment at the furthest remove from the narrative present, is depicted in Salabert's novel as the origin of adult trauma, and this will also be the case in Luisa Castro's *La fiebre amarilla*. Unlike Castro's novel, however, *Arde lo que será* foregrounds two adult subjects who finally transcend, albeit momentarily, their own times such that the event of saying dislocates the synchrony of things said.

As one of the most complex, and arguably the most ludic, of the narrative texts considered in the present chapter, *Arde lo que será* shuttles among competing and complementary times and perspectives throughout the three discrete sections, differentiated as the "First Part," the "Second Part," and an untitled third part.[15] The first of these introduces the alternating first-person perspectives of the two protagonists, Ander and Nerea, as they fortuitously reunite after a decade apart. During those ten years of separation, both have suffered because of their responses to the literal and figurative crimes of their parents. In the more extensive second part, Ander's past-tense narration frames the protracted disclosure of Nerea's fictitious childhood as Ariadna Balzzi, the adopted daughter of a Uruguayan couple connected to the country's repressive military. And the concise third segment displays an omniscient third-person narrator who knits together the multiple versions of the separate and shared histories of the protagonists against the backdrop of their passionate reunion. Because the harrowing legacies of postwar Francoism in Spain and the so-called Dirty War in Uruguay bear down upon the primordial memories of Ander and Nerea, try though they might, they cannot completely transcend their violent (and violated) histories in the present tense of their recollections.[16] But they do finally face toward one another and acknowledge saying, which is not reducible to content, as the ethical gesture that marks their suffering-for-the-other.

Like other novels by Gen X writers, *Arde lo que será* is undeniably relational, founded upon the ethical responses and responsibilities of subjects toward others through time. In a text so rigorously dedicated to history and chronology, the present- and future-inflected title registers as potentially dissonant. The novel's epigraph, featured in French and Spanish, references four lines of a poem by Louis Aragon from which Salabert's title is extracted: "*Avenir, souvenir / Nuances si légères / au feu de ce qui fut / brûle ce qui sera. (Porvenir, recuerdo / matices tan leves / en el fuego de lo que fue / arde lo que será)*" [Future, I remember / touches so light / in the fire of what was / burns what will be].[17] As the reader learns, early in the first section, the title contains only the second half of the original citation (in French), as told to Nerea by her current lover, Jon, and then retold to Ander, who recaptures the last two lines in order to insert them into his own history: "Fue él quien te leyó, contaste, esos versos prodigiosos" [He was the one who read to you, you said, those prodigious verses].[18] Within the context of the protracted time line of the narrative, the title alludes to the troubled role of time in the novel; the violence of the past "burns" through any possible future just as Ander and Nerea's own stories, extended to the other, provoke an initial welcome by inciting love but then double back on themselves to eclipse diachrony. This lapse of time can only be glimpsed in the final sentences of the novel and in the last few words exchanged before they embrace separate futures.

The novel sets up at least four divergent chronologies that overlap with and interrupt one another in the temporal style of a set of nested Chinese boxes. In the remembered "now" of the most recent time period that edges the first section, Ander waits for his estranged wife at the same restaurant where Nerea happens to be playing the piano (and may even have been waiting for him). After the two former confidants recognize one another, they retreat to a hotel for three days to finally consummate their mutual sexual desire, and they simultaneously begin to speak about, and thus fill in, the temporal gaps since their last meeting some ten years earlier. During the considerably lengthier "Second Part," which commences with the date-and-place stamp of "November 1986. Madrid,"[19] Ander and Nerea separately recall the interlude of several months during which they met, fell in love, and unexpectedly parted from one another. And in the brief third section, they revisit the "present" together in order to finalize both the retelling of their chronologies and the reconstruction of their separate selves, both of which cancel any future encounter with the Other.

Crucial to Ander's three chronologies of "long ago, then, and now" is the trauma that he endured during his distant childhood in Valcarlos, a remote town on the Spanish side of the French border. After spying on his mother for months, he witnessed the murder of her clandestine lover, a guerrilla rebel, at the hands of pro-Franco gunmen and with the active collusion of his jealous (and zealous) father. Extravagant and illicit passion and an obsession with verbal invention, both of which he inherited from his maternal line, have indelibly marked "Carlos," as Ander refers to his younger self, since that moment. He elects to transfer both onto Nerea, after she begs him, early in their conjoined chronology, "*Invéntame un pasado, Ander. Por favor. . . . Sólo quiero un pasado, Ander. Nunca lo he tenido. Por favor*" [Invent a past for me, Ander. Please. . . . I only want a past, Ander. I've never had one. Please].[20] In response, he bestows upon her the name of Nerea (from the Basque word for "mine") and bequeaths his own history to her by recounting the story of his childhood and by inserting her (you) into the story in his time. The basis of their amorous relationship, then, rests on the discovery and manipulation of his remote past, a past that has separated him from himself and thrown him out of time. When he tries to use that history to acknowledge and respond to the other, in the person of Nerea, temporal disjunction proves wildly insufficient to sustain diachrony. His time converts her into a subject and gives her a weapon with which to defend herself against the return of her own violent history. Because Ander cannot move beyond his previous trauma and Nerea cannot recast someone else's chronology into her own, neither can sustain a face-to-face welcome of the other or accept the debt of suffering for the other. Instead, the twin narrators are doomed to loop their unresolved chronologies through ever-more contemporary versions of their encounters with one another until they finally commit to impossible proximity in an unknowable future.

For her part, Nerea also harbors ancient trauma, and it erupts into the time of the story that she shares with Ander. After she spends several months in peaceful domesticity with him and his extended community of urban squatters (the *okupa*, as they are known in colloquial Spanish), her adopted grandfather, an officer in the Uruguayan military, dispatches a detective, and later his henchmen, to locate the fugitive and forcefully return her to her parents. Although she quickly disappears, revealing her future plans to no one, "the Coronel" kidnaps and tortures Ander for information concerning his granddaughter, information that the other man does not have. When his captors finally release him, Ander cannot overcome the resulting brokenness and guilt. He superficially reconciles with his odious father, reenters middle-class society, becomes a hack screenwriter, and after a decade of emotional numbness and professional mediocrity, is on the precipice of his first divorce when he chances upon Nerea for the second time.

Nerea also disturbs, in the second section, Ander's double narration of the past (his and theirs) with her fragmentary account of intergenerational violence. As the narrative action advances, she reaches back into her own past to recount how she has repeatedly attempted to uncover her true origins, long hidden and revised by her adoptive family. As the only daughter of an unmarried Uruguayan woman who may have been involved in revolutionary activities, the two-year-old child, renamed Ariadna, had been given to Esteban and Miriam Balzzi after the child's mother died while being tortured by Esteban's father, "the Coronel." In a desperate pursuit for knowledge about her biological mother, and to exert the only power that she considered effective, the fourteen-year-old Ariadna had seduced her "father." Though their incestuous affair had persisted for five years, Esteban had refused to concede any details about her real mother, and Ariadna had fled into anonymity at the age of nineteen, at which point he had turned to his powerful father for help in "restoring" his errant daughter to their family.

At this point in her narration, Ariadna had taken refuge with Ander and his *okupa* friends in Madrid, she had deleted all signs of her prior history, and she had metamorphosed into Nerea. As she retells her more recent history to Ander from the vantage point of their shared present, when her past threatened to destroy her new community, Nerea abandoned her friends and sought out Esteban in order to compel him to finally confess the name and biography of her mother. Unfortunately, he admitted to either knowing very little or having forgotten whatever he had once known, save for the prisoner's first name (Ángela), a hazy supposition as to why she may have been captured, and the horrendous details surrounding her brutal murder. In response, Nerea fatally shot him before quitting the scene to an unknown destination.

The ephemeral final section, introduced with a one-line epigraph from Saint-John Perse's poem "Exil,"[21] returns to, and proceeds forward from, the temporal interval that unfolds during the "First Part"; the lovers reveal their alternative pasts to one another and try unsuccessfully to face the other in the present until Ander intuits, and Nerea confirms, her departure against the promise of a third reunion. But before she leaves, and after they have made love over and over again in the course of the three days, he intuits in her "la rabia de antaño" [yesterday's anger][22] that nothing can diminish, while she acknowledges in him her former salvation. For he had known, though perhaps not consciously, where she had gone after killing Esteban and where she had remained for the elapsed decade; he had known because he had given the idea to her in the story of his past, which became her past. After her crime, she had traveled to Valcarlos and adopted Ander's birthplace, and the site of his origin, as her own, renaming herself Nerea Valcarlos.

Once they have pursued the other through time, "buscándonos del lado otro en el interior contrario, tú, sí, precisamente tú, mi *alter ego* como alguien te llamó" [searching for ourselves from the other side in the opposite inside, you, yes, precisely you, my *alter ego* like someone called you],[23] they coincide on the dangers of verbal invention: "No se puede amar las palabras y no equivocarse" [One cannot love words and not make mistakes].[24] They also gesture toward a hypothetical tomorrow, one in which Nerea will finally discern her true name, the name that her deceased mother gave to her, and she will return to whisper it to Ander. The last line of *Arde lo que será* encapsulates all of the temporal play and proximity that have crisscrossed the novel; as he waits on the threshold of a doorway for Nerea to walk away from him and toward an impossible future in which she will discover her history, Ander tells her, "Vendré entonces. Aunque a lo mejor, o a lo peor, no me haya ido, aunque esté muerto. Seguro" [I will come back then. Even if for better, or for worse, I haven't gone, even if I am dead. Without a doubt].[25] His concluding words suggest something beyond that which is thematizable, an opening to the unknown other that Nerea might one day become. Levinas might call the origin that Nerea seeks a version of "the immemorial past." As perceiving subjects caught up in the trauma of alterity, however, we cannot experience or know the immemorial past through either memory or history because, according to Levinas, "this past is without reference to an identity naively—or naturally—assured of its right to presence, where everything must have begun. In this [ethical anteriority of] responsibility I am thrown back toward what has never been my fault or my deed, toward what has never been in my power or in my freedom, toward what has never been my presence, and has never come into memory."[26] The immemorial past lies before and beyond "clock time" and the memories that such time foments.

Both Ander and Nerea, as present narrators and as the victims of totalizing histories, try to articulate themselves and each other as *the other*. It is too late to accomplish this because each cannot transcend his or her own suffering; they become temporarily unstuck from their pasts by transferring their memories to one another in order to nurture their desire for one another in the present. Their separate presents eclipse any future; each adult narrates her or his childhood, and thus the story of their memories, to the other. Nerea does this in the present of their reencounter, while Ander did the same in their shared past. The goal of their narrations, and of their discourse, lies in imagining diachrony while imposing synchrony, converting the time of the other into their shared time, but as Levinas theorizes, the welcoming face-to-face anticipates "any moment of recollection, recovery, or synthesis."[27] Though they may have moved beyond the compulsion to map the other's suffering onto their own, thanks to the confessional impetus of their narratives, they have yet to acknowledge that the other's suffering precedes and substitutes for their own. The final lines, uttered by Ander to Nerea, intimate that this might happen beyond the language of the said and in some other time. The next novel will imagine ethical proximity as even more removed from the language of synchrony.

Sergi Pàmies's third novel, *Sentimental*, was originally written and published in Catalan in 1995.[28] It is unusual in some respects, not the least of which involves the introduction of extraterrestrial beings into the narrative, which in turn disrupts the synchrony of the subject. Pàmies installs the protagonist within a narrative that alternates between cohesion and disjunction and between a series of "presents" (with occasional incursions into the intelligible future) and a series of "pasts." Once the protagonist has been engulfed by the aliens, who are depicted as a "gelatinous mass," time and discourse start to unwind the subject toward ethical obligation. *Sentimental* also explores the temporal experience of human consciousness that becomes graspable through otherness. Although the protagonist is firmly ensconced in his own subjectivity at the outset of the novel, he is gradually "undone" and "unsaid" by his obligation to those he has left behind and to the "being" that has absorbed him into their time.

On an otherwise ordinary day in an unnamed city in Belgium, an unnamed man walks from his home to the neighborhood bar to buy a pack of cigarettes. The bar is closed, the nearby store is on fire, and at his next destination, a hotel, the clerk lies dead from a gunshot to the head. After smoking a cigarette and collecting his wits, the man inexplicably decides to take a commercial flight to Oporto, Portugal. When his plane suddenly crashes into the ocean, the man dons his lifejacket and escapes through the emergency exit. The only survivor, he is rescued and taken to an Oporto hospital, from which he also flees. After wandering the streets for two days, the man sneaks into the empty trailer of a truck headed for Lisbon. When he arrives in Lisbon, he stows away on a merchant ship destined for Rio de Janeiro, Brazil. On the ship, he is discovered and befriended by the cook, Nelson Horácio, who procures a passport and a new identity, that of Lourenço Oliveira, for the man once they reach Horácio's home in Rio. In addition, he welcomes "Lourenço" into his home, introduces him to his family, and arranges a job for him as a truck driver, a job that he retains for many years.

Soon after starting his new life in Brazil, the man falls in love with a feminine voice that he hears over the loudspeaker at an airport. When Lourenço shows up at her office, the woman summarily rebuffs him as crazy. After a gap of ten years, the narration resumes on the occasion of the man's forty-second birthday. He and Iris, the woman with the seductive voice, have now been together for a decade, in spite of the fact that she is eighteen years older than him. After his party, he falls asleep and awakes to the sight and sound of invisible beings who surround him and absorb him into their gelatinous "body." In the process, his own physical body is transformed into a perceiving voice, part of a larger organism from which he cannot separate. Time loses meaning and distinction. The former man is allowed to become aware of, and suffer as a result of, the death of his friend and employer, Antunes. He also "sees," from within the consciousness that he shares with the beings, a series of people who are leaving their loved ones, just as he abandoned his family some ten years previously. He is also permitted to observe, but not communicate with or affect in any way, a young Belgian woman who may be his adult daughter as she breaks the world record for the hundred-meter dash. Her final words, and the final words of the novel, are an echo of the words that Lourenço would have used to describe his friend's coffee: "No es pot descriure amb paraules" [You can't describe it with words].[29]

Divided into six sequentially numbered chapters, *Sentimental* unspools from a third-person omniscient narrator who mostly privileges the protagonist's perspective and only occasionally delves briefly into the perceptions of secondary characters such as Iris and the young Belgian sprinter. The narrator also mostly narrates in the present but occasionally anticipates a hypothetical future outcome from the man's actions, thoughts, and decisions. It could be argued that he trails his ego into and out of the unlikely situations in which he finds himself—in some instances not projecting much beyond his present needs and in others assuming that strangers will respond to *him*. He is self-absorbed without necessarily being deeply self-conscious or self-reflective, and the present-tense episodic quality of the narrative confirms this disjunction. He is also absorbed into the alien other such that, paradoxically, he is self- and other-absorbed.

One of the early sequences of events illustrates this quality. The man is compelled, for reasons that he does not necessarily understand or even question, to satisfy his need for a cigarette. His addiction propels him forward here, and other unseen causes will again move him forward in the future. When his first action does not produce a cigarette, he moves on to the next available opportunity. When that choice likewise fails, he leaves the scene of an all-consuming fire without offering assistance. His third option, that of a familiar hotel, yields a dead body and a pack of cigarettes. He does not know what to do about the corpse, but after finally smoking a cigarette from the pack that lies near the bloody body, he runs away. In light of all the examples and expressions of intersubjectivity thus far analyzed, the main character of *Sentimental* is strangely isolated and willfully solitary.

The narrative abruptly switches to the future tense here, indicating that the man *will* run although no one is pursuing him, he *will* go back to the hotel bar and jump from one of the windows, he *will* twist his ankle and not care, he *will* cross streets and narrowly avoid an accident, and he *will* feel lost, at which point he will light another cigarette, realize that he is close to his house, and drive his car in the other direction. A complementary version of this temporal exchange is previewed in the first sentence of the novel: "L'home que fa un moment ha dit: 'Vaig a comprar tabac' no tornarà mai més a casa seva" [The man who one minute ago said "I'm going to buy tobacco" will never return to his house].[30] In spite of this prophetic beginning, time unfolds successively and episodically in accordance with the major events of the protagonist's life. He does not evince any emotional or mental progression; rather, the months during which he leaves Belgium, survives a plane crash, travels from Oporto to Lisbon to Rio, and, thanks to Horácio, receives a new identity and embarks on another life unspool as a string of events that happen to him. He demonstrates little agency or awareness of his relationships with others or the passage of time.

One might expect that the decade he spends in the company of Iris might result in some kind of extended self-reflection, but the narration jumps from the event of his first problematic encounter with Iris to his forty-second birthday ten years later. Their courtship is described as a historical event, punctuated by cause and effect: the man's repeated efforts to achieve his goal, Iris's capitulation, their sexual initiation, and the slide into a comfortable routine. The narration returns to the present only when the protagonist wakes up to the arrival of the "beings" (*ens* in Catalan) who are described as "subjunctively invisible," silent, reminiscent of geometrical units. When the man is absorbed into their aggregate being, he remains in exactly the same position and no longer experiences time or aging. His consciousness now prevails over all of the successive descriptions.

The man now understands and expresses his new experience in light of prior erroneous assumptions. He has not been transported to a spaceship but instead occupies space as both outside and inside the "gelatinous mass." Light-years transpire in an instant; the intersected beings evince a hierarchy, uniformity, and most surprisingly, "una immensa extensió de timidesa" [an immense extension of timidity].[31] The protagonist attributes their timidity, which also now applies to him, to the force of necessity and to the proximity of the one to the other. Further revelations have to do with the conversion of all present events into history and with the protagonist's decision to collaborate with these "others." Collaboration induces the transmutation of the suffering of others into his suffering; the protagonist literally takes on and feels the suffering, and even the death, of Antunes as if it were his own. He relives his abandonment of his family through "thousands" of similar betrayals: "Fugen per terra, mar i aire, i l'Oliveira té el privilegi de sentir-los com si els veiés tots junts al mateix temps. Molts tenen una idea precisa d'on volen anar. La majoria, no. Sembla que provin fins on poden arribar amb l'estímul de no saber si arriba-ran enlloc" [They flee by earth, water and air, and Oliveira has the privilege of sensing them as if he were seeing them all together at the same time. Many have exact ideas about where they want to go. The majority doesn't. It seems that they try to imagine how far they can get with the stimulus of ignoring whether they will arrive anywhere].[32] This process reaches its apex with the young woman, who is in all likelihood the man's daughter. Thanks to his new form, and the passive awareness that comes with it, he suf-fers when she suffers and he triumphs when she triumphs. All this occurs, however, against the backdrop of his sure knowledge that he will never return, that she will never know him, that her future exceeds him, and that his future has already happened. By the end of the novel, the alien beings have receded and the narrative con-denses into all that the woman cannot put into words but has left its trace in the diachrony of alterity. In the next novel, diachrony will approach alterity through death.

Luisa Castro Legazpi's second novel, *La fiebre amarilla* (1994),[33] is paradoxically the most conventional of the three novels analyzed insofar as it features an omniscient narrator and displays the plot principally organized according to objectively verifiable details and dialogue. Castro also offers up a facile explanation, by way of Vir-ginia's illness, for the temporal confusion that governs the plot. The novel is unusual, nonetheless, in that past, present, and future meet at mortality, and death inhabits the novel as a person, as a kind of vision, as a place, as paternity, and as a metaphor for that which cannot be known or narrated.

The plot of *La fiebre amarilla* unfolds in sixteen numbered chapters by means of at least three enmeshed temporal planes, each with its corresponding, yet divergent, perspective. In the first time zone, Virginia Legazpi, a seventy-year-old woman who has always lived in a small village in Spain, tumbles down the stairs in her home just before she is scheduled to join a widow's excursion to the Shrine of Fátima in Portugal.[34] In spite of the fact that she is not really a widow, she had intended to make the pilgrimage in order to finally fulfill a decades-old promise to her dying mother, Amadora. When she goes to the hospital to have her broken arm set (again), the doctor informs Virginia that she has inoperable cancer and sends her home. She floats in and out of delirium for two weeks and then apparently dies.

In the second time zone, generally corresponding to Virginia's childhood, her father, Jesús Legazpi, abandons his daughter and his wife, Amadora, when Virginia is ten years old to emigrate to Cuba with a mysterious woman, presumably his lover. One year later, mother and daughter receive the astonishing news that Legazpi has expired from yellow fever,[35] but Virginia apparently ignores the telegram to spend the next six decades awaiting both her father's explanation and his bodily return. Legazpi's arrival at his daughter's bedside coincides, in the first time zone, with her delirium, during which she believes that, like her father, she suffers from yellow fever. He repeatedly begs Virginia to recognize him, approve of his impending marriage, and meet his future wife, who has accompanied him. When she finally agrees to his pleas, "death," in the guise of a woman, enters Virginia's room and requests that she return with them to Cuba. And in the third time zone, Ladislao Atare, the taxi driver who transported Legazpi and his lover to Ferrol in the first time, collects the couple in the second time at the dock, prior to their departure for Cuba, and drives them back to Virginia's village.

The three temporal strands carry equal narrative authority and interweave the supplementary stories of Virginia; her husband, Francisco Pena; her adult daughter, Juana; Amadora; Jesús Legazpi; the village priest, don Sergio; the village doctor, don Pablo; Ladislao Atare; and a peripatetic countess. All these characters convene across competing times in order to inflect how one might recognize and enact ethical responsibility to the other in time. Virginia, as the connecting thread, presents the self who is summoned by the Other to account for death. To glimpse that mystery, which escapes resolution, Virginia must be on the verge of—but not in—the future. On the cusp of the futural moment throughout the novel, it gradually dawns on her that in dying (and thus surviving yellow fever), she must return to the moment of trauma in which she was called to take responsibility for her father's death.

The text commences in the present moment, recounted in the completed past of the preterit tense, when Virginia believes that she has contracted yellow fever and, several days later, "conoció por primera vez a su padre" [she met her father for the first time].[36] Her memories of Jesús Legazpi are based entirely on her mother's stories and the single photograph of her parents' wedding, which adorns the wall of her bedroom next to a bizarre painting in which a devil consumes the feet of a Christ figure. Significantly, when they meet, Legazpi calls his daughter by her first name, and instead of acknowledging him, she "sees" the village physician. The two temporal planes, embodied by Legazpi and don Pablo, will coexist throughout both Virginia's present and the remainder of the novel.

Although Virginia's perspective predominates in the first chapter, the narrator-as-gatherer merges the protagonist's self-directed memories of the past and her other-directed attentiveness to the present. Disease, old age, and imminent death afford a reasonable motivation for her delusion, but no narrative authority ever confirms this explanation. However, Virginia's pull to recover her father's imaginary past, and thus to hold him accountable for her current distress, is really about her own impending expression of Levinasian diachrony. Whereas the other two novels represent what might be termed "memorial encounters," the effect of which is to remind the subjects of themselves, *La fiebre amarilla* works through an immemorial encounter to rehearse the impossible meeting of self and other in the future of death.

In response to the "where" of such a future, the movement of "othering" displays in Castro's text as departing to and returning from the unknowable future destinations of Coimbra and Cuba. The Shrine of Fátima signals a site of maternal longing so fierce that Virginia's own mother has guaranteed her daughter's pilgrimage in several ways: Amadora bequeaths to her daughter a sum of money to make the journey that Amadora could never realize,

Virginia recollects the reported appearance of the Virgin of Fátima (and thus the reason for the shrine) as a direct effect of her father's exodus to Cuba, and before her proposed trip, she imagines that she need never to return from Coimbra to her family, her village, and her present life. The potential resonances among Virginia's own name, the requisite virginal status of Fátima, Amadora's (remembered) eschewal of sexual relations with her husband, and the seemingly miraculous birth of their daughter all suggest that Virginia may be the literal manifestation of her mother's own temporal drive toward ethical alterity. Because most textual references to Amadora are filtered through someone else's consciousness, it is difficult to confirm such a move. Likewise, throughout the novel, Virginia is fixated on her father's departure and return, with all that both of these actions imply, and she habitually summons the memory of her mother in support of what might be considered the primary paternal mystery. As a partial response to this mystery, she associates Cuba with refuge, yearning, and foreignness, and she assumes that her father can and will rescue her from her present circumstances precisely because he has already traveled so far that, in Virginia's mind, his only recourse is to turn around, return "home," and reclaim his daughter.

In a peculiarly affirmative interrogation of the art of time in a Levinasian approximation, *La fiebre amarilla* links the narrative to the microhistory of the painting that faces Virginia's bed, which was her mother's bed before her. The painting, periodically described by Virginia and the other characters, reveals a supposedly ethical confrontation between good and evil, Christ and the devil.[37] It also connects daughter and father. In one temporal strand, Ladislao delivers Legazpi and the unnamed woman to the dock in time to board the ship that will take them to Cuba, only to subsequently be directed to drive them back to Amadora's house (which is now Virginia's house) because Legazpi cannot depart without saying good-bye to his only daughter. When the taxi arrives, and in a clear case of disjunctive time, Legazpi gives the painting to Amadora as a final gift for Virginia, with instructions to hang it in their bedroom.

When Virginia returns from the hospital to see that in the painting good now consumes evil, she deduces that she cannot possibly have cancer. Rather, she claims for herself the disease of yellow fever, which she has forever associated with her father. Given that he could have contracted yellow fever, so the story goes, only by leaving the brisk, rainy climate of Northern Spain for a tropical country such as Cuba, Virginia's self-diagnosis also anticipates her definitive departure for Cuba (instead of the original destination of the Shrine of Fátima) in the company of her father and his supposed mistress. The altered painting, in Virginia's mind, corroborates her father's mission of salvation, and it inspires her to reconsider the terms of her initial abandonment. As the sole artistic object in the novel, given that the wedding photograph is presented as nothing more than a record, the religious iconography is the only visual stimulus in Virginia's ordinary domestic environment, and it moves her to reevaluate and reinhabit her own time and the conflicting times of her parents. In sum, she sees in the painting a possible cipher for another time and the time of the Other—a time in which she embraces death, in a variety of literal and metaphorical manifestations—and recognizes ethicality.

By the end of the novel, the fate of the painting corroborates the temporal movement that has "undetermined" the future of death: "Así, como la voltereta del cuadro, tan enigmática en apariencia, el mundo podía revolverse de la noche a la mañana, y las casas, y las cabezas de los hombres, y hasta las palabras dentro de las cabezas de los hombres. Pues sí que podían. Podían eso y mucho más" [Thus, like the somersault of the painting, with its enigmatic appearance, the world could have turned upside down from night to morning, and the houses and the minds of men and even the words inside the minds of men. Surely they could have. They could have done that and much more].[38] The turnaround of the world and the words refers to the about-face of time, or the art of time, whereby the future and the past, across the present, trade places. In the time(s) of the novel, Amadora grows ever younger, and death is not an occurrence but a human subject who accompanies Virginia into the immemorial past and the unknowable future.[39] But before she can meet death, Virginia must "recognize" her father and become willing to assume prior responsibility, through the time of narration, for his death. Once she finally acknowledges Jesús Legazpi, and once he removes the telegram from the painting and insistently names himself to and for her, she is prepared to meet his companion, who, not coincidentally, is referred to as death only once and only in the final paragraphs of Castro's novel. On the brink of their long-awaited trip to Cuba, as the place of no-time, the personification of death lingers while don Pablo stands in for her father. His parting words of advice extend protection and comfort and sustain the mystery of alterity: "Llevad ropa de verano—le oyó—, no creo que paséis frío" [Take your summer clothes—she heard him say—I don't think you'll get cold].[40] Under the semblance of parental care, Virginia hears the unknowable, and yet familiar, tomorrow.

Because the futurity of death is unnarratable and beyond the chronology of time, as Levinas has theorized, *La fiebre amarilla* does not follow Virginia into death, although it does suggest that she follows her father into *his* death. She finally accepts responsibility for the Other by discarding "her" past, present, and future and by giving up her claims to grievance. In so doing, she marks her future identity as fundamentally other-wise and in direct opposition to the self-obsessed futures displayed in *Veo veo*, *El frío*, and *Mensaka* and the reiterated failures of the past in *El secreto de Sara*, *Arde lo que será*, and *Tocarnos la cara*. When Virginia finally hears and responds to the call of the other—prior to all rationality, all memory, and all discourse—she refigures her paternal history; she becomes the parent and her father becomes the child, and death links them to one another. To reiterate Levinas's position, "The very relationship with the other is the relationship with the future,"[41] and that relationship is exposed, in Castro's novel, through the future of death and, more particularly, through Virginia's transcendently "always already" devotion to another, which is the time of alterity. This other not only is her father or his female companion but also includes everything about her father (and, by extension, the future) that has always escaped her comprehension and her present and everything that makes the stranger unknowable and temporally immeasurable. Time traps the experiencing subjects in the texts discussed in the previous chapters, but in *Anatol y dos más*, *Sentimental*, and *La fiebre amarilla*, time liberates, to varying degrees, the self to approach and even encounter the Other in saying.

Afterword

As I draft these words, Cataluña is grappling with the possibilities and consequences of succession; illegal immigration, domestic violence, and terrorism are on the rise in Spain and elsewhere; North Korea threatens nuclear aggression and the United States, with the largest military arsenal in the world, threatens to retaliate; definitive proof exists that national elections have been manipulated for personal, corporate, and state profit; reports of sexual assault, harassment, and cover-ups in the U.S. entertainment industry and politics multiply daily; gun violence reaches agonizingly further into schools, stores, and public festivals; and climate change threatens human sustainability and negatively impacts global health, food sovereignty, and the survival of countless living species. The reality of difference, and the violent reactions that fears of difference generate, are not merely theoretical or philosophical. They are painfully tangible and potentially catastrophic—indeed, apocalyptic—and every day they become more so.

Which stories of difference get told to whom, why some of these endure and others do not, and how storytelling engages and is engaged by ethics are all questions that cultural workers, and literary critics among them, have debated and rehearsed for centuries. I unknowingly took my first steps toward *The Art of Time* several decades ago when I decided to relentlessly believe, and to endeavor to persuade others to believe, that fictional narrative matters—that it matters in ways that are inseparable from the articulation and sustainability of what it means to be human across all cultures, across all historical periods. Without stories, we do not exist;

without the capacity to tell and hear stories, we are diminished in the world, and the world is extinguished within us.

I was initially drawn to the philosophical arguments of Levinas because his work foregrounds, in ways that I shall perhaps always be striving to comprehend, the dynamic significance of the Other, others, and otherness in the elaboration and movement of human subjectivity. Drawing his theories into my own inevitably partial perspective, I have always known that my awareness and perception unfold in time and in relation to a multitude of others. In embarking upon the present scholarly enterprise, I have sought to pursue some sense, albeit inconclusive and selective, of how we as human subjects reject, suppress, defer, colonize, define, approach, and/or embrace alterity.

The project at hand is rooted in the intersection between intersubjectivity, alterity, and temporality. In order to allegorize three (from among the myriad) approaches to Levinas's theory of alterity, I have elected to analyze specific novels from a cohort of Peninsular novelists born after 1960 and who published their work in Spain during the 1990s. At the same time, I try to show how narrative fiction exceeds the limits of Levinas's philosophy because of its overt engagement with time. In *Veo veo*, *El frío*, and *Mensaka*, the characters embark upon the tragedy of solipsistic subjectivity as an antidote to present trauma. The time of the other must be subsumed again and again through the fiction of synchrony; suffering is aligned with the ego, forges coherence, and forswears futurity. The novels ultimately critique egology, however, by emphasizing consciousness as repetition and stasis.

The novels discussed in chapter 4, *El secreto de Sara*, *Anatol y dos más*, and *Tocarnos la cara*, exhort and then postpone alterity indefinitely. It is significant that these three novels track the relations of writers who project chronology onto the Other even as they try to face toward alterity. If, as Levinas postulates, diachrony is the work of the face-to-face relationship, then time eventually returns the narrating subjects to themselves. The subjects also assume consciousness to be the origin, as opposed to the result, of ethical responsibility. When they remember, they are catapulted into suffering and lament, which consequently positions them *after* their awareness of their responsibility. *Arde lo que será*, *Sentimental*, and *La fiebre amarilla*, by contrast, open ethical responsibility toward the future. In the traces of saying, one may discern the diachrony of speaking, the anteriority of obligation, and the dislocation of sameness in favor of the one-for-the-other. In these three novelistic expressions of the art of time, then, we glimpse three very disparate relationships to alterity. Taken together, the nine novels exhort us to consider again and always the price of temporal mastery and the promise of ethical responsibility.

I have not explicitly addressed the act of reading, our acts of reading, or Levinas's understanding of reading and the reader because to do so would significantly exceed the self-imposed limitations of my argument, the literary texts that I have chosen to analyze, and the broad outlines of Levinas's philosophy of alterity. Colin Davis has posited that "the act of reading brings into play the most important issue of [Levinas's] ethical philosophy, namely the possibility of a transforming encounter with someone or something entirely other."[1] In his analysis of Levinas's 1947 essay on Proust, Davis concludes that Levinas has sketched a potential phenomenology of reading in which text and reader renew each other. Seán Hand makes an even stronger case for the ethical exigency of literature in Levinas's philosophy: "For Levinas [artistic characters and dilemmas] are the necessary dramatization of ethical being which has become elsewhere fatally compromised and reduced in the philosophical process of the comprehension of Being. They operate then as the ethical shadow within ontological language, as an aesthetic of the face-to-face relation otherwise threatened with suppression in the work of the metaphysician."[2]

Neither have I overtly attended to the nexus between Levinas and politics, although this very nexus is inevitably expressed throughout the Gen X narrative.[3] It is nonetheless my contention that Gen X novels demonstrate a clear political project in exploring ethical engagement as a prerequisite to consciousness and to essence. Some accomplish this goal by showcasing spectacular failures. Others reverse the order of alterity and sameness, thereby unhinging synchrony from subjectivity. And yet others animate otherness as a discursive event, acutely accessible and discernable in fictional narrative. The art of time, the ethics of time, and the narrative of time all coincide in the Gen X novels that I have here (and now) analyzed. Other novels by other authors from the same cohort may provoke other readings of Levinas's theory. Only time will tell.

Acknowledgments

Acknowledgments extend to authors the opportunity to publicly recognize those who, in profound and meaningful ways, have offered themselves to us and who have, in turn, allowed us to offer ourselves to them. My list of acknowledgments is necessarily partial, but I am nonetheless indebted to the following people and institutions.

For refuge, constancy, and tribal connection over the years, I am grateful to my Colorado, California, and Washington families, past and present: Elle, Emme, Jenn, Joe, Tony; Brianna, Davey, Vivian; Brad, Campbell, Elise, Jenny; Gail and Sue; David Whitney and Judy; Florence Belle and Ralph Donald; and the Tuininga clan. My words, here and throughout my professional life, bear witness to the countless interventions of teachers who have nurtured my intellect and my soul in equal measure. In particular I remember Jane Drummond, Jack Moninger, and Bill Stough for their gentle discipline and sharp intelligence; Monique Chefdor, Michael C. Harper, and Thaïs Lindstrom for their vibrant thoughtfulness; Ruth El-Saffar, Susan Noakes, Elizabeth Schultz, and Janet Sharistanian for being strong and brilliant women; and John Brushwood, Andrew Debicki, Michael Doudoroff, George Woodyard, and most of all, Robert C. Spires, to whom this book is dedicated, for their intellectual openness, community, and joyful wonder.

Beyond the classroom, ours is often a solitary vocation, punctuated occasionally by remarkable encounters—some brief and some sustained over time—with remarkable colleagues. I share a home, in the Department of Spanish and Portuguese at the

University of Colorado Boulder (UCB), with formidable scholars and committed educators, and I name them here: Julio Baena, Anne Becher, Esther Brown, Juan Pablo Dabove, Peter Elmore, Leila Gómez, Susan Hallstead, Juan Herrero-Senés, Javier Krauel, Mary K. Long, Tania Martuscelli, Susanna Pérez-Pàmies, Andrés Prieto, Javier Rivas Rodríguez, Marcelo Schincariol, and Núria Silleras-Fernández. Luis T. González-del-Valle has carefully shepherded my career and my professional formation in more ways than I can count or imagine, and I also gratefully dedicate this monograph to him. Juli Highfill and all of my fellow "spirals" (you know who you are!) make me proud to call myself a Hispanist. Malcolm, David, Roberta, and Geraldine have all steadfastly encouraged me for forever, and their research has inspired and elevated my own across the miles and over the years. Donald R. Wehrs has made all the difference, from start to finish, to this project in particular. Alan Hart is a scholar, a gentleman, and my philosophy guru, and to him and Judith Hart I am infinitely thankful for our long friendship.

Without financial support from the following institutional entities, I could have neither commenced nor concluded the current project: the Council on Research and Creative Work at UCB awarded me a Faculty Fellowship in 2003–2004, UCB also granted me three sabbaticals during the prolonged gestation and realization of this book, and I received an Individual Growth Grant from the Leadership Education for Advancement and Promotion at UCB in spring 2016, which allowed me to complete the project. In addition, writers frequently require space and quiet, and I am fortunate to have found both in abundance at Dayton Memorial Library (DML). My thanks to the librarians at DML and to Regis University. It has been both an honor and a pleasure to work with Greg Clingham, Pam Dailey, and the editorial and copyediting staff at Bucknell University Press, and I formally extend my thanks (yet again) to them.

Finally, I run up against the inadequacies of language in sounding the depth and breadth of my debt to Daryl W. Palmer, whose faith, creativity, good humor, and thoughtful acumen continue to sustain my work and my life well into a fourth decade. More. Again. Still. Always.

Notes

Unless otherwise noted, all translations are my own.

1. Ethics, Alterity, and Levinas

1. Colin Davis notes that Emmanuel Levinas's term *l'éthique* can be translated as both "ethics" and "the ethical," with the second term referring to "a domain from which nothing human may be excluded" (*Levinas: An Introduction* [Notre Dame, Ind.: University of Notre Dame Press, 1996], 3). In a related vein, Edith Wyschogrod and Gerald P. McKenny suggest that "the ethical" refers to "not only who says what, when and under what circumstances, but also what could be said under specifiable conditions, in short the 'about'" (Introduction to *The Ethical* [Malden: Blackwell, 2003], 1). I might add that "the ethical," throughout Levinas's texts, consistently adjectivizes both discourse and the human subject and is therefore appropriate as a descriptor of his project.

2. The following scholars have published book-length monographs on diverse facets and categories of contemporary Peninsular narrative and culture in light of ethical concerns: Txetxu Aguado, *La tarea política: Narrativa y ética en la España posmoderna* (Barcelona: Viejo Topo, 2004); Katarzyna Beilin and William Viestenz, eds., *Ethics of Life: Contemporary Iberian Debates* (Nashville: Vanderbilt University Press, 2016); Ángel G. Loureiro, *The Ethics of Autobiography: Replacing the Subject in Modern Spain* (Nashville: Vanderbilt University Press, 2000); and Peregrina Pereiro, *La novela española de los noventa: Alternativas éticas a la postmodernidad* (Madrid: Pliegos, 2002). These authors do not, however, discuss either Spain's Generación X or temporality. Of all of them, only

Loureiro turns briefly to Levinas (among many other theorists) in his exploration of Spanish autobiography as an ethical act. Katarzyna Olga Beilin also mentions Levinas in passing in her book on the theme of otherness in contemporary Spanish narrative and film (*Del infierno al cuerpo: La otredad en la narrativa y en el cine español contemporáneo* [Madrid: Ediciones Libertarias, 2007], 351–352). See also Jessica A. Folkart's cogent article for an application of Levinas's theory of alterity to short stories by Spanish writer Cristina Fernández Cubas ("The Ethics of Spanish Identity and In-difference," *Philosophy and Literature* 35, no. 2 [2011]: 216–232).

3. Because Levinas attempts to revise the Western ethical tradition, I have chosen to concentrate on certain strands of Western philosophy. In no way do I intend, however, to suggest that other equally valid and influential ethical traditions do not exist and have not significantly affected the history of humanity.

4. Historically speaking, formal logic emerged as a fourth branch of philosophy with the work of Aristotle. Because Levinas does not engage formal logic either methodologically or conceptually, I do not consider it here.

5. See Julia Annas's "Ethics and Morality," in *Encyclopedia of Ethics*, ed. Lawrence C. Becker and Charlotte B. Becker (New York: Garland Press, 1992), 1:329–331, for a concise summary of the historical differences between conceptions of ethics and conceptions of morality. For reasons that I will subsequently discuss, Levinas typically prefers the term *ethics*, but he occasionally uses *morality* and *ethics* interchangeably, and in ordinary language use, they are frequently considered synonymous.

6. Emmanuel Levinas, *Totality and Infinity: An Essay on Exteriority*, trans. Alphonso Lingis (Pittsburgh: Duquesne University Press, 1969), 43.

7. Tina Chanter, *Time, Death, and the Feminine: Levinas with Heidegger* (Stanford: Stanford University Press, 2001), 1. In addition to the sources quoted within my monograph, other relevant discussions of Levinas and time include Yael Lin's *The Intersubjectivity of Time: Levinas and Infinite Responsibility* (Pittsburgh: Duquesne University Press, 2013); and Christophe Bouton's *Temps et liberté* (2008), published as *Time and Freedom*, trans. Christopher Macann (Evanston, Ill.: Northwestern University Press, 2014). Most books on Levinas's philosophy address the concept of

time to some extent. See the bibliographies in Chanter's *Time, Death, and the Feminine*; Lin's *Intersubjectivity of Time*; and Eric Severson's *Levinas's Philosophy of Time: Gift, Responsibility, Diachrony, Hope* (Pittsburgh: Duquesne University Press, 2013), for a relatively complete list of essays related to time and alterity.

8. See, for example, William R. Schroeder's classification of Levinas as a Continental philosopher who "offers a new type of ethical theory, one which roots ethics in a fundamental relationship to other people." Schroeder also emulates the resistance among some philosophers to Levinas's work by declaring that "for Levinas, there are no founding values and no basic principles. . . . Moreover, there are few arguments" (Schroeder, "Continental Ethics," in *The Blackwell Guide to Ethical Theory*, ed. Hugh LaFollette and Ingmar Persson [Chichester: Wiley Blackwell, 2013], 477, 480).

9. I here reference the division favored by LaFollette and Persson, *Blackwell Guide to Ethical Theory*.

10. Peter Singer is one of the most vocal and well-known proponents of practical ethics, having published early contributions to the subdiscipline with *Animal Liberation: A New Ethics for Our Treatment of Animals* (New York: HarperCollins, 1975); and *Practical Ethics* (Cambridge: Cambridge University Press, 1979). Some of his recent discussions include *The Life You Can Save: Acting Now to End World Poverty* (New York: Random House, 2009); *The Most Good You Can Do: How Effective Altruism Is Changing Ideas about Living Ethically* (New Haven, Conn.: Yale University Press, 2015); and *Ethics in the Real World: 82 Brief Essays on Things That Matter* (Princeton: Princeton University Press, 2016).

11. See John Llewelyn, *The HypoCritical Imagination: Between Kant and Levinas* (London: Routledge, 2000), for a superb analysis of the "double axis" of Kant's notion of the imagination and Levinas's notion of saying.

12. Scholars have dedicated considerable attention to Levinas's distinction between *autrui* and *autre*, both of which he occasionally capitalizes. I follow Lingis's translation, in which he notes, in Levinas's preface to *Totality and Infinity*, that "with the author's permission, we are translating '*autrui*' (the personal Other, the you) by 'Other,' and '*autre*' by 'other.' In doing so, we regrettably sacrifice the possibility of reproducing the author's use of capital or small letters with both these terms in the

French text" (24–25). Additionally, in the translator's note to Levinas's *Ethics and Infinity*, trans. Richard A. Cohen (Pittsburgh: Duquesne University Press, 1985), Cohen indicates that he has followed Lingis's convention and adds that "*Autrui*, in French, refers to the personal other, the other person; *autre* refers to otherness in general, to alterity" (17).

In his summary and discussion of the key tenets of *Totality and Infinity*, Seán Hand further expounds on the variants of *other* within the text: for Levinas, "the metaphysical other (*autre*) is also both the absolutely other (*l'absolument Autre*) and the Other (*Autrui*). In addition, this other or Other is also personified as 'the Stranger who disturbs the being at home with oneself,' or 'the free one' who is not wholly 'in my site'" (*Emmanuel Levinas* [London: Routledge, 2009], 40).

13. Two recent volumes, Mark Payne, *The Animal Part: Human and Other Animals in the Poetic Imagination* (Chicago: University of Chicago Press, 2010); and William Edelglass, James Hatley, and Christian Diehm, eds., *Facing Nature: Levinas and Environmental Thought* (Pittsburgh: Duquesne University Press, 2012), examine some practical applications of Levinas's philosophy. See also the essays collected in Peter Atterton and Matthew Calarco, eds., *Radicalizing Levinas* (Albany: State University of New York Press, 2010).

14. *Shoah* derives from the Hebrew word for "catastrophe" and refers to the mass extermination of European Jews by the Nazis and their accomplices between 1939 and 1945. Some Jewish writers (and Levinas among them) prefer *the Shoah* to *the Holocaust* because the first term eschews the religious connotations of the second. Regarding his own intimately painful experience of the Shoah, Levinas enlisted in the French army in 1932, returned to military service as a French officer at the outbreak of World War II in 1939, and was taken prisoner by the Germans in 1940. He was saved from execution by virtue of being in French uniform, but all members of his family, save his wife and young daughter, perished in concentration camps. The definitive biography of Levinas remains Salomon Malka's *Emmanuel Levinas: His Life and Legacy*, trans. Michael Kigel and Sonja M. Embree (Pittsburgh: Duquesne University Press, 2006), first published in French in 2002 as *Emmanuel Lévinas: La vie et la trace*. Malka, who both studied with Levinas and knew him and his immediate family, discusses Levinas's life as a series

of encounters organized according to place and as a series of influences organized according to historical personages.

15. The theoretical roots of classical ethics may be generally located in the tensions between preclassical Homeric society, which dated roughly from the eighth to the sixth century BCE, and Socratic society, which originated in approximately 500 BCE. The former is depicted in the canonical epics of Homer's *The Iliad* and its successor, *The Odyssey*, both of which celebrate the male hero as morally superior to all other human beings because of the ways in which he complies with his assigned social function. The Greek word ἀγαθός, an early version of the contemporary concept of "goodness," initially functioned, according to Alasdair MacIntyre, as a predicate directly attached to the role of a Homeric nobleman and was synonymous with the words that characterized the qualities of the Homeric ideal (*A Short History of Ethics* [London: Routledge, 1966], 6). Furthermore, adjectives of appraisal such as ἀγαθός expressed facts, supported by the previous performance of the hero in question, which were then attached to societal expectations regarding future performances. A cognate of αγαθός, ἀρετή is often, and perhaps mistakenly, translated as "virtue" (and its opposite as αἰδώς, or "shame") and attached to the man who accomplished (or, in the case of shame, failed to accomplish) his social role. Each social role had a different ἀρετή, or "virtue," but a man was ἀγαθός if he had the ἀρετή of his particular function (7–8).

16. These dramatic and historical texts included, among others, Aristophanes's *Clouds* (performed 423 BCE), Euripides's tragedies (438–405 BCE), and Thucydides's *History of the Peloponnesian War* (431–404 BCE). Although Levinas, in consonance with Plato and in contrast to Heidegger, consistently rejects art as derivative and deformative, he relies heavily on literary examples and tropes throughout his work. For a lucid explanation of the nexuses between literature and Levinas's work, see Jill Robbins, *Altered Reading: Levinas and Literature* (Chicago: University of Chicago Press, 1999); and Alain P. Toumayan, *Encountering the Other: The Artwork and the Problem of Difference in Blanchot and Levinas* (Pittsburgh: Duquesne University Press, 2004). For varied and provocative considerations of Levinas's relevance for particular literary texts, see Steven Shankman, *Other Others: Levinas, Literature,*

Transcultural Studies (Albany: State University of New York Press, 2010); Ann W. Astell and J. A. Jackson, eds., *Levinas and Medieval Literature: The "Difficult Reading" of English and Rabbinic Texts* (Pittsburgh: Duquesne University Press, 2009); Donald R. Wehrs and David P. Haney, eds., *Levinas and Nineteenth-Century Literature: Ethics and Otherness from Romanticism through Realism* (Newark: University of Delaware Press, 2009); and Donald R. Wehrs, ed., *Levinas and Twentieth-Century Literature: Ethics and the Reconstruction of Subjectivity* (Newark: University of Delaware Press, 2013).

17. Jean-Marc Narbonne examines in detail the links between Platonism, Neoplatonism, and Levinas's ethics, and he strikingly concludes the following: "'The Other' resides already in Plato's ἐπέκεινα, the Biblical already in the Greek, but more simply that they participate, in a certain manner, one in the other, and that, it follows, the primacy of the ethical can be read already just beneath the surface of the Platonic project, and that, in a sense, it has borne it forever" (Narbonne, *Levinas and the Greek Heritage* [Leuven: Peeters, 2006], 97). See also the essays in Brian Schroeder and Silvia Benso, eds., *Levinas and the Ancients* (Bloomington: Indiana University Press, 2008), in which the contributors explicate Levinas's theory in relation to the pre-Socratics, Socrates, Plato, Aristotle, the Stoics, Pyrrho of Elis, St. Paul, Plotinus, Neoplatonism, and St. Augustine. Sarah Allen's *The Philosophical Sense of Transcendence: Levinas and Plato on Loving beyond Being* (Pittsburgh: Duquesne University Press, 2009) compares Platonic Eros and Levinasian desire in the movement of transcendence and the good beyond being, whereas Wendy C. Hamblet's *The Lesser Good: The Problem of Justice in Plato and Levinas* (Lanham, Md.: Lexington Books, 2009) links the analyses of justice and goodness by Plato and Levinas. Tanja Staehler, in *Plato and Levinas: The Ambiguous Out-Side of Ethics* (New York: Routledge, 2010), also surveys the intersections between ancient philosophy and Levinas's theories. I found particularly helpful her comparison of the structural similarities between Plato's understanding of speech and writing and Levinas's understanding of the saying and the said (chap. 9, 151–163).

In a related vein, Oona Ajzenstat traces Levinas's thought through the Bible, the Kabbalah, the Talmud, and the Holocaust, the last of which she equates with "night space." She describes her intent thus: "To watch Levinas reading certain of the foundational texts of the Jewish tradition in an effort to determine how he reads and why he reads the way he does. . . . And we see that he reads . . . in a particular way, a way that is almost devoid of historical concern but is deeply philosophical and deeply ethical, a way of reading the goal of which is to tell the truth, or rather the *truths*, of human existence in relation" (*Driven Back to the Text: The Premodern Sources of Levinas's Postmodernism* [Pittsburgh: Duquesne University Press, 2001], 4–5). Taken together, the aforementioned volumes productively thread through Levinas's markedly contemporary project influences and sources from premodern philosophy and theology.

18. Whereas in Homeric society there existed a single cosmic order, applicable to both gods and humans, in which the natural order and the moral order were roughly coterminous, when this unified order metamorphosed—due to invasion, colonization, and the acceleration of travel and trade—into a range of competing social orders, moral assessments turned nostalgically toward the "golden age" with the goal of recuperating a desirable society. Citizens began to question whether "the good," in specific and general instances, pertained to local conventions or to universal nature. I have relied here and elsewhere on MacIntyre's concise summary of ancient ethics (*Short History*, chaps. 2–7).

19. Emmanuel Levinas, *Entre nous: Thinking-of-the-Other*, trans. Michael B. Smith and Barbara Harshav (London: Continuum, 2006), 83.

20. John M. Cooper, "History of Western Ethics: 2. Classical Greek," in *Encyclopedia of Ethics*, ed. Becker and Becker, 1:462. For a detailed analysis of ancient Greek philosophy and philosophers, see the relevant sections in W. K. C. Guthrie, *History of Greek Philosophy*, 3 vols. (Cambridge: Cambridge University Press, 1962–1969).

21. Cooper, "History of Western Ethics," 1:463.

22. Cooper, 1:464.

23. MacIntyre, *Short History*, 61.

24. After Aristotle's death in 322 BCE, Hellenistic philosophers formulated Stoicism and Epicureanism, among other philosophical movements, as continuations and critiques of the earlier debates on ethics. From 323 BCE to approximately 150 BCE, they shared Socrates's vision of the exceptionality and autonomy of human beings, and they viewed

happiness as independent of chance and uncontrollable circumstances. To an even greater degree than their precursors, these philosophers strove to assign complete control to human beings in their present situations. In both ethical platforms, individual choice and responsibility, in opposition to inherited privileges and the vagaries of fate, assumed a greater role than in previous theories. Indeed, one's ethics or happiness was the purview of one's will—one's view of external circumstances—rather than linked to the facts or objects themselves. Levinas regularly theorizes against human choice because it can derive from and lead to asphyxiating self-interest; he instead embraces immanent responsibility, specifically for the Other, as the key to all ethical considerations.

25. Menachem Kellner, "Jewish Ethics," in *A Companion to Ethics*, ed. Peter Singer (Oxford: Blackwell, 1991), 87. In *The Guide for the Perplexed* (written ca. 1190 in Judeo-Arabic and translated into Hebrew in 1204), Maimonides claimed that the imitation of God includes both intellectual perfection, or metaphysical speculation, and right behavior, or ethics. Kellner identifies four main categories in Jewish ethics: biblical, rabbinic, medieval, and modern. See his chapter, referenced above, for a fuller treatment of both Maimonides's ethics and Jewish ethics more generally. Levinas will incorporate, to greater and lesser degrees, all these traditions into his contemporary notion of alterity and into his multiple volumes of commentaries on the Talmud. Scholars have extensively investigated Levinas's relationship to Judaism. See, among others, Claire Elise Katz, *Levinas and the Crisis of Humanism* (Bloomington: Indiana University Press, 2013); her *Levinas, Judaism, and the Feminine* (Bloomington: Indiana University Press, 2003); and Aryeh Botwinick, *Emmanuel Levinas and the Limits to Ethics: A Critique and a Re-appropriation* (London: Routledge, 2014).

26. J. B. Schneewind, "History of Western Ethics: 8. Seventeenth and Eighteenth Century," in *Encyclopedia of Ethics*, ed. Becker and Becker, 1:507–508.

27. Emmanuel Levinas's published dissertation was translated into English by André Orianne in 1973 as *The Theory of Intuition in Husserl's Phenomenology*. The original 1930 text constituted the first book on Husserl in French, and Levinas's fascination with his mentor's work continued

throughout his long philosophical career; it is not coincidental that in a late collection of essays titled *Outside the Subject*, trans. Michael B. Smith (London: Athlone, 1993) and published originally in French as *Hors sujet* (1987), Levinas again takes up Husserlian subjectivity. See also Silvia Benso, *The Face of Things: A Different Side of Ethics* (Albany: State University of New York Press, 2000); Chanter, *Time, Death, and the Feminine*; and Richard A. Cohen, *Ethics, Exegesis and Philosophy: Interpretation after Levinas* (Cambridge: Cambridge University Press, 2001), among others, for comprehensive discussions of the relationship between Levinas's philosophy and the ideas of Husserl and Heidegger.

28. Franz Clemens Brentano stressed intentionality and intrinsic value, both of which would prove to be key concepts for future phenomenologists, and he also paved the way for value realism. Following Descartes, Brentano concurred that "all mental phenomena are directed upon the objects of our ideas" and that the appropriate relationship between our attitudes toward the objects and the objects themselves determines correctness, which is in turn linked to goodness (Roderick M. Chisholm, "Brentano, Franz Clemens [1838–1917]," in *Encyclopedia of Ethics*, ed. Becker and Becker, 1:97–98). In accordance with Plato, he also advocated for goodness in itself: if an object is intrinsically good, then it is appropriate to affirm or love that object, and if the object is intrinsically bad, then it is appropriate to deny or hate that object.

29. Schroeder, "Continental Ethics," 529.

30. See Kris Sealey's discussion of Levinas and Sartre in *Moments of Disruption: Levinas, Sartre, and the Question of Transcendence* (Albany: State University of New York Press, 2013), chap. 5, 117–150, in which she elaborates upon the following premise: "As is the case in other descriptions, their (concrete) phenomenologies of alterity are similar in many respects. However, there is significant divergence in their interpretations of this alterity of the Other. . . . The explicitly political commitments through which Sartre formalizes his phenomenology of alterity are quite absent in Levinas's work" (117). While explicit political commitment might have been absent from Levinas's early work, it undeniably informs his later writing.

31. The adolescent Levinas also witnessed firsthand the Russian Revolution, although scholars and biographers tend to focus almost exclusively

on Levinas's statements regarding the influence of World War II on his own thought. After World War II, however, Levinas increasingly distanced himself from other ethical theories in order to critique the Western ethical tradition and conceptualize an alternative ethics based on our encounters with and moral obligations to the other person as radically other.

32. Emmanuel Levinas, "Martin Buber and the Theory of Knowledge," in *The Levinas Reader*, ed. Séan Hand (Oxford: Blackwell, 1989), 74. Levinas's essay on Buber, written in 1958, was originally published in German in 1963, it was subsequently translated by Levinas himself into French, and the French version was published posthumously in 1976. The English-language translation of the essay dates from 1967. Levinas mentions Buber in *Totality and Infinity*, 68–69, 115; and again in *Otherwise Than Being, or Beyond Essence*, trans. Alphonso Lingis (Pittsburgh: Duquesne University Press, 1981), 13. For a treatment of Levinas's shifting relationship with Buber's philosophical position, see, among others, Robert Bernasconi's essay on "'Failure of Communication' as a Surplus: Dialogue and Lack of Dialogue between Buber and Levinas," in *The Provocation of Levinas: Rethinking the Other*, ed. Robert Bernasconi and David Woods (London: Routledge, 1988), 100–135.

33. Commentators have identified many more feasible links, particularly regarding the impact of Judaism on formulations of time, between Levinas and Franz Rosenzweig. In his preface, Levinas acknowledges his unequivocal debt to Rosenzweig: "We were impressed by the opposition to the idea of totality in Franz Rosenzweig's *Stern der Erlösung*, a work too often present in this book to be cited" (Levinas, *Totality and Infinity*, 28). For a complete treatment of the relationship between Levinas and Rosenzweig, see the texts by Susan Handelman, "Facing the Other: Levinas, Perelman, Rosenzweig," in *Divine Aporia: Postmodern Conversations about the Other*, ed. John C. Hawley (Lewisburg, Pa.: Bucknell University Press, 2000), 263–285; Richard A. Cohen, *Elevations: The Height of the Good in Rosenzweig and Levinas* (Chicago: University of Chicago Press, 1994); Robert Gibbs, *Correlations in Rosenzweig and Levinas* (Princeton: Princeton University Press, 1992); Cohen, *Ethics, Exegesis and Philosophy*; and Richard A. Cohen, ed., *Face to Face with Levinas* (Albany: State University of New York Press, 1986).

34. See John E. Drabinski, *Sense and Sensibility: The Problem of Phenomenology in Levinas* (Albany: State University of New York Press, 2001); and the first three essays in Joëlle Hansel, ed., *Levinas in Jerusalem: Phenomenology, Ethics, Politics, Aesthetics* (Amsterdam: Springer, 2009), 3–57, for analyses of Levinas's intellectual relationship to phenomenology.

35. Michael Hammond et al., *Understanding Phenomenology* (Oxford: Basil Blackwell, 1991), 1.

36. Because Levinas works within the first subfield, I have chosen to focus on transcendental phenomenology in my summary. For a discussion of the existential manifestations of phenomenology, see chapters 11 and 12—on Sartre and Merleau-Ponty, respectively—in Dermot Moran's *Introduction to Phenomenology* (London: Routledge, 2000), 354–434. Moran includes a chapter on Levinas's contributions to phenomenology, which he characterizes as "reminding Western philosophy of the manner in which the other person and 'otherness' in general intervenes in and subverts all our attempts to provide global and totalising explanations" (320).

37. Husserl employs the concept of "apodicticity," or "absolute indubitability," which he opposes to nonapodictic evidence: "Any evidence is a grasping of something that is, or is thus, a grasping in the mode of 'it-itself,' with full certainty of its being, a certainty that accordingly excludes every doubt. . . . An *apodictic* evidence, however, is not merely certainty of the affairs . . . evident in it; rather it discloses itself, to a critical reflection, as having the signal peculiarity of being *at the same time* [i.e., as well as being certain] *the absolute unimaginableness* (inconceivability) of their *non-being*, and thus excluding in advance every doubt as 'objectless,' empty" (quoted in Hammond et al., *Understanding Phenomenology*, 21; emphasis in the original).

38. Hammond et al., 2–3; emphasis in the original.

39. Severson, *Levinas's Philosophy of Time*, 33.

40. Hammond et al., *Understanding Phenomenology*, 5; emphasis in the original.

41. Levinas, *Ethics and Infinity*, 30.

42. Levinas, *Outside the Subject*, 152.

43. Emmanuel Levinas, *Time and the Other (and Additional Essays)*, trans. Richard A. Cohen (Pittsburgh: Duquesne University Press, 1987), 39.

44. It is perhaps worth noting that Husserl himself proposed Heidegger as his successor at the University of Freiburg and that Heidegger inherited Husserl's chair at that same institution in 1928.

45. Hand, *Emmanuel Levinas*, 13. Current scholars of Levinas's work are fortunate to benefit from numerous superb introductions to his philosophy. Among these, I have relied principally on four texts, which have proved immeasurably helpful and clear: Davis, *Levinas*; Simon Critchley and Robert Bernasconi, eds., *The Cambridge Companion to Levinas* (Cambridge: Cambridge University Press, 2002); Hand, *Emmanuel Levinas*; and Severson, *Levinas's Philosophy of Time*.

46. Martin Heidegger, *Being and Time*, trans. John Macquarrie and Edward Robinson (New York: Harper & Row, 1962), 35; emphasis in the original.

47. Davis, *Levinas*, 16.

48. Severson, *Levinas's Philosophy of Time*, 28; emphasis in the original.

49. Davis, *Levinas*, 21.

50. Richard A. Cohen, "Translator's Introduction," in *Time and the Other*, by Levinas, 4.

51. I refer, in particular, to the essays collected under the titles *De l'existence à l'existant* (translated by Alphonso Lingis into English and published as *Existence and Existents* [1947; repr., Dordrecht: Kluwer, 1978]), "Le temps et l'autre," and *En découvrant l'existence avec Husserl et Heidegger* (1949). "Le temps et l'autre" originally appeared in a collection of essays edited by Jean Wahl and titled *Le choix, le monde, l'existence* (Grenoble: Arthaud, 1947) and was republished in French, with a new preface by Levinas, in 1979. It was translated into English by Cohen and included in *Time and the Other*. An abbreviated version of the third text was translated into English by Richard A. Cohen and Michael B. Smith and published as *Discovering Existence with Husserl* (Evanston, Ill.: Northwestern University Press, 1998). See Davis's *Levinas* for a list of Levinas's texts, together with the publication information for their English-language translations.

52. Levinas, *Time and the Other*, 43. As the translator of this work, Cohen provides a concise etymology—citing D. J. O'Connor's "Substance and Attribute" (1972)—of the Greek origin of *hypostasis*; he also notes that Levinas employs the term to refer to both "the origin of an entity that is

neither substantial nor insubstantial" and "the individuation of existence" (43–44n6).

53. Levinas, 52.

54. Severson, *Levinas's Philosophy of Time*, 190.

55. Levinas, *Discovering Existence*, 144–145. In one of many acute gestures of commemoration undertaken throughout his career, Levinas inserts a note after "the mystery of intentionality" in which he acknowledges and praises Yvonne Picard's published master's thesis; alludes to her death "for having participated in the Resistance, without her origin having been able to be the cause of her martyrdom"; and "render[s] a pious homage—imprescriptible—by evoking her thought and thus moving the lips of the dead" (192). This commemorative drive perhaps reaches its apotheosis with the double dedication, in French and in Hebrew, of *Otherwise Than Being* to "the memory of those who were closest among the 6 million assassinated by the National Socialists, and of the millions on millions of all confessions and all nations, victims of the same hatred of the other man, the same anti-semitism" (Levinas, *Otherwise Than Being*, v).

56. *A l'heure des nations* includes five Talmudic readings that Levinas presented at the annual colloquium of French-speaking Jewish intellectuals during the 1980s, supplemented by essays on Judaism and exegesis. Subsequent volumes appearing under Levinas's name feature, in the main, previously published essays collected into single volumes; interviews and discussions with Levinas, such as Jill Robbins, ed., *Is It Righteous to Be? Interviews with Emmanuel Levinas* (Stanford: Stanford University Press, 2001); and translations of earlier works.

57. James R. Mensch's *Levinas's Existential Analytic: A Commentary on* Totality and Infinity (Evanston, Ill.: Northwestern University Press, 2015) comprises, to my knowledge, the most recent monograph, as of 2017, that is dedicated entirely to explicating Levinas's first volume.

58. While I cannot pretend to actively dialogue, either directly or indirectly, with all of the vast corpus of secondary criticism on Levinas's thought, I would be remiss not to recognize some of the earliest English-language considerations of Levinas's philosophy: the essays collected in Cohen, *Face to Face with Levinas*; and Bernasconi and Wood, *Provocation*

of Levinas; together with Alphonso Lingis's *Libido: The French Existentialist Theories* (Bloomington: Indiana University Press, 1985); and Mark C. Taylor's *Altarity* (Chicago: University of Chicago Press, 1987).

59. Levinas, *Totality and Infinity*, 26.

60. Levinas, 26–27.

61. Levinas, 43.

62. Three years after the publication of *Totalité et infini*, Jacques Derrida published the first, and still arguably the most influential, critique of Levinas's thought in *Revue de métaphysique et de morale* (and subsequently as chap. 4 in *L'écriture et la différence* [1967] / *Writing and Difference* [1978]). There he takes Levinas to task concerning at least two types of problems in Levinas's work: apparent inconsistencies in his thinking and blind spots in his readings of other philosophers, including Kant, Kierkegaard, Buber, and most importantly, Husserl and Heidegger. In characteristic fashion, Derrida further argues that "by making the origin of language, meaning, and difference the relation to the infinitely other, Levinas is resigned to betraying his own intentions in his philosophical discourse" (Derrida, *Writing and Difference*, trans. Alan Bass [Chicago: University of Chicago Press, 1978], 151). Instead of finding ample indications of the spuriousness of Levinas's project, however, Derrida argues that "Levinas's precursors already share the respect for the Other which he apparently fails to find in them. Ultimately, Levinas's fundamental problem concerns the language of philosophy itself. Levinas's recourse to a language rooted in the primacy of the Same necessarily defeats his desire for a discourse fully exposed to the strangeness of the Other" (Davis, *Levinas*, 66). In 1973, Levinas published an essay titled "Tout Autrement" in which he underscored Derrida's own dependence on ontological language in the latter's 1967 essay. Levinas's 1973 essay was translated into English by Simon Critchley in 1991 as "Wholly Otherwise" and is included as the first chapter in Robert Bernasconi and Simon Critchley, eds., *Re-reading Levinas* (Bloomington: Indiana University Press, 1991). See Critchley's *The Ethics of Deconstruction: Derrida and Levinas* (Oxford: Blackwell, 1992), among many other fine discussions, for a cogent analysis of the two French philosophers. See also Derrida's published eulogy, *Adieu to Emmanuel Levinas*, trans.

Pascale-Anne Brault and Michael Naas (Stanford: Stanford University Press, 1999), for his final homage to Levinas.

63. Hand, *Emmanuel Levinas*, 46.

64. Although *Otherwise Than Being* was first published in French in 1974, it was based in part on articles and lectures delivered between 1967 and 1974.

65. Hand, *Emmanuel Levinas*, 49.

66. Levinas, *Otherwise Than Being*, 46.

67. Levinas, 37–38.

68. Levinas, 47.

69. Levinas, 111.

70. Davis, *Levinas*, 81.

71. Levinas, *Entre nous*, 201.

2. Spain's Generación X

1. Julián Casanova and Carlos Gil Andrés's *Twentieth-Century Spain: A History* (Cambridge: Cambridge University Press, 2014) includes a helpful bibliography for all the major periods in the history of twentieth-century Spain, together with a list of pertinent general references.

2. Casanova and Gil Andrés, 3.

3. Casanova and Gil Andrés, 9.

4. See José Álvarez Junco's 1996 essay for an expansive discussion of *caciquismo* in Spain and its impact on twentieth-century politics ("Redes locales, lealtades tradicionales y nuevas identidades colectivas en la España del siglo XIX," in *Política en penumbra: Patronazo y clientelismo políticos en la España contemporánea*, ed. Antonio Robles Ejea [Madrid: Siglo XXI, 1996], 71–94).

5. Among many compelling and lucid book-length studies of Basque and Catalonian nationalisms, see Xosé Manoel Núñez Seixas, *Los nacionalismos en la España contemporánea: Siglos XIX y XX* (Madrid: Hipòtesi, 1999); Antonio Elorza, *Un pueblo escogido: Génesis, definición y desarrollo del nacionalismo vasco* (Madrid: Crítica, 2001); and Angel Smith, *The Origins of Catalan Nationalism, 1770–1898* (Basingstoke: Palgrave Macmillan, 2014).

6. Casanova and Gil Andrés, *Twentieth-Century Spain*, 23–24.

7. These included the appointment of the prime minister and all other ministers; the sharing of legislative power with the Cortes, which the king had the power to summon and dissolve; the direction of diplomatic relations and the administration of justice; and the position as commander in chief of the armed forces, with the authority to appoint, dismiss, and decorate members of the army.

8. Historians alternatively cite July 25 to August 2, 1909, as the relevant dates.

9. Antonio Maura served as the prime minister of Spain on five separate occasions between 1903 and 1922: 1903 to 1904, 1907 to 1909, 1918 (seven months), 1919 (three months), and 1921 to 1922 (eight months).

10. Casanova and Gil Andrés, *Twentieth-Century Spain*, 59.

11. José Luis Gómez Navarro has observed that the imposition of a military dictatorship during the early part of the twentieth century in Spain paralleled similar events in Portugal, Greece, Poland, Romania, Bulgaria, Hungary, and Yugoslavia. He further identifies the factors common to all these countries that resulted in the imposition of military dictatorships during the initial decades of the twentieth century: "La fragmentación y descomposición política de los sectores sociales dominantes, la situación de crisis latente en la que una minoría gobierna ante la indiferencia o el divorcio de las masas y haciéndolo de forma que amplios sectores de ellas odian pero no pueden destruir, el predominio militar en las relaciones civiles-militares, la permanencia de una legitimidad tradicional vinculada al Monarca, la falta de consolidación de una nueva legitimidad con base en la soberanía popular y que se exprese a través de los partidos politicos, y la pérdida de la legitimidad y el fracaso en la gestión de los gobiernos" [The political fragmentation and decomposition of the dominant social sectors, the situation of the latent crisis in which a minority governs in the face of the indifference or divorce of the masses, and doing so in a way that many sectors hate but cannot destroy, military dominance in civilian-military relations, the permanence of a traditional legitimacy connected to the Monarchy, the lack of consolidation of a new legitimacy with a base in popular sovereignty that is expressed via political parties, and the loss of legitimacy and the failure of the creation of governments] (Gómez Navarro, *El régimen de Primo de Rivera: Reyes, dictaduras y dictadores* [Madrid: Cátedra, 1991], 58).

For a comparative analysis of the emergence of dictatorial regimes in Europe during the early twentieth century, see also chapters 1 and 2 in this text. Gómez Navarro also provides an extensive bibliography of scholarship on Primo de Rivera's dictatorship.

12. María Teresa González Calbet, *La dictadura de Primo de Rivera: El Directorio Militar* (Madrid: El Arquero, 1987), 12.

13. See, among other relevant discussions, the essays collected in Sebastian Balfour and Paul Preston, eds., *Spain and the Great Powers in the Twentieth Century* (London: Routledge, 1999), for a comprehensive treatment of the evolving role of Spain vis-à-vis the international community from 1900 to 1975. Published four years earlier, the essays in Richard Gillespie, Fernando Rodrigo, and Jonathan Story, eds., *Democratic Spain: Reshaping External Relations in a Changing World* (London: Routledge, 1995), examine Spain's place in the international community after 1975.

14. Casanova and Gil Andrés, *Twentieth-Century Spain*, 102.

15. See Paul Preston, *The Spanish Holocaust: Inquisition and Extermination in Twentieth-Century Spain* (New York: W. W. Norton, 2012), for an insightful and far-reaching discussion of this issue.

16. Casanova and Gil Andrés, *Twentieth-Century Spain*, 161.

17. Bruce Lincoln has noted that religion proved exceedingly useful as the only cause to systematically generate international sympathy for the Nationalists (Lincoln, "Revolutionary Exhumations in Spain, July 1936," *Comparative Studies in Society and History* 27, no. 2 [1985]: 231–260). By contrast, because of widespread international media coverage of selected violence on the part of the Republican forces (and drastically limited international media exposure to Nationalist violence), the anticlericalism associated with the Republic side yielded no international support whatsoever.

18. Casanova and Gil Andrés, *Twentieth-Century Spain*, 211.

19. Other sources put the number of executions during the Spanish Civil War as high as half a million.

20. Casanova and Gil Andrés, *Twentieth-Century Spain*, 220.

21. Franco's declared policy of nonintervention did not, however, impede him from supporting the Nazi cause by establishing the División Azul [Blue Division], which was composed of some forty-seven thousand Spanish troops who accompanied the German army when they invaded

the Soviet Union in June 1941. See Jorge M. Reverte, *La División Azul: Rusia 1941–1944* (Madrid: RBA, 2011), for a detailed account of this military collaboration.

22. Javier Tussell, *Carrero: La eminencia gris del régimen de Franco* (Madrid: Temas de Hoy, 1993), 461, quoted in Casanova and Gil Andrés, *Twentieth-Century Spain*, 271.

23. Fernando de Santiago served as the interim prime minister for three days (July 1, 1976–July 3, 1976) during the transition.

24. See Casanova and Gil Andrés, *Twentieth-Century Spain*, 301–306, for a summary of Suárez's political career, accomplishments, and challenges.

25. It could be argued that Calvo Sotelo's rise to prominence represented a step backward in the political evolution of Spain: he had worked as a lawyer in the Cortes during Franco's final years, had maintained firm ties with the business world, was in favor of the monarchy, and had worked closely with Suárez. On the one hand, when Calvo Sotelo was elected to the post of prime minister, he also formed a cabinet made up entirely of UCD deputies as opposed to a coalition government, but he excluded, for the first time during the twentieth century, military ministers from the cabinet. On the other hand, during his short tenure, he accomplished very little—other than shepherding Spain into the North Atlantic Treaty Organization (NATO), largely due to the internal disintegration of his political party. Casanova and Gil Andrés cite as the fatal flaw of the UCD its inability to create "a true party of the masses, a solid structure, a defined ideology and an unquestioned leadership" (326). Felipe González and the PSOE, by contrast, achieved all these goals during the subsequent fourteen years.

26. Casanova and Gil Andrés, *Twentieth-Century Spain*, 341.

27. Casanova and Gil Andrés, 342.

28. Santos Alonso has linked the far-flung prosperity that characterized 1990s Spain with the extended success of Aznar and the PP during the same decade: "El mismo Aznar destacó en su primera campaña electoral su apoyo indiscutible siempre y cuando la cultura fuera rentable. . . . Es decir, se trataba de transformar las manifestaciones artísticas—a imagen y semejanza de los modelos americanos—no en actividades destinadas a la formación humanística e integral del ciudadano, sino en industrias que debían revertir sus beneficios en la economía española. Y así fue"

[Aznar himself emphasized in his first electoral campaign his undeniable support when, and only when, the culture was profitable. . . . In other words, the point was to transform artistic manifestations—in the image and like the American models—not into activities destined toward the humanistic and holistic formation of citizens, but into industries that should return their benefits to the Spanish economy. And this is what happened] (*La novela española en el fin de siglo: 1975–2001* [Madrid: Mare Nostrum, 2003], 179).

29. Carmen de Urioste, "La narrativa española de los noventa: ¿Existe una 'Generación X'?," *Letras Peninsulares* 10, no. 3 (1997–1998): 457.

30. See Carmen de Urioste, *Novela y sociedad en la España contemporánea (1994–2009)* (Madrid: Fundamentos, 2009), 41–72; and Christine Henseler, *Spanish Fiction in the Digital Age: Generation X Remixed* (New York: Palgrave Macmillan, 2011), for further discussions of the narrative of Spain's Gen X as interventions in youth culture.

31. Tara Brabazon, *From Revolution to Revelation: Generation X, Popular Memory and Cultural Studies* (Aldershot: Ashgate, 2005), 10.

32. José María Izquierdo, "Narradores españoles novísimos de los años noventa," *Revista de Estudios Hispánicos* 35, no. 2 (2001): 293–294.

33. Toni Dorca, "Joven narrativa en la España de los noventa: La generación X," *Revista de Estudios Hispánicos* 31, no. 2 (1997): 309–324; Urioste, "Narrativa española," 457.

34. Izquierdo, "Narradores españoles," 295.

35. Alonso, *Novela española*, 50. Alonso focuses primarily on the novels of the last three of these seven generations, which he links, in the subtitles of the pertinent chapters, to "the expectations of narrative change" (1975–1981; chap. 3), "the normalization of narrative change" (1982–1990; chap. 4), and "between literary autonomy and commerce" (1991–2001; chap. 5). See chapters 2 and 5 in his *Novela española* for a broader justification of the generational divisions utilized and a wide-ranging discussion of novels published by authors from various generations during the 1990s. Among the texts and authors that I consider, Alonso briefly mentions Belén Gopegui, *Tocarnos la cara* (Barcelona: Anagrama, 1995); José Ángel Mañas, *Historias del Kronen* (Barcelona: Destino, 1994); and several novels by Juana Salabert, including *Arde lo que será* (Barcelona: Destino, 1996).

36. As only two among the many cogent recent attacks on the "generational approach" long employed by Hispanists, see the essay by C. Christopher Soufas Jr., who posits the following: "What I consider to be an unproductive model has been assimilated into the collective consciousness of Hispanists for more than half a century and, primarily because of the simplicity and convenience of the model, has been made to seem neutral and even natural" (Soufas, "Origins and Legacy of the Spanish Literary Generation," *Anales de la literatura española contemporánea* 36, no. 1 [2011]: 209). In the realm of critics who work with Gen X writers, José F. Colmeiro arguably set the bar for the "antigeneration" position vis-à-vis these authors in his 2001 essay, in which he minces no words in statements such as the following: "Se produce la 'feliz' coincidencia de la inercia crítica nacional y del mimetismo y dependencia cultural del extranjero, especialmente de la industria cultural del cine, la television, la música y la literatura de los Estados Unidos, que son fomentados por la hegemonía cultural producto de la globalización económica" [The "happy" coincidence is produced involving national critical inertia and mimeticism and cultural dependence on the foreign, especially on the part of the cultural industry associated with the film, television, music, and literature of the United States, which is fomented by the hegemonic cultural product of economic globalization] ("En busca de la 'Generación X': ¿Héroes por un día o una nueva generación perdida," *España Contemporánea* 14, no. 1 [2001]: 8–9).

37. I list the seventy-nine authors here alphabetically, together with their years of birth and, in the two pertinent cases, the years in which they died: Mercedes Abad (b. 1961), Antonio Álamo (b. 1964), Leopoldo Alas Mínguez (1962–2008), Joaquín Albaicín (b. 1965), Javier Azpeitia (b. 1962), Nuria Barrios (b. 1962), Lola Becarria (b. 1963), Felipe Benítez Reyes (b. 1960), Ricardo Emilio Bofill (b. 1965), Juan Bonilla (b. 1966), Gabriela Bustelo (b. 1962), Emilio Calle (b. 1963), Cuca Canals (b. 1962), Luis María Carrero (b. 1967), Martín Casariego (b. 1962), Nicolás Casariego (b. 1970), Francisco Casavella (b. 1963), Luisa Castro (b. 1966), Javier Cercas (b. 1962), Lucía Etxebarria (b. 1966), José Fernández de la Sota (b. 1960), Antonio Fontana (b. 1964), Espido Freire (b. 1974), Ángel García Galiano (b. 1961), Ignacio García-Valiño (1968–2014), Marcos Giralt Torrente (b. 1968), Pablo González Cuesta (b. 1968), Belén

Gopegui (b. 1963), Almudena Grandes (b. 1960), Ismael Grasa (b. 1968), Josan Hatero (b. 1970), Enrique de Hériz (b. 1964), Begoña Huertas (b. 1965), Andrés Ibañez (b. 1961), Paula Izquierdo (b. 1962), María Jaén (b. 1962), Ángela Labordeta (b. 1967), Elvira Lindo (b. 1962), Marisa Lorenzo (b. 1961), Ray Loriga (b. 1967), José Machado (b. 1974), Pedro Maestre (b. 1967), Luis Magrinyá (b. 1960), José Ángel Mañas (b. 1971), Luis G. Martín (b. 1962), José Ramón Martín Largo (b. 1960), Ignacio Martínez de Pisón (b. 1960), Caimán Montalbán (no dates), Carmen Montalbán Mansilla (b. 1963), Daniel Múgica (b. 1967), Antonio Orejudo Ultrilla (b. 1963), David Pallol (b. 1966), Sergi Pàmies (b. 1960), Maria de la Pau Janer (b. 1966), Francisco Peregil (b. 1967), Tino Pertierra (b. 1964), Beatriz Pottecher (b. 1961), Juan Manuel de Prada (b. 1970), Benjamín Prado (b. 1961), Rafael Reig (b. 1963), Blanca Riestra (b. 1970), Ana Rioja (b. 1962), Marta Rivera de la Cruz (b. 1970), Félix Romeo (1968–2011), Fernando Royuela (b. 1963), Luis Manuel Ruiz (b. 1973), Juan Manuel Salmerón (b. 1971), Juana Salabert (b. 1962), Care Santos (b. 1970), Marta Sanz (b. 1967), Francisco J. Satué (b. 1961), Javier Sebastián (b. 1962), Lorenzo Silva (b. 1966), Eloy Tizón (b. 1964), David Trueba (b. 1969), Pedro Ugarte (b. 1963), Clara Usón (b. 1961), Eduardo Vilas (b. 1971), Roger Wolfe (b. 1962).

38. As is the case with any rule, there are inevitable exceptions to this claim. As only three instances, both Juana Salabert and Sergi Pàmies were born in Paris, although all of their published novels have been written in Spanish and Catalan, respectively, and were published initially in Spain; Roger Wolfe, born in Westerham, England, has resided in Spain since the age of five and also publishes primarily in Spanish. I am also acutely aware that my selection of 1960 and 1974 (in consonance with the dates chosen by most critics) as the birth-year margins for the generation signifies the exclusion of countless superb writers such as Susana Fortes (b. 1959), Inma Monsó (b. 1959), and Olga Guirao (b. 1959) on one end of the chronological divide and Elvira Navarro (b. 1978) on the opposite edge of the same.

39. See Candice L. Bosse, *Becoming and Consumption: The Contemporary Spanish Novel* (Lanham, Md.: Lexington Books, 2007); Henseler, *Spanish Fiction*; and Eva Navarro Martínez, *La novela de la Generación X* (Granada: Universidad de Granada, 2008), for further discussions

of the intertwined roles of advertising and youth culture within this demographic. Henseler, in particular, analyzes in great detail new media technologies in the context of Spain's Gen X, and she concludes, among other provocative observations, that "the remixing of Generation X is the interpretive result of a process of cultural and media hybridization that centers not only on the connections between old and new content but also on old and new techniques" (*Spanish Fiction*, 221–222).

40. In addition, 1996 also saw the publication of Santos Sanz Villanueva's "Así pasaron veinte años," *República de las Letras* 50 (1996): 19–24; and Ángel García Galiano and Ándrés Sánchez Magro, during the same year, offered their assessment in "Narrativa española de los noventa: La sociedad literaria," *Reseña* 277 (1996): 2–7.

41. Ramón Acín, "El comercio en la literatura: Un difícil matrimonio," *Ínsula* 589–590 (1996): 6.

42. Many of the novelists who regularly comprise Spain's Gen X have also published short stories. All the authors anthologized or mentioned in Sabas Martín, ed., *Páginas amarillas* (Madrid: Lengua de Trapo, 1997), with the exception of F. M. (the pseudonym of Pablo Bullejos) and José Fernández-Cavia, published novels in Spain during the 1990s. Because I do not consider short fiction in the present study, I exclude F. M. and Fernández-Cavia from my provisional list of Gen X writers. In addition to the thirty-seven novelists whose short fiction is profiled in the anthology, Martín also refers, in his introduction, to twenty-six authors whose short fiction he does not include but who published at least one novel in the 1990s.

Javier Calvo, ed., *After Hours: Una muestra de cult fiction* (Barcelona: Mondadori, 1999), is likewise composed of short stories—in this instance by twenty-three Gen X writers, eight of whom are also featured in *Páginas amarillas*: Gabriela Bustelo, Nicolás Casariego, Francisco Casavella, F. M., Marcos Giralt Torrente, Josan Hatero, Félix Romeo, and Juan Manuel Salmerón. Calvo also introduces stories by José Fernández de la Sota, Marisa Lorenzo, Rafael Reig, Luis Manuel Ruiz, Clara Usón, and Roger Wolfe, all of whom also published novels in the 1990s. The other writers anthologized (Ruth Baza, Eloy Fernández Porta, Mariano Gistaín, Juan Gracia, Jesús Llorente, F. M., Eduard

Márquez, Vicente Mora, and Jordi Puntí) have either published no
novels or did not publish their first novel until after 2000. I therefore
do not include, for the purpose of my study, this latter subset of authors
among Gen X writers.

For her part, Noemí Montetes Mairal's volume *Qué he hecho yo para
publicar esto (XX escritores* jóvenes *para el siglo XXI)* (Barcelona: DVD
Ediciones, 1999) presents interviews with eleven of the authors named
in *Páginas amarillas*: Antonio Álamo, Felipe Benítez Reyes, Francisco
Casavella, Luisa Castro, Javier Cercas, Almudena Grandes, Juan Manuel
de Prada, Benjamín Prado, Juana Salabert, Javier Sebastián, and Eloy
Tizón. Of the remaining nine interviewees, Carlos Castán Andolz and
Vicente Gallego have published no novels; José Ángel Cilleruelo, Carlos
Marzal, and Vicente Valero published their first novels in 2001, 2005,
and 2014, respectively; and finally, Pablo García Casado, Luis García
Montero, José María Micó, and Jorge Riechmann are primarily poets
and do not, to my knowledge, write narrative fiction.

I derive the seventy-nine names enumerated previously from the
sixty-three applicable authors discussed and/or anthologized by Martín
and the six writers featured in Calvo's *After Hours* but not mentioned
by Martín (Fernández de la Sota, Lorenzo, Reig, Ruiz, Usón, Wolfe). In
addition, Carles Bernadell highlights the narrative of Ricardo Emilio
Bofill throughout his essay on the new literary generation, which
appeared in the pages of *Quimera* in 1996; Carmen de Urioste includes
Espido Freire, Elvira Lindo, and Marta Rivera de la Cruz in her 2001
article on the Spanish women who belong to the Gen X—and I would
also add Carmen Montalbán Mansilla and Maria de la Pau Janer (who
publishes in Catalan and Spanish) to Urioste's roster. Finally, Eloy
Fernández Porta mentions Caimán Montalbán and Enrique de Hériz in
his discussion of the Gen X (Fernández Porta, "Poéticas del Prozac: Tres
líneas en la novela española de los noventa," *Quimera* 145 [1996]: 35–37),
and Francisco Peregil and Eduardo Vilas appear in Luis Mancha San
Esteban's roster of relevant authors (Mancha San Esteban, *Generación
Kronen: Una aproximación antropológica al mundo literario en España*
[Alcalá de Henares: Universidad de Alcalá, 2006]). All the writers
included on my roster of Gen X writers were born between 1960 and

1974 and published at least one novel in Spain during the 1990s. My list is by no means complete, and I leave it to future scholars to amplify and revise the parameters of the Gen X.

43. All the literary journals thus far mentioned feature essays on Spain's Gen X by well-known critics in Spain—among them, Ramón Acín, Santos Alonso, Eloy Fernández Porta, José Antonio Fortes, Germán Gullón, and Santos Sanz Villanueva. The noteworthy critical articles that appeared in scholarly outlets between 2000 and 2010, many of which I cite throughout the current project and all of which are included in the bibliography, include those by Athena Alchazidu, José F. Colmeiro, Toni Dorca, Enrique Ferrari, Santiago Fouz-Hernández, José María Izquierdo, Jason E. Klodt, Matthew J. Marr, Nina L. Molinaro, Virginia Newhall Rademacher, H. Rosi Song, Nathan Richardson, and Robert C. Spires, together with the essays collected in Ángeles Encinar and Kathleen M. Glenn, eds., *La pluralidad narrativa: Escritores españoles contemporáneos (1984–2004)* (Madrid: Biblioteca Nueva, 2005); and Christine Henseler and Randolph D. Pope, eds., *Generation X Rocks: Contemporary Peninsular Fiction, Film, and Rock Culture* (Nashville: Vanderbilt University Press, 2007). Numerous scholars in Spain and the United States also published book-length monographs on this same group of novelists, either as Gen X writers or in light of other critical lenses, during the first decade of the twenty-first century. These scholars, some of whom I cite throughout the monograph, include (but certainly are not limited to) the following: Yaw Agawu-Kakraba, Santos Alonso, Candice L. Bosse, José F. Colmeiro, Kathryn Everly, Antonio Gutiérrez Resa, Christine Henseler, Luis Mancha San Esteban, Gonzalo Navajas, Eva Navarro Martínez, Dorothy Odartey-Wellington, Peregrina Pereiro, Jorge Pérez, Cintia Santana, and Carmen de Urioste.

As evidence of the cultural prominence and challenges of this specific group of writers in Spain, the scholarship on Spain's Gen X has continued to expand and increase. Relevant book-length monographs published since 2010 include Henseler's *Spanish Fiction*; Jorge Pérez's *Cultural Roundabouts: Spanish Film and Novel on the Road* (Lewisburg, Pa.: Bucknell University Press, 2011); and Yvonne Gavela-Ramos's *El espejo de Perseo: Cultura visual en la narrativa y el cine español* (Vigo: Editorial Academia del Hispanismo, 2015). In my lengthy catalog, I have opted to forego recognition of the vast critical commentary, in the form of discrete essays and monographs, on individual writers associated with the Gen X. I will reference some of these in successive chapters during my discussions of particular novels.

44. Germán Gullón, "Cómo se lee una novela de la última generación (Apartado X)," *Ínsula* 589–590 (1996): 31. At the other end of the critical spectrum, Santos Alonso complained, in the pages of *Leer* during the same year, of the spectacular lack of maturity and artistic sensibility that characterized the generation: "A los jóvenes precoces de hoy se les ha hecho creer que si una novela vende, al margen de como esté escrita, puede alcanzar la inmortalidad, y ellos, sus autores, pueden ser considerados unos maestros de la pluma y del ordenador. Pero la realidad es muy otra. La mayoría, ni son maestros de nada y hacen nada por serlo" [The precocious youth of today has been made to believe that if a novel sells, independently of how it is written, immortality can be achieved, and they, the authors of said novels, can consider themselves to be masters of the pen and the computer. But the reality is something else altogether. The majority are masters of nothing and do nothing to become so] ("El revuelo de la juventud," *Leer* 83 [1996]: 29).

45. Santos Sanz Villanueva, "El archipiélago de la ficción," *Ínsula* 589–590 (1997): 4.

46. Urioste, "Narrativa española"; and Dorca, "Joven narrativa."

47. Urioste, "Narrativa española," 457.

48. Andrés Carabantes, "La tribu del Kronen," *Leer* 80 (1995–1996): 30.

49. Izquierdo, "Narradores españoles," 296. Izquierdo notes that "cofradía del cuero" [leather brotherhood] was coined by Jorge Herralde, director of Anagrama, in reference to the subgroup of hard realists who utilized the poetics of rock music and the Beat Generation in their narratives. "Generación J.A.S.P." (the initials stand for "Joven Aunque Sobradamente Preparado," or "Young Although Extremely Prepared") emerged as part of a publicity campaign to market a particular kind of car. Sabas Martín traces the origins of "juventud caníbal" [cannibal youth] to an Italian group of writers who came to prominence through the publication of the anthology *Juventud caníbal*, published first in Italian by Einaudi and then in Spanish by Mondadori in 1998 ("Narrativa española tercer milenio [guía para usuarios]," in *Páginas amarillas*, xii).

50. Christine Henseler, "Pop, Punk, and Rock & Roll Writers: José Ángel Mañas, Ray Loriga, and Lucía Etxebarria Redefine the Literary Canon," *Hispania* 87, no. 4 (2004): 692.

51. Antonio Gutiérrez Resa, *Sociología de valores en la novela contemporánea española* (Madrid: Fundación Santa María, 2003); Henseler and Pope, *Generation X Rocks*; Dorothy Odartey-Wellington, *Contemporary Spanish Fiction: Generation X* (Newark: University of Delaware Press, 2008); Navarro Martínez, *Novela de la Generación X*; Henseler, *Spanish Fiction*.

52. See, in addition to the critics discussed previously, Martín, "Narrativa española," x–xiv; Montetes Mairal, *Qué he hecho yo*, 20; and Dorca, "Joven narrativa," 310. Among the many superb discussions of this dimension of the Gen X, I might also single out in Gavela-Ramos, *Espejo de Perseo*, chaps. 1 and 2.

53. Dorca, "Joven narrativa," 310.

54. Cited in Colmeiro, "En busca," 9 (no original attributions given).

55. Odartey-Wellington, *Contemporary Spanish Fiction*, 21.

56. Quoted in Odartey-Wellington, 22 (no author given).

57. Urioste, *Novela y sociedad*, 11–12.

58. Urioste, 13.

59. See Maria T. Pao, "Sex, Drugs, and Rock & Roll: *Historias del Kronen* as Blank Fiction," *Anales de la literatura española contemporánea* 27, no. 2 (2002): 245–260, 531–546, for an insightful review of the terminology associated with "hard realism" or "dirty realism." See also Cintia Santana, *Forth and Back: Translation, Dirty Realism, and the Spanish Novel (1975–1995)* (Lewisburg, Pa.: Bucknell University Press, 2013), for a more recent examination of dirty realism, its antecedents, and its reception vis-à-vis Spain's Gen X writers. Santana cites Casavella's novel *El triunfo* [*Triumph*] (1990) as the earliest manifestation in Spain of the aesthetic, and she names Loriga, Mañas, and Prado as the primary practitioners of dirty realism (*Forth and Back*, 107–110).

   As a notable subgenre of criticism on, and about, the novelists associated with dirty realism in Spain, some scholars have linked the novelistic tendency with *neo-tremendismo*, harkening back to Spanish novels published in the 1940s. See, in particular, Athena Alchazidu, "Generación X: Una modalidad finisecular del tremendismo," *Études Romanes de Brno* 32, no. 23 (2002): 99–108.

60. See Bill Buford, "Editorial," *Granta* 8 (1983): 4–5, for one of the earliest descriptions of dirty realism. Critics also apply the term *neorealism* to the subgroup of contemporary Peninsular novelists. See, for example, Germán Gullón, "Introducción," in *Historias del Kronen*, by José Ángel Mañas (Barcelona: Destino, 1994), v–xxxviii.

61. Douglas Coupland, *Generation X: Tales for an Accelerated Culture* (New York: St. Martin's Press, 1991). In addition to the ever-expanding base of articles devoted to the topic of the Gen X in an international arena, see the following for book-length commentaries on the origins and manifestations of the "Generation X" in the United States and the United Kingdom: Joe Austin and Michael Nevin Willard, eds., *Generations of Youth: Youth Cultures and History in Twentieth-Century America* (New York: New York University Press, 1998); Brabazon, *From Revolution to Revelation*; Bernard Carl Rosen, *Masks and Mirrors: Generation X and the Chameleon Personality* (Westport, Conn.: Praeger, 2001); Douglas Rushkoff, ed., *The Gen X Reader* (New York: Ballantine, 1994); and John M. Ulrich and Andrea L. Harris, eds., *GenXegesis: Essays on " Alternative" Youth (Sub)Culture* (Madison: University of Wisconsin Press, 2003). Interestingly, John M. Ulrich expands the time frame associated with the moniker: "Since [the early 1950s], 'Generation X' has always signified a group of young people, seemingly without identity, who face an uncertain, ill-defined (and perhaps hostile) future" ("Introduction," in *GenXegesis*, 3). For a wide-ranging discussion of the Generation X in the international context, see, among other sources, the essays in Christine Henseler, ed., *Generation X Goes Global: Mapping a Youth Culture in Motion* (New York: Routledge, 2013).

62. Martín, "Narrativa española," xiii.

63. Izquierdo, "Narradores españoles," 293.

64. Urioste actually lists twenty-five women writers in "Narrative of Spanish Women Writers of the Nineties: An Overview," *Tulsa Studies in Women's Literature* 20, no. 2 (2001): 279–295, but several of these were born before 1960. I consider only those writers born after 1960: Mercedes Abad, Nuria Barrios, Lola Becarria, Gabriela Bustelo, Luisa Castro, Lucía Etxebarria, Espido Freire, Belén Gopegui, Almudena Grandes, Begoña Huertas, Ángela Labordeta, Blanca Riestra, Juana Salabert, and Clara Usón. For his part, Izquierdo names Abad, Becarria, Bustelo, Castro,

Etxebarria, Gopegui, Grandes, Huertas, Labordeta, Riestra, and Salabert. He also adds Cuca Canals, Paula Izquierdo, María Jaén, Beatriz
Pottecher, Marta Rivera de la Cruz, and Marta Sanz. I have included all
of the aforementioned in my own list of Gen X novelists.

65. Dorca, "Joven narrativa," 310.

66. Colmeiro, "En busca," 11.

67. Izquierdo, "Narradores españoles," 296.

3. Repeating the Same Violence, or The Failure of Synchrony

1. Gabriela Bustelo, *Veo veo* (Barcelona: Anagrama, 1996); Marta Sanz, *El
frío* (Madrid: Debate, 1995); and José Ángel Mañas, *Mensaka* (Barcelona:
Destino, 1995).

2. Alain P. Toumayan, "Levinas and French Literature," in *Levinas and
Nineteenth-Century Literature: Ethics and Otherness from Romanticism
through Realism*, ed. Donald R. Wehrs and David P. Haney (Newark:
University of Delaware Press, 2009), 129. Toumayan follows the cited
statement with a series of explanatory claims organized around the
Hebrew *tohubohu* [without form], which he equates with the fundamental foreignness of the uncreated. See his *Encountering the Other: The Artwork and the Problem of Difference in Blanchot and Levinas* (Pittsburgh:
Duquesne University Press, 2004) for an extended treatment of Levinas's
view of art in relation to that of Maurice Blanchot.

3. Emmanuel Levinas, "Reality and Its Shadow," in *The Levinas Reader*, ed.
Seán Hand (Oxford: Blackwell, 1989), 130.

4. Emmanuel Levinas, *Totality and Infinity: An Essay on Exteriority*, trans.
Alphonso Lingis (Pittsburgh: Duquesne University Press, 1969), 140.

5. Emmanuel Levinas, *Time and the Other (and Additional Essays)*, trans.
Richard A. Cohen (Pittsburgh: Duquesne University Press, 1987), 72.

6. Jill Robbins, *Altered Reading: Levinas and Literature* (Chicago: University of Chicago Press, 1999), 154. Robbins here threads her analysis
through readings of a chronologically inverted series of philosophical
texts by Levinas: *Totality and Infinity* (1961), "The Other in Proust"
(1947), "Reality and Its Shadow" (1948), and "The Transcendence of
Words" (1949). See her book for a cogent, provocative, and productively

literary exploration of Levinas's own, largely unacknowledged, ambivalence toward literature.

7. Levinas, *Totality and Infinity*, 213.

8. Levinas, 203; emphasis mine.

9. Sam B. Girgus, *Levinas and the Cinema of Redemption: Time, Ethics, and the Feminine* (New York: Columbia University Press, 2010), 4.

10. Levinas, *Time and the Other*, 45.

11. Levinas, 32; emphasis in the original.

12. In the context of *Time and the Other*, Levinas discusses *dia-chrony* in his preface, written and published in 1979 on the occasion of the French-language reissue of the volume, and he utilizes both *dia-chrony* and *diachrony* in "Diachrony and Representation," written in 1982 and included, together with "The Old and the New," in the English-language translation of *Time and the Other*, published in 1987. In his 1982 essay, he suggests that *dia-chrony* corresponds to "the 'difference' of diachrony" (*Time and the Other*, 118). He seems to employ *dia-chrony* and *diachrony* interchangeably in the four essays originally included in *Time and the Other*. I include these details because they seem to confirm that Levinas's thought was continually both evolving and returning to its sources. I have elected to use *diachrony* throughout my argument.

13. Levinas, *Time and the Other*, 99.

14. Levinas, *Totality and Infinity*, 46.

15. Levinas, *Time and the Other*, 100.

16. Levinas, 54–55.

17. Christine Henseler considers Spain's Gen X texts as "realist projects" in order to underscore their "underlying genre hybridity." See her *Spanish Fiction in the Digital Age: Generation X Remixed* (New York: Palgrave Macmillan, 2011) for an elegant and fascinating reading of Gen X narratives, both fiction and film, in terms of reality TV.

18. Following James Annesley, Maria T. Pao's "Sex, Drugs, and Rock & Roll: *Historias del Kronen* as Blank Fiction," *Anales de la literatura española contemporánea* 27, no. 2 (2002): 245–260, 531–546 analyzes José Ángel Mañas's *Historias del Kronen* (Barcelona: Destino, 1994) as an example of blank fiction, a term that may, I believe, usefully be extended to the works of other Gen X writers in Spain who choose realism as their dominant narrative strategy.

19. Henseler reports that Bustelo in fact considers herself to be postfeminist, defined as "a more mature, autocritical, and ironic take on feminism . . . that goes beyond divisionary gender boundaries to include men into life's cycle" (*Spanish Fiction*, 134, first inset box). The author of *Veo veo* thus counters Lucía Etxebarria's more exclusionary perspective regarding gender.

20. In addition to *Veo veo*, Bustelo has authored *Planeta hembra* (2001) and *La historia de siempre jamás* (2007). She also works as a professional translator and has translated a number of children's books and English-language classics, such as Rudyard Kipling's *The Jungle Book*, from English into Spanish. More recently, she has translated well-known contemporary popular memoirs and biographies, including Elizabeth Gilbert's *Eat, Pray, Love* (2006) and Brent Schlender and Rick Tetzeli's *Becoming Steve Jobs* (2015), from English into Spanish.

21. Henseler, *Spanish Fiction*, 145. Henseler underscores Misha Kavka and Amy West's distinction between "located" and "unlocated" time in reality TV: "The time given for the completion of a task in reality television, whether five seconds or a month, are viewed as units disengaged from historical time and may be counted backward or forward. Therefore, one of the most important features of time in reality TV is its finiteness and its renewability" (139, inset box). Her reading of the novel—and indeed, of the cultural and technological dynamics of Spain's Gen X—offers a vibrant and, in many ways, complementary alternative to my own.

22. *Veo veo* has received notable critical attention since its publication in 1996. Dorothy Odartey-Wellington compares Bustelo's inaugural novel to Ismael Grasa's *De Madrid al cielo* regarding the ways in which both novels "ingeniously adapt the detective genre to show how agency is undermined by the changing parameters of urban space in 1990s Spain" (Odartey-Wellington, *Contemporary Spanish Fiction: Generation X* [Newark: University of Delaware Press, 2008], 49). In his dissertation on the interface between space and character in Gen X novels by Spanish authors, Corey Michael Rubin likewise interprets *Veo veo* according to its urban themes and strategies (Rubin, "Rats in the City: Mapping a Space-Character Interface in the Narratives of Spain's Generation X" [PhD diss., University of Iowa, 2014]). In a parallel vein, Henseler, *Spanish Fiction*; and Candice L. Bosse, *Becoming and Consumption: The Contemporary*

Spanish Novel (Lanham, Md.: Lexington Books, 2007), highlight Bustelo's fascination with image production and consumerism. Henseler relates the novel to the techniques of remixing common to "reality projects" (*Spanish Fiction*, 132–145), whereas Bosse follows the gendered proliferation of consumption through the novel. Morella Ortiz, "Espacios para la subjetividad femenina en *Veo veo*, de Gabriela Bustelo," *Céfiro* 11, nos. 1–2 (2011): 84–95, also concentrates on gender in Bustelo's first novel. See also Bosse's 2005 interview with Bustelo for an additional consideration of these same themes in "El sujeto femenino y las culturas de consumo: Una entrevista con Gabriela Bustelo," *Letras Hispanas* 2, no. 2 (2005): 102–108. Finally, Yvonne Gavela-Ramos examines the referential and structural functions of cinematographic discourse in the novel in both her essay "La retórica de lo icónico en la narración fílmica de *Veo veo* de Gabriela Bustelo," *Revista de Estudios Hispánicos* 45, no. 2 (2011): 307–328, and more generally, her book *El espejo de Perseo: Cultura visual en la narrativa y el cine español* (Vigo: Editorial Academia del Hispanismo, 2015). In my essay "Watching, Wanting, and the Gen X Soundtrack of Gabriela Bustelo's *Veo veo*," in *Generation X Rocks: Contemporary Peninsular Fiction, Film, and Rock Culture*, ed. Christine Henseler and Randolph D. Pope (Nashville: Vanderbilt University Press, 2007), 203–215, I discuss these same functions in terms of the musical intertextuality of *Veo veo*. Shorter discussions of Bustelo's debut novel include those by Marina Villalba Álvarez, "Dos narradoras de nuestra época: Gabriela Bustelo y Marta Sanz," in *Mujeres novelistas: Jóvenes narradoras de los noventa*, ed. Alicia Redondo Goicoechea (Madrid: Narcea, 2003), 123–130; and Carmen de Urioste, "Narrative of Spanish Women Writers of the Nineties: An Overview," *Tulsa Studies in Women's Literature* 20, no. 2 (2001): 279–295. *Veo veo* was reviewed by Santos Sanz Villanueva, "Review of *Veo veo*, by Gabriela Bustelo," *Cuadernos Hispanoamericanos* 559 (1997): 117–118; and Carmen Ferrero, "Review of *Veo veo*, by Gabriela Bustelo," *España Contemporánea* 12, no. 1 (1999): 113–115, among others.

23. As one example of the intense intertextuality at work in the novel, Bustelo incorporates some thirty-seven musical references, indicated in the chronological order in which they appear in *Veo veo*: "I'll Be Your Mirror," Lou Reed; "Ella es un volcán," La Unión; "Como una ola," Rocío

Jurado; "Little Red Corvette," Prince; "Nothin' but a Woman," Robert Cray; "Spanish Stroll," Mink Deville; FYC (Fine Young Cannibals); Ernie Isley; "Live and Let Die," Wings; "Beds Are Burning," Midnight Oil; "My Baby Just Cares for Me," Nina Simone; "Slow Love," Prince; "The Mystery," Van Morrison; Teddy Pendergrass; David Sanborn [*sic*]; Mike River; the Cars; the Motels; the Pretenders; Steve Miller; Lou Reed; the Rolling Stones; the Mammas and Papas; the Supremes; "Me colé en una fiesta," Mecano; Anna Domino; Patricia Kraus; "I'm Your Man," Leonard Cohen; "Crazy River," Robbie Robertson; "Change My Mind," Martha Davis; Guy Béart; "Cigarette of a Single Man," Squeeze; "Faith," George Michael; Nat King Cole; "The End," the Doors; "La vie en rose"; "You Can't Always Get What You Want," the Rolling Stones. See my article "Watching, Wanting," 203–115, for a discussion of these references, and of music more generally, in Bustelo's debut novel.

24. The title of the novel alludes to a children's game, the translation of which is "I spy with my little eye." The game often occurs in a moving car, in which the lead player elects a visible object that corresponds to a letter of the alphabet, the letter provides the only clue to the object, and the other players must discern the identity of the mystery object (Bustelo, quoted in Henseler, *Spanish Fiction*, 134).

25. Bustelo, *Veo veo*, 175.

26. Bosse, *Becoming and Consumption*, 131.

27. Henseler, *Spanish Fiction*, 134.

28. See Mark Allinson, "The Construction of Youth in Spain in the 1980s and 1990s," in *Contemporary Spanish Cultural Studies*, ed. Barry Jordan and Rikki Morgan-Tamosunas (New York: Oxford University Press, 2000), 265–273, for a fuller treatment of this topic.

29. Bustelo, *Veo veo*, 9.

30. Bustelo includes the Spanish translation in brackets: "Seré tu espejo. / Reflejaré lo que eres, por si no lo sabes" (*Veo veo*, 7). Given my current argument, it bears remarking that the author chose to translate "reflect what you are" as *reflejaré* [I will reflect] instead of the second-person command *refleja* [reflect]. She also opted for the indicative "por si no lo sabes" [in case you don't know] instead of the subjunctive "por si no lo sepas" [in case you might not know], although Reed's original lyrics allow for either option.

31. Bustelo, 9.

32. Henseler attributes Vania's lack of meaningful social relationships to Bustelo's critique of "contemporary capitalist culture's social fabric" (*Spanish Fiction*, 134).

33. Bustelo, *Veo veo*, 19.

34. Bustelo, 20.

35. Bustelo, 143.

36. Bustelo, 160.

37. Toni Dorca, "Joven narrativa en la España de los noventa: La generación X," *Revista de Estudios Hispánicos* 31, no. 2 (1997): 312.

38. Bustelo, *Veo veo*, 172.

39. The author's full name is Marta Sanz Pastor, but she publishes under the shortened name of Marta Sanz. In addition to edited volumes, books of poetry, and two collections of essays, Sanz has published eleven novels since the appearance of *El frío* in 1995: *Lenguas muertas* (1997), *Los mejores tiempos* (2001, Premio Ojo Crítico de Narrativa), *Animales domésticos* (2003), *Susana y los viejos* (2006, finalist for Premio Nadal), *La lección de anatomía* (2008), *Black, black, black* (2010), *Un buen detective no se casa jamás* (2012), *Amour fou* (2013), *Daniel Astor y la caja negra* (2013), *Farándula* (2015, Premio Herralde de Novela), and *Clavícula* (2017).

Scholarship on *El frío* is limited. I have published three essays on the novel: "Facing Towards Alterity and Spain's 'Other' New Novelists," *Anales de la literatura española contemporánea* 30, nos. 1–2 (2005): 301–324; "Looking for the Other: Peninsular Women's Fiction after Levinas," in *Women in the Spanish Novel Today: Essays on the Reflection of Self in the Works of Three Generations*, ed. Kyra A. Kietrys and Montserrat Linares (Jefferson, N.C.: McFarland, 2009), 133–351; and "The Art of Time: Levinasian Alterity and the Contemporary Spanish Novel," in *Levinas and Twentieth-Century Literature: Ethics and the Reconstruction of Subjectivity*, ed. Donald R. Wehrs (Newark: University of Delaware Press, 2013), 255–277. See also David Becerra Mayor, "Marta Sanz: Del realismo a la posmodernidad," in *Convocando al fantasma: Novela crítica en la España actual*, ed. David Becerra Mayor (Madrid: Tierradenadie, 2015), 107–159; and Villalba Álvarez's "Dos narradoras," in which she briefly mentions *El frío* in her commentary on Bustelo and Sanz. Christine Henseler dedicates a chapter in her *En sus propias palabras:*

Escritoras españolas ante el mercado literario (Madrid: Torremozas, 2003) to Sanz, and both María del Mar López-Cabrales's *Palabras de mujeres: Escritoras españolas contemporáneas* (Madrid: Narcea, 2000); and Carmen de Eusebio's "Entrevista a Marta Sanz," *Cuadernos Hispanoamericanos* 768 (2014): 114–124, include published interviews with the author. *El frío* was reviewed by Ignacio Echevarría, "Contra el sufrimiento. Marta Sanz, *El frío*," *El País Babelia*, 1995, 22–27.

40. Sanz, *El frío*, 46–47.

41. Levinas, *Totality and Infinity*, 264–265.

42. My interpretation of Sanz's inaugural novel runs counter to the reading postulated by Becerra Mayor, in which he maintains that "la protagonista se ve a sí misma como el *otro* aniquilado que es incapaz de enfrentarse a los demás sujetos que habitan este mundo" [The protagonist sees herself as an annihilated *other* who is incapable of confronting the other subjects who inhabit this world] ("Marta Sanz," 111). The problem, in my interpretation, is precisely that the protagonist considers herself to be an Other.

43. Sanz, *El frío*, 7.

44. Levinas, *Time and the Other*, 55.

45. Sanz, *El frío*, 11.

46. Sanz, 101.

47. Sanz, 118.

48. Levinas, "Reality and Its Shadow," 139.

49. Sanz, *El frío*, 121.

50. Levinas, *Time and the Other*, 55.

51. During the 1990s, Mañas was arguably one of the most recognizable authorial forces among the novelists associated with Spain's Gen X thanks to his early publishing success; at the tender age of twenty-three, his first novel, *Historias del Kronen* (1994), was a finalist for the prestigious Premio Nadal. The novel was subsequently translated into numerous other languages and served as the basis for a 1995 film directed by Montxo Armendáriz. Since the publication, in 1998, of the fourth novel in his Kronen tetralogy, Mañas has published seven novels, a series of novellas (with Antonio Domínguez Leiva), and most recently, a collection of aphorisms illustrated and inspired by French artist Franciam Charlot.

While *Historias del Kronen* has received the lion's share of the scholarly attention dedicated to Mañas's work, considerations of *Mensaka* are frequently included in discussions of the Kronen tetralogy. See, in particular, essays by the following scholars: Carmen de Urioste, "Punk y ruido en la 'Tetralogía Kronen' de José Ángel Mañas," *España Contemporánea* 16, no. 2 (2003): 29–52; and her "Cultura punk: La 'Tetralogía Kronen' de José Ángel Mañas o el arte de hacer ruido," *Ciberletras* 11 (2004), http://www.lehman.cuny.edu/ciberletras/vii/urioste.html (accessed July 2, 2018); Pablo Gil Casado, "Tetralogía Kronen: Realismo, dimensión críticosocial y postmodernidad," *Ojáncano* 26 (2004): 77–102; Jorge Pérez, "Suspiros de España: El inconsciente político nacional en la narrativa de José Ángel Mañas," *España Contemporánea* 18, no. 1 (2005): 33–51; and Carter E. Smith, "Social Criticism or Banal Imitation? A Critique of the Neo-realist Novel Apropos the Works of José Ángel Mañas," *Ciberletras* 12 (2004), http://www.lehman.cuny.edu/ciberletras/vi2/smith.htm (accessed March 18, 2016). Urioste's monograph also includes a lucid discussion of *Mensaka* (*Novela y sociedad en la España contemporánea [1994–2009]* [Madrid: Fundamentos, 2009]). Christine Henseler's treatment of Mañas's punk aesthetics, in her essay "Pop, Punk, and Rock & Roll Writers: José Ángel Mañas, Ray Loriga, and Lucía Etxebarria Redefine the Literary Canon," *Hispania* 87, no. 4 (2004): 692–702; and her monograph, *Spanish Fiction*, are certainly applicable to *Mensaka*. Criticism on the film adaptation of Mañas's second novel comprises an additional area of current research. See Vicente José Benet, "El malestar del entretenimiento," *Archivos de la Filmoteca* 39 (2001): 40–53; Danielle Tsibulsky, "Análisis pragmático de *Mensaka*," *Gaceta Hispánica de Madrid* 7 (2005): 1–30; and Matthew J. Marr, "Generation X and Its Discontents: The Girl Aggressor and Youth Subjectivity in the Cinematic Adaptation of *Mensaka*," *Revista de Estudios Hispánicos* 42, no. 1 (2008): 131–155; and his *The Politics of Age and Disability in Contemporary Spanish Film: Plus Ultra Pluralism* (New York: Routledge, 2013).

52. Mañas, *Mensaka*, 11; emphasis in the original.

53. Mañas, 11; emphasis in the original.

54. Mañas, 11; emphasis in the original.

55. Mañas, 12; emphasis in the original.

56. Mañas, 20.

57. Mañas, 15.

58. Mañas, 165.

59. Mañas, 165.

60. Mañas, 42.

4. The Betrayal of Diachrony

The quotation from Emily Dickinson at the beginning of this chapter serves as the epigraph to Tino Pertierra's *El secreto de Sara* (Barcelona: Alba, 1996). The epigraph features the first two lines from Dickinson's poem "LXXXIX," written around 1884 and published in "Nature: Part Two." The original English-language text reads, "Not knowing when the Dawn will come, / I open every Door" (*The Poems of Emily Dickinson*, ed. Thomas H. Johnson [Cambridge, Mass.: Belknap Press of Harvard University Press, 1958], 3:1111).

1. Emmanuel Levinas, *Totality and Infinity: An Essay on Exteriority*, trans. Alphonso Lingis (Pittsburgh: Duquesne University Press, 1969), 237.

2. Jacques Derrida famously critiqued Levinas's reliance on spatial imagery in his 1964 essay titled "Violence and Metaphysics," in which Derrida deftly maintained that the tension that Levinas hones throughout *Totality and Infinity* between exteriority and interiority underscores the "traditional logos governed by the structure of 'inside-outside,' 'interior-exterior'" (quoted in Eric Severson, *Levinas's Philosophy of Time: Gift, Responsibility, Diachrony, Hope* [Pittsburgh: Duquesne University Press, 2013], 143–144). Severson, among other commentators, critiques Levinas's use of spatial imagery throughout *Totality and Infinity* (*Levinas's Philosophy*, 144–171). Characterizing Levinas's approach as "Hegelian," Severson writes, "In *Totality and Infinity*, the other disturbs the system primarily by introducing a *distance* or *transcendence* too exterior for assimilation into the system. . . . The notion of infinity as developed here by Levinas proposes radical difference as insurmountable *spatial* separation" (144–145; emphasis in the original).

3. Levinas, *Totality and Infinity*, 202.

4. Emmanuel Levinas, *Otherwise Than Being, or Beyond Essence*, trans. Alphonso Lingis (Pittsburgh: Duquesne University Press, 1981).

5. Levinas, *Totality and Infinity*, 49.

6. Severson, *Levinas's Philosophy*, 144.

7. In section 2 of *Totality and Infinity*, Levinas theorizes the intentionality of enjoyment and the problematically gendered metaphor of feminine habitation from which alterity, as the separation between self and other, emerges. In personalizing "the home" as feminine, and in explicitly instrumentalizing the concept via the embodiment of woman (or, as Seán Hand notes, the wife), Levinas introduces one of the fundamental aporias of his thought: woman effectively occupies the role of "handmaid to an implicitly masculine effort of expression" (Hand, *Emmanuel Levinas* [London: Routledge, 2009], 42). Levinas only deepens this breach with his ensuing discussion of maternity. Because of limitations of space, I cannot examine the contradictions introduced by Levinas's gendering, albeit metaphorically, of fundamental concepts within his philosophy. The comprehensive critiques by Stella Sandford in *The Metaphysics of Love: Gender and Transcendence in Levinas* (London: Athlone, 2000); and Tina Chanter in *Time, Death, and the Feminine: Levinas with Heidegger* (Stanford: Stanford University Press, 2001) of Levinas's conceptualization of the feminine remain, to my mind, the standard against which all subsequent scholarship on the topic must be considered. Other relevant book-length discussions include those by Lisa Guenther and Lisa Baraitser, included in my bibliography. See also my essay "Looking for the Other: Peninsular Women's Fiction after Levinas," in *Women in the Spanish Novel Today: Essays on the Reflection of Self in the Works of Three Generations*, ed. Kyra A. Kietrys and Montserrat Linares (Jefferson, N.C.: McFarland, 2009), 133–151, for a pertinent discussion of gender, Levinasian alterity, and Gen X narrative by Peninsular women writers.

8. Levinas, *Totality and Infinity*, 223.

9. Levinas, 224.

10. See Severson, *Levinas's Philosophy*, 120.

11. Levinas, *Totality and Infinity*, 225.

12. Emmanuel Levinas, *Time and the Other (and Additional Essays)*, trans. Richard A. Cohen (Pittsburgh: Duquesne University Press, 1987), 77.

13. Levinas, *Totality and Infinity*, 80–81; emphasis in the original.

14. Levinas, 81.

15. Levinas, 206–207.

16. Tino Pertierra is the pseudonym of Celestino Pertierra Álvarez, a prolific journalist and currently an editor with the newspaper *La Nueva España*, located in Oviedo, the capital of Asturias. In addition to *El secreto de Sara*, to date Pertierra has published five novels as well as short story collections, plays, young-adult fiction, travel books on Asturias, and collections of essays and journalism. To my knowledge, no formal scholarship exists on *El secreto de Sara* or on Pertierra's narrative fiction more generally. The first edition of *El secreto de Sara* does include an appendix by Susana Rafart Corominas, in which she discusses the author's biography as well as the themes, genre, structure, characters, language, and style of the novel.

17. The name of the fictitious town in the novel corresponds to the first-known settlement in Gijón, Asturias (600–500 BCE).

18. Pertierra, *Secreto de Sara*, 44.

19. As a further indication of the eventual temporal suppression of alterity, the chronology of the chapters is as follows: prólogo, lunes, uno, dos, tres, martes, cuatro, miércoles, cinco, seis, jueves, siete, viernes, ocho, sábado, nueve, domingo, diez, once, lunes, doce, martes, trece, epílogo [prologue, Monday, one, two, three, Tuesday, four, Wednesday, five, six, Thursday, seven, Friday, eight, Saturday, nine, Sunday, ten, eleven, twelve, thirteen, epilogue]. Five chapters (uno, dos, miércoles, cinco, and diez [one, two, Wednesday, five, and ten]) feature two sections, distinguished by the equivalent of an asterisk and a shift in narrative theme or perspective.

20. In yet another indication of the author's exploration of the relationship between past and present, the prologue and the numbered chapters all display epigraphs extracted from a range of literary sources. These sources vary widely and include the following, in chronological order: Walt Whitman's *Leaves of Grass*, Charles Baudelaire's *Les fleurs du mal*, Jean-Arthur Rimbaud's *Une saison en enfer*, John Keats (no text noted), Emily Dickinson (no text noted), Rubén Darío's *Celeste carne*, Dorothy Parker's *Threnody*, Peter Handke's *Der Chinese des Schmerzes*, *Medea*, William Wordsworth (no text noted), Rainer Maria Rilke (no text noted), Alfred Tennyson (no text noted), Johann Wolfgang von Goethe (no text

noted), and William Faulkner's *The Wild Palms*. All of the epigraphs included in Pertierra's novel appear in Spanish.

21. Pertierra, *Secreto de Sara*, 62.

22. Pertierra, 115.

23. Pertierra, 10.

24. Pertierra, 11.

25. For an alternative reading of the cultural dynamics of "being forgettable" in Spain's Gen X narrative more generally, see Nathan Richardson's cogent essay, "The Art of Being Forgettable: Ray Loriga's *Lo peor de todo*, the *Generación X*, and the New Cultural Field," *Arizona Journal of Hispanic Cultural Studies* 9 (2005): 207–217.

26. Pertierra, *Secreto de Sara*, 119.

27. Pertierra, 120.

28. Levinas, *Totality and Infinity*, 282.

29. Jeffrey Dudiak, *The Intrigue of Ethics: A Reading of the Idea of Discourse in the Thought of Emmanuel Lévinas* (New York: Fordham University Press, 2001), 281–282.

30. Pertierra, *Secreto de Sara*, 126.

31. Blanca Riestra, *Anatol y dos más* (Barcelona: Anagrama, 1996). Blanca Riestra Rodríguez-Losada has published, under the name of Blanca Riestra, nine novels in Spanish, one novel in Galician, and one volume of poetry to date. Her fictional narrative has received several awards: Premio de Novela Ateneo Joven de Sevilla (2001), Premio Tigre Juan (2004), Premio Internacional de Novela Ciudad de Barbastro (2013), Premio de Narrativa Torrente Ballester (2015), and most recently, Premio de Novela por Entregas de *La voz de Galicia* (2016). To my knowledge, only Javier Vargas has published scholarship on *Anatol y dos más* ("*Anatol y dos más*, de Blanca Riestra: La insuficiencia del cuerpo como expresión identitaria," *Letras Femeninas* 28, no. 2 [2002]: 35–47), although the novel was reviewed by, among others, Belén Ginart, in "Blanca Riestra describe una iniciación a la vida en su novela *Anatol y dos más*," *El País*, December 5, 1996, https://elpais.com/diario/1996/12/05/cultura/849740407_850215.html (accessed October 5, 2017). The corresponding page for Blanca Riestra on Wikipedia (https://es.wikipedia.org/wiki/Blanca_Riestra) includes quotations from reviews of *Anatol*

y dos más that appeared in *El Periódico de Catalunya, Sur,* ABC, and *El País,* but I have been unable to locate any of these.

32. In a further indication of the illusory prominence of place, Riestra dedicates her novel to four people and, lastly, "a mi Santiago ya perdido" [to my now lost Santiago] (*Anatol y dos más,* 7). Nostalgia weighs heavily on the narrative and on the time of alterity, as I will subsequently analyze.

33. Levinas, *Otherwise Than Being,* 4.

34. My reading is in direct contrast to Vargas's premise that Pepe strives, throughout the novel, to give voice to his latent homosexuality. I find no textual evidence for this component of Vargas's interpretation, although my subsequent discussion does overlap, albeit in an entirely distinct context, with his discussion of "el continuo viaje de ida y vuelta que se realiza entre exterioridades e interioridades, entre lo individual y lo compartido, entre lo propio y lo común" [the continual journey of departure and arrival that is realized between exteriorities and interiorities, between what is singular and what is shared, between ownership and commonality] ("*Anatol y dos más,*" 36).

35. Riestra, *Anatol y dos más,* 152.

36. Juana Salabert, *Arde lo que será* (Barcelona: Destino, 1996); and Sergi Pàmies, *Sentimental* (Barcelona: Quaderns Crema, 1995), likewise employ epigraphs, which I will discuss in chapter 5. Interestingly, as another sign of their entanglement in far-flung issues of anteriority, six of the nine novelists analyzed throughout the project also "begin" their respective novels with a dedication (Bustelo, Salabert, and Pàmies are the exceptions), and Mañas adds a third category, acknowledgments, to his dedication and epigraph in *Mensaka.*

37. Riestra, *Anatol y dos más,* 9.

38. Riestra, 9.

39. Riestra, 11.

40. Riestra, 13.

41. Riestra, 56.

42. Riestra, 16.

43. Riestra, 17.

44. Riestra, 18; emphasis mine.

45. Riestra, 27.

46. Riestra, 21; emphasis in the original.

47. Riestra, 134; emphasis in the original.

48. Riestra, 135; emphasis in the original.

49. Riestra, 135; emphasis in the original.

50. Riestra, 129.

51. Riestra, 147.

52. Riestra, 151–152.

53. Riestra, 152.

54. Riestra, 152.

55. Belén Gopegui, *Tocarnos la cara* (Barcelona: Anagrama, 1995). Gopegui has thus far published thirteen novels, as well as screenplays, short story collections, and several volumes of essays. In contrast to the scant criticism to date on Pertierra's *El secreto de Sara* and Riestra's *Anatol y dos más*, scholars have enthusiastically embraced Gopegui's novels. *Tocarnos la cara* was reviewed by, among others, Ángel García Galiano, "Review of *Tocarnos la cara*, by Belén Gopegui," *Reseña* 264 (1995): 29; and Janet Pérez, "Review of *Tocarnos la cara*, by Belén Gopegui," *España Contemporánea* 10, no. 2 (1997): 117–119. Hayley Rabanal devotes an entire chapter to Gopegui's second novel in her superb monograph *Belén Gopegui: The Pursuit of Solidarity in Post-transition Spain* (Woodbridge: Tamesis, 2011). In addition to Rabanal's study of political solidarity in Gopegui's fiction, Nuria Cruz-Cámara, "Notas sobre un 'Bildungsroman' posmoderno: *Tocarnos la cara* de Belén Gopegui," *Crítica Hispánica* 26, nos. 1–2 (2004): 41–48; and Eva Legido Quigley, "La superación de una 'episteme' posmoderna saturada: El caso de Belén Gopegui en *Tocarnos la cara*," *Monographic Review / Revista Monográfica* 17 (2001): 146–164, have insightfully analyzed *Tocarnos la cara* in light of its potential links to postmodernism, and Janet Pérez, "Belén Gopegui, la nueva novela femenina y el neo-realismo postmoderno," *Letras Femeninas* 31, no. 1 (2005): 42–48, has discussed the novel in the context of the emerging "feminine narrative" of the 1990s in Spain. Finally, Ignacio Soldevila Durante, "La obra narrativa de Belén Gopegui," in *Mujeres novelistas: Jóvenes narradoras de los noventa*, ed. Alicia Redondo Goicoechea (Madrid: Narcea, 2003), 79–95; and Biruté Ciplijauskaité, *La construcción del "yo" femenino en la literatura* (Cádiz: Universidad de Cádiz, 2004), locate the novel within Gopegui's narrative corpus as a whole.

56. Soldevila Durante, "Obra narrativa," 83.

57. In her elegant consideration of *Tocarnos la cara*, Rabanal comments
    briefly on Levinasian alterity as an effect of solidarity: "The calling into
    question of the self which occurs in the *Probador* can be understood as
    designed to foster a sense of solidarity by awakening an already existing
    responsibility towards the other" (*Belén Gopegui*, 71). While I agree with
    much of her formulation, I emphasize temporality to the exclusion of
    solidarity. See chapter 1 (22–77) in Rabanal's monograph for a lucid and
    far-reaching discussion of the novel in light of the tactics and strategies
    of solidarity.

58. Rabanal, *Belén Gopegui*, 69–70. It is worth noting that Rabanal attaches
    a note to the passage that I here quote, in which she declares that "the
    encounter with the other is not an event or relationship that can be situ-
    ated in time, or the history of the subject." She then cites Colin Davis's
    claim that such an encounter is instead "a structural possibility that
    precedes and makes possible all subsequent experience" (70). Insofar as
    she understands time as synonymous with the history of the subject, I
    agree with her assessment, but I maintain that time is much more com-
    plex and multifaceted in Levinas's philosophical examination of alterity.

59. Gopegui, *Tocarnos la cara*, 54.

60. Levinas again minces few words in his condemnation of art in *Totality
    and Infinity* when he compares congealing "in isolation the terms that
    constitute the plurality" to "the gods immobilized in the between-time
    of art, left for all eternity on the edge of the interval, at the threshold of
    a future that is never produced, statues looking at one another with
    empty eyes, idols which, contrary to Gyges, are exposed and do not see"
    (221–222). The echoes from Plato are unmistakable, as are both Levinas's
    reduction of "art" to poetry and his own problematic dependence on
    "empty" imagery and rhetorical tropes.

61. Although a consideration of Gopegui's constantly expanding novelistic
    corpus lies far beyond the scope of my analysis, Eva Legido-Quigley's
    enumeration, from a 1998 interview with the author, of many of the
    ideas that traverse all of Gopegui's work nonetheless bears repeating in
    the context of my argument: "La clemencia, la piedad frente al dolor, los
    bálsamos, el consuelo, ese 'consolatrix aflictorum', la noción de imá-
    genes salvíficas. En la misma línea, ideas como la necesidad del otro,
    esa 'humana dependencia de ser abrazado'. La benevolencia para con

uno mismo y con los demás, la benignidad. El respeto por los otros, por la fragilidad de ciertos modos de ser" [Mercy, pity in the face of pain, balms, solace, that "consolatrix aflictorum," the notion of salvational images. In the same vein, ideas like the necessity for the other, that "human dependence of being embraced." Benevolence with oneself and with others, kindness. Respect for others, for the fragility of certain ways of being] ("Conversación con Belén Gopegui: La necesidad de una vía política," *Ojáncano* 16 [1999]: 103). For additional interviews with Gopegui in which the author discusses *Tocarnos la cara*, see María del Mar López-Cabrales, *Palabras de mujeres: Escritoras españolas contemporáneas* (Madrid: Narcea, 2000); and Marta Rivera de la Cruz, "Belén Gopegui: Cada vez hay menos gente que quiere asumir la responsabilidad de saber más que otro," *Espéculo* 7 (1997), https://webs.ucm.es/info/especulo/numero7/gopegui.htm (accessed June 4, 2004).

62. Gopegui, *Tocarnos la cara*, 11.

63. Levinas, *Totality and Infinity*, 46.

64. Levinas, 283.

65. A rehearsal of the aggressive history between Spain and the Middle East, while relevant, is far beyond the scope of my current project. I would, however, be remiss not to note that the name of Fátima appears to anchor Gopegui's novel and Luisa Castro's *La fiebre amarilla*, which I discuss in chapter 5. Fátima is both the name of Mohammed's daughter and a common Islamic female name. Whereas the two Fátimas in *Tocarnos la cara* appear to embody Simón's recurring sexual fantasy of the unattainable female object, Castro emphasizes the spiritual and religious associations of the name by referencing the "real" Shrine of Fátima. However, the more abstract version of Fátima featured in Castro's novel is just as illusory (if not more so) than the two carnal women in Gopegui's novel.

66. Gopegui, *Tocarnos la cara*, 210.

67. Gopegui, 213–214.

68. Levinas, *Totality and Infinity*, 21.

69. Gopegui, *Tocarnos la cara*, 26.

70. Gopegui, 11.

5. Diachrony and Saying

The quotation from Sergi Pàmies also serves as the epigraph for his *Sentimental* (Barcelona: Quaderns Crema, 1995) and may be translated into English as "We know that magnets attract magnetite [ferrous ferric oxide], but we do not know if magnetite also attracts the magnet or if the magnet is dragged by the magnetite against its will." Pàmies attributes the quotation to a twelfth-century Arab doctor.

1. Emmanuel Levinas, *Totality and Infinity: An Essay in Exteriority*, trans. Alphonso Lingis (Pittsburgh: Duquesne University Press, 1969), 22; emphasis in the original.

2. Levinas, 30.

3. Diane Perpich, *The Ethics of Emmanuel Levinas* (Stanford: Stanford University Press, 2008), 117.

4. Emmanuel Levinas, *Otherwise Than Being, or Beyond Essence*, trans. Alphonso Lingis (Pittsburgh: Duquesne University Press, 1981), 9.

5. Levinas, 10.

6. I follow Levinas (and his English-language translator, Alphonso Lingis) in utilizing the lowercase *said* and *saying* throughout my book, unless the terms are capitalized in the original. In addition to the sources already cited, I have been immeasurably aided by the following discussions concerning *saying* and *said*: Steve McCaffery, *Prior to Meaning: The Protosemantic and Poetics* (Evanston, Ill.: Northwestern University Press, 2001), 204–229; Michael B. Smith, *Toward the Outside: Concepts and Themes in Emmanuel Levinas* (Pittsburgh: Duquesne University Press, 2005), 43–56; and Bernhard Waldenfels, "Levinas on the Saying and the Said," in *Addressing Levinas*, ed. Sean Nelson, Antje Kapust, and Kent Still (Evanston, Ill.: Northwestern University Press, 2005), 86–97.

7. Levinas, *Otherwise Than Being*, 5.

8. Levinas, 34.

9. Levinas, 36; emphasis in the original.

10. Levinas, 37–38.

11. Levinas, 41.

12. Levinas, 48.

13. Levinas, xlviii.

14. Salabert's *Arde lo que será* (Barcelona: Destino, 1996), published only weeks after Salabert's first novel, *Varadero* (1996), was a finalist for Spain's prestigious Premio Nadal, awarded that year to another Gen X novelist, Pedro Maestre, for his *Matando dinosaurios con tirachinas.* To date, Salabert has published eight novels, a novel for children, a collection of short stories, a volume of essays, and a travelogue.

15. Scholars have considered Salabert's novels, but they tend to focus on her *Velódromo de invierno* (2001) to the exclusion of her other narrative texts. *Arde lo que será* was reviewed by Javier Goñi, "Sólo creo en los escritores que son lectores fanáticos," *El País,* January 14, 1996, https://elpais.com/diario/1996/01/14/cultura/821574001_850215.html (accessed September 18, 2017); Guadalupe Grande, "Review of *Arde lo que será*, by Juana Salabert," *El Urogallo* 120 (1996): 75–76; Víctor Molina, "De textura y talante tan distintos," *Quimera* 145 (1995): 61–64; and Francisco Solano, "Review of *Arde lo que será*, by Juana Salabert," *Reseña* 271 (1996): 35. The following authors all comment briefly on Salabert's second novel in light of her other novels: Santos Alonso, *La novela española en el fin de siglo: 1975–2001* (Madrid: Mare Nostrum, 2003); M. Mar Langa Pizarro, *Del franquismo a la posmodernidad: La novela española (1975–1999)* (Alicante: Universidad de Alicante, 2002); María del Mar Mañas Martínez, "Juana Salabert o la persistencia de la memoria," in *Mujeres novelistas: Jóvenes narradoras de los noventa*, ed. Alicia Redondo Goicoechea (Madrid: Narcea, 2003), 59–78; and Álvaro Romero Marco, "Melodrama, laberinto y memoria en la novelística de Juana Salabert," in *La pluralidad narrativa: Escritores españoles contemporáneos (1984–2004)*, ed. Ángeles Encinar and Kathleen M. Glenn (Madrid: Biblioteca Nueva, 2005), 107–118. Although she does not examine *Arde lo que será*, Tabea Alexa Linhard's essay on nostalgia in Salabert's narrative more generally, "The Maps of Nostalgia: Juana Salabert's *Velódromo de invierno*," *Revista Hispánica Moderna* 60, no. 1 (2007): 61–77, is pertinent to my discussion of temporal alterity. Finally, María del Mar López-Cabrales's 2000 interview with Salabert, to which I refer in my analysis of the novel, includes a number of illuminating comments by both interviewer and interviewee (*Palabras de mujeres: Escritoras españolas contemporáneas* [Madrid: Narcea, 2000], 63–72).

16. Though I do not address the political or sociocultural ramifications of the state-enforced violence depicted in Salabert's novel, Levinas might suggest that such violence derives, in no small part, from the metaphysical violence of sameness and the totalizing impulses of normative subjectivity.

17. Salabert, *Arde lo que será*, 7; emphasis in the original.

18. Salabert, 34.

19. Salabert, 59.

20. Salabert, 101; emphasis in the original.

21. "J'habiterai mon nom," which the author herself has translated into Spanish as "Habitaré mi nombre" [I will inhabit my name] (Salabert, 255).

22. Salabert, 257.

23. Salabert, 259–260.

24. Salabert, 269.

25. Salabert, 271.

26. Emmanuel Levinas, *Time and the Other (and Additional Essays)*, trans. Richard A. Cohen (Pittsburgh: Duquesne University Press, 1987), 111.

27. Eric Severson, *Levinas's Philosophy of Time: Gift, Responsibility, Diachrony, Hope* (Pittsburgh: Duquesne University Press, 2013), 228.

28. Pàmies's *Sentimental* was translated into Spanish by Marcelo Cohen, and the Spanish-language edition of the novel was also published in 1995. In addition to writing fiction, Pàmies is a translator, journalist, and television and radio presenter. He published two novels, *La primera pedra* (1990) and *L'instint* (1993), prior to *Sentimental*. Since 1995, Pàmies has published only short story collections. *Sentimental* was positively reviewed by Belén Ginart, "Anagrama publica *Sentimental*, tercera novela de Sergi Pàmies," *El País*, September 10, 1996, https://elpais.com/diario/1996/09/10/cultura/842306403_850215.html (accessed October 3, 2017), and is mentioned briefly in Jordi Marrugat's *Narrativa catalana de la postmodernitat* (Barcelona: Universidad de Barcelona, 2014).

29. Pàmies, *Sentimental*, 142.

30. Pàmies, 9.

31. Pàmies, 135.

32. Pàmies, 166.

33. Luisa Castro has published six novels (the last of these with Raúl del Pozo), a collection of short stories, two volumes of essays, and eight collections of poetry (in both Spanish and Galician). Her narrative fiction has been analyzed by Béatrice Rodríguez, "Luisa Castro o la escritura doble," in *Mujeres novelistas*, ed. Redondo Goicoechea, 97–107; Kirsty Hooper, "Alternative Genealogies? History and the Dilemma of 'Origin' in Two Recent Novels by Galician Women," *Arizona Journal of Hispanic Cultural Studies* 10, no. 1 (2006): 45–58; and Rubén Peinado Abarrio, "La narrativa minimalista de Luisa Castro," *Corrientes* 1 (2011): 92–111. I have previously analyzed Castro's *La fiebre amarilla* (Barcelona: Anagrama, 1994) in the following essays: "The Art of Time: Levinasian Alterity and the Contemporary Spanish Novel," in *Levinas and Twentieth-Century Literature: Ethics and the Reconstruction of Subjectivity*, ed. Donald R. Wehrs (Newark: University of Delaware Press, 2013), 255–277; "Facing Towards Alterity and Spain's 'Other' New Novelists," *Anales de la literatura española contemporánea* 30, nos. 1–2 (2005): 301–324; and "Looking for the Other: Peninsular Women's Fiction after Levinas," in *Women in the Spanish Novel Today: Essays on the Reflection of Self in the Works of Three Generations*, ed. Kyra A. Kietrys and Montserrat Linares (Jefferson, N.C.: McFarland, 2009), 133–151. In addition to my discussions, Katarzyna Moszczyska compares Castro's first and second novels in her essay "Entre '*Cuatro Calles*': Hacia el análisis sociodiscursivo de *La fiebre amarilla* y *El somier* de Luisa Castro," in *Gonzalo Torrente Ballester y los escritores nacidos en Galicia*, ed. Manuel Ángel Candelas Colodrón and Magda Potok (Vigo: Editorial Academia del Hispanismo, 2009), 197–208.

34. The Nossa Senhora do Rosário da Fátima [Shrine of Our Lady of Fátima], located seventy-five kilometers to the South of Coimbra, Portugal, is a highly celebrated Marian shrine visited by some four million people each year. The shrine commemorates the apparition of the Virgin Mary to three local shepherd children in 1917. It is significant that in *La fiebre amarilla*, neither the protagonist nor her mother has ever traveled outside of their village. The two characters erroneously place the shrine in the city of Coimbra when it is in fact housed in the city of Fátima. Geographical reality has little currency in Castro's novel. Rather, the

importance of the Shrine of Our Lady of Fátima rests on its metaphorical and temporal suggestiveness.

35. The disease of yellow fever suggests a number of associations that are relevant to Castro's novel. As an acute viral hemorrhagic illness, it is highly contagious and transmitted primarily through the bite of the female mosquito. Yellow fever occurs almost exclusively in tropical or subtropical climates and has played a crucial role in Cuban history. During the nineteenth century, it was considered one of the most dangerous infectious diseases in the world—in no small part because it figured prominently as the primary cause of death during the Spanish American War of 1898. Some sources indicate that yellow fever was responsible for thirteen times more deaths than the military casualties that resulted from Cuba's so-called War of Independence. Moreover, a Cuban doctor named Carlos Finlay was the first to correctly propose, in 1881, that yellow fever was transmitted by mosquitoes rather than by direct human contact.

In the context of the novel, Galicia, the geographical site of the narrative, has historically been associated with the highest indices of migration, particularly during the late nineteenth and early twentieth centuries, of any area in Spain. In addition to other countries in South America, Galicians frequently emigrated to Cuba. Fidel Castro was in fact the son of Galician émigrés. Cuba represents a highly charged symbolic locale in Galician national culture as both exotic and familiar, a Spanish colony and a radically independent country, a tropical island paradise in contrast to the rainy, cool climate of Northern Spain. Although the racial differences among the early twentieth-century populations of Cuba and Galicia are never mentioned in the novel, the African presence in Cuba constitutes a provocative counterpart to the Muslim connotations of Fátima. The disease of yellow fever, over the course of the narration, acquires potential links to voluntary and involuntary exodus, heroic actions, contagion, political independence, and otherworldly paradise.

36. Castro, *Fiebre amarilla*, 9.

37. Other than a vague account of the exaggerated features of the two religious figures, the details of the painting remain oblique. There is no information in the novel concerning its origins, its artistic quality, or the

size of the canvas. Virginia recalls the artwork as the only keepsake from her father and hides his death notice behind the frame. The untitled image is thus initially assigned a synecdochical position vis-à-vis Legazpi.

38. Castro, *Fiebre amarilla*, 165.

39. It has rightly been suggested that Castro may be revisiting the traditional Spanish folk motif of death as a woman, and often a female pilgrim, who appears in physical form in order to help human beings finalize their lives before accompanying them on their final journeys. This motif permeates Spanish literature, from the medieval "Romance del enamorado y la muerte" ["Romance of the lover and death"] through Alejandro Casona's canonical play *La Dama del Alba* [*The Lady of Dawn*] (1944). In Castro's version, the woman is of secondary importance to Jesús Legazpi and figures principally as a corporeal explanation for Legazpi's abandonment of his family. Other potential personifications of this folk motif in the novel include Amadora, a mysterious countess, and even (or perhaps especially) Virginia herself.

40. Castro, *Fiebre amarilla*, 171.

41. Levinas, *Time and the Other*, 77.

Afterword

1. Colin Davis, *Critical Excess: Overreading in Derrida, Deleuze, Levinas, Žižek and Cavell* (Stanford: Stanford University Press, 2010), 81. I cannot hope to summarize, at this late juncture, Davis's intricate exploration of Levinas's Talmudic commentaries and the distinctions between Levinas's own approach to sacred texts and to secular texts other than to suggest that Levinas treats Talmudic texts as many of us might treat literary texts. He seeks and finds ambiguity, a surplus of meanings, and a certain degree of interpretive freedom. For additional considerations of Levinas and the practice (and ethics) of reading, see Robert Eaglestone, *Ethical Criticism: Reading after Levinas* (Edinburgh: Edinburgh University Press, 1997); and Roland A. Champagne, *The Ethics of Reading According to Emmanuel Lévinas* (Amsterdam: Rodopi, 1998), among many other sources.

2. Seán Hand, "Shadowing Ethics: Levinas's View of Art and Aesthetics," in *Facing the Other: The Ethics of Emmanuel Levinas*, ed. Seán Hand (Surrey: Curzon Press, 1996), 83.

3. For three examinations of the applicability of Levinas's thought to political theories and praxis, see the essays included in Asher Horowitz and Gad Horowitz, eds., *Difficult Justice: Commentaries on Levinas and Politics* (Toronto: University of Toronto Press, 2006); William Paul Simmons, *An-archy and Justice: An Introduction to Emmanuel Levinas's Political Thought* (Lanham, Md.: Lexington Books, 2005); and Victoria Tahmasebi-Birgani, *Emmanuel Levinas and the Politics of Non-violence* (Toronto: University of Toronto Press, 2014).

Bibliography

Acín, Ramón. "La biblioteca del mañana." *Leer* 83 (1996): 30–35.

———. "El comercio en la literatura: Un difícil matrimonio." *Ínsula* 589–590 (1996): 5–7.

Agawu-Kakraba, Yaw. *Postmodernity in Spanish Fiction and Culture.* Cardiff: University of Wales Press, 2010.

Aguado, Txetxu. *La tarea política: Narrativa y ética en la España posmoderna.* Barcelona: Viejo Topo, 2004.

Ajzenstat, Oona. *Driven Back to the Text: The Premodern Sources of Levinas's Postmodernism.* Pittsburgh: Duquesne University Press, 2001.

Alchazidu, Athena. "Generación X: Una modalidad finisecular del tremendismo." *Études Romanes de Brno* 32, no. 23 (2002): 99–108.

Allen, Sarah. *The Philosophical Sense of Transcendence: Levinas and Plato on Loving beyond Being.* Pittsburgh: Duquesne University Press, 2009.

Allinson, Mark. "The Construction of Youth in Spain in the 1980s and 1990s." In *Contemporary Spanish Cultural Studies,* edited by Barry Jordan and Rikki Morgan-Tamosunas, 265–273. New York: Oxford University Press, 2000.

Alonso, Santos. "Así pasaron veinte años." *República de las Letras* 50 (1996): 19–24.

———. *La novela española en el fin de siglo: 1975–2001.* Madrid: Mare Nostrum, 2003.

———. "El revuelo de la juventud." *Leer* 83 (1996): 24–29.

Alonso Zaldívar, Carlos, and Manuel Castells. *Spain beyond Myths.* Madrid: Alianza, 1992.

Altisent, Marta E., ed. *A Companion to the Twentieth-Century Spanish Novel.* Woodbridge: Tamesis, 2008.

Álvarez Junco, José. "Redes locales, lealtades tradicionales y nuevas identidades colectivas en la España del siglo XIX." In *Política en penumbra: Patronazo y clientelismo políticos en la España contemporánea*, edited by Antonio Robles Ejea, 71–94. Madrid: Siglo XXI, 1996.

Annas, Julia. "Ethics and Morality." In *Encyclopedia of Ethics*, vol. 1, edited by Lawrence C. Becker and Charlotte B. Becker, 329–331. New York: Garland Press, 1992.

Astell, Ann W., and J. A. Jackson, eds. *Levinas and Medieval Literature: The "Difficult Reading" of English and Rabbinic Texts*. Pittsburgh: Duquesne University Press, 2009.

Atterton, Peter, and Matthew Calarco, eds. *Radicalizing Levinas*. Albany: State University of New York Press, 2010.

Austin, Joe, and Michael Nevin Willard, eds. *Generations of Youth: Youth Cultures and History in Twentieth-Century America*. New York: New York University Press, 1998.

Balfour, Sebastian, and Paul Preston, eds. *Spain and the Great Powers in the Twentieth Century*. London: Routledge, 1999.

Baraitser, Lisa. *Maternal Encounters: The Ethics of Interruption*. London: Routledge, 2009.

Becerra Mayor, David, ed. *Convocando al fantasma: Novela crítica en la España actual*. Madrid: Tierradenadie, 2015.

———. "Marta Sanz: Del realismo a la posmodernidad." In *Convocando al fantasma: Novela crítica en la España actual*, edited by David Becerra Mayor, 107–159. Madrid: Tierradenadie, 2015.

Becker, Lawrence C., and Charlotte B. Becker, eds. *Encyclopedia of Ethics*. 2 vols. New York: Garland Press, 1992.

Beilin, Katarzyna Olga. *Del infierno al cuerpo: La otredad en la narrativa y en el cine español contemporáneo*. Madrid: Ediciones Libertarias, 2007.

Beilin, Katarzyna Olga, and William Viestenz, eds. *Ethics of Life: Contemporary Iberian Debates*. Nashville: Vanderbilt University Press, 2016.

Benet, Vicente José. "El malestar del entretenimiento." *Archivos de la Filmoteca* 39 (2001): 40–53.

Benso, Silvia. *The Face of Things: A Different Side of Ethics*. Albany: State University of New York Press, 2000.

Bergo, Bettina. "Levinas's Weak Messianism in Time and Flesh, or the Insistence of Messiah Ben David." *Journal for Cultural Research* 13, nos. 3–4 (2009): 225–248.

Bernadell, Carles. "Los que no son de Cuenca: Retrato de un artista adolescente." *Quimera* 145 (1996): 38–39.

Bernasconi, Robert. "'Failure of Communication' as a Surplus: Dialogue and Lack of Dialogue between Buber and Levinas." In *The Provocation of Levinas: Rethinking the Other*, edited by Robert Bernasconi and David Wood, 100–135. London: Routledge, 1988.

Bernasconi, Robert, and Simon Critchley, eds. *Re-reading Levinas*. Bloomington: Indiana University Press, 1991.

Bernasconi, Robert, and David Wood, eds. *The Provocation of Levinas: Rethinking the Other*. London: Routledge, 1988.

Bosse, Candice L. *Becoming and Consumption: The Contemporary Spanish Novel*. Lanham, Md.: Lexington Books, 2007.

———. "El sujeto femenino y las culturas de consumo: Una entrevista con Gabriela Bustelo." *Letras Hispanas* 2, no. 2 (2005): 102–108.

Botwinick, Aryeh. *Emmanuel Levinas and the Limits to Ethics: A Critique and a Re-appropriation*. London: Routledge, 2014.

Bouton, Christophe. *Time and Freedom*. Translated by Christopher Macann. Evanston, Ill.: Northwestern University Press, 2014.

Brabazon, Tara. *From Revolution to Revelation: Generation X, Popular Memory and Cultural Studies*. Aldershot: Ashgate, 2005.

Buford, Bill. "Editorial." *Granta* 8 (1983): 4–5.

Bustelo, Gabriela. *Veo veo*. Barcelona: Anagrama, 1996.

Calvo, Javier, ed. *After Hours: Una muestra de cult fiction*. Barcelona: Mondadori, 1999.

Candelas Colodrón, Manuel Ángel, and Magda Potok, eds. *Gonzalo Torrente Ballester y los escritores nacidos en Galicia*. Vigo: Editorial Academia del Hispanismo, 2009.

Carabantes, Andrés. "La tribu del Kronen." *Leer* 80 (1995–1996): 30–33.

Casanova, Julián, and Carlos Gil Andrés. *Twentieth-Century Spain: A History*. Cambridge: Cambridge University Press, 2014.

Castro, Luisa. *La fiebre amarilla*. Barcelona: Anagrama, 1994.

Champagne, Roland A. *The Ethics of Reading According to Emmanuel Lévinas*. Amsterdam: Rodopi, 1998.

Chanter, Tina. *Ethics of Eros: Irigaray's Rewriting of the Philosophers*. New York: Routledge, 1995.

———, ed. *Feminist Interpretations of Emmanuel Levinas*. University Park: Pennsylvania State University Press, 2001.

———. "Introduction." In *Feminist Interpretations of Emmanuel Levinas*, edited by Tina Chanter, 1–27. University Park: Pennsylvania State University Press, 2001.

———. *Time, Death, and the Feminine: Levinas with Heidegger*. Stanford: Stanford University Press, 2001.

Chisholm, Roderick M. "Brentano, Franz Clemens (1838–1917)." In *Encyclopedia of Ethics*, vol. 1, edited by Lawrence C. Becker and Charlotte B. Becker, 97–98. New York: Garland Press, 1992.

Ciplijauskaité, Biruté. *La construcción del "yo" femenino en lu literatura*. Cádiz: Universidad de Cádiz, 2004.

Cohen, Richard A. *Elevations: The Height of the Good in Rosenzweig and Levinas*. Chicago: University of Chicago Press, 1994.

———. *Ethics, Exegesis and Philosophy: Interpretation after Levinas*. Cambridge: Cambridge University Press, 2001.

———, ed. *Face to Face with Levinas*. Albany: State University of New York Press, 1986.

———. "Translator's Introduction." In *Time and the Other (and Additional Essays)*, by Emmanuel Levinas, 1–27. Translated by Richard A. Cohen. Pittsburgh: Duquesne University Press, 1987.

———. "Translator's Note." In *Ethics and Infinity*, by Emmanuel Levinas, 17–18. Translated by Richard A. Cohen. Pittsburgh: Duquesne University Press, 1985.

Colmeiro, José F. "En busca de la 'Generación X': ¿Héroes por un día o una nueva generación perdida?" *España Contemporánea* 14, no. 1 (2001): 7–26.

Cooper, John M. "History of Western Ethics: 2. Classical Greek." In *Encyclopedia of Ethics*, vol. 1, edited by Lawrence C. Becker and Charlotte B. Becker, 461–467. New York: Garland Press, 1992.

Coupland, Douglas. *Generation X: Tales for an Accelerated Culture*. New York: St. Martin's Press, 1991.

Critchley, Simon. *The Ethics of Deconstruction: Derrida and Levinas*. Oxford: Blackwell, 1992.

Critchley, Simon, and Robert Bernasconi, eds. *The Cambridge Companion to Levinas*. Cambridge: Cambridge University Press, 2002.

Cruz-Cámara, Nuria. "Notas sobre un 'Bildungsroman' posmoderno: *Tocarnos la cara* de Belén Gopegui." *Crítica Hispánica* 26, nos. 1–2 (2004): 41–48.

Davis, Colin. *Critical Excess: Overreading in Derrida, Deleuze, Levinas, Žižek and Cavell*. Stanford: Stanford University Press, 2010.

———. *Levinas: An Introduction*. Notre Dame, Ind.: University of Notre Dame Press, 1996.

Derrida, Jacques. *Adieu to Emmanuel Levinas*. Translated by Pascale-Anne Brault and Michael Naas. Stanford: Stanford University Press, 1999.

———. *Writing and Difference*. Translated by Alan Bass. Chicago: University of Chicago Press, 1978.

Dickinson, Emily. *The Poems of Emily Dickinson*. Vol. 3. Edited by Thomas H. Johnson. Cambridge, Mass.: Belknap Press of Harvard University Press, 1958.

Dorca, Toni. "Joven narrativa en la España de los noventa: La generación X." *Revista de Estudios Hispánicos* 31, no. 2 (1997): 309–324.

Drabinski, John E. *Sense and Sensibility: The Problem of Phenomenology in Levinas*. Albany: State University of New York Press, 2001.

Dudiak, Jeffrey. *The Intrigue of Ethics: A Reading of the Idea of Discourse in the Thought of Emmanuel Levinas*. New York: Fordham University Press, 2001.

Eaglestone, Robert. *Ethical Criticism: Reading after Levinas*. Edinburgh: Edinburgh University Press, 1997.

Echevarría, Ignacio. "Contra el sufrimiento: Marta Sanz, *El frío*." Review of *El frío*, by Marta Sanz. *El País Babelia*, 1995, 22–27.

Edelglass, William, James Hatley, and Christian Diehm, eds. *Facing Nature: Levinas and Environmental Thought*. Pittsburgh: Duquesne University Press, 2012.

Elorza, Antonio. *Un pueblo escogido: Génesis, definición y desarrollo del nacionalismo vasco*. Madrid: Crítica, 2001.

Encinar, Ángeles, and Kathleen M. Glenn, eds. *La pluralidad narrativa: Escritores españoles contemporáneos (1984–2004)*. Madrid: Biblioteca Nueva, 2005.

Eusebio, Carmen de. "Entrevista a Marta Sanz." *Cuadernos Hispanoamericanos* 768 (2014): 114–124.

Everly, Kathryn. *History, Violence, and the Hyperreal: Representing Culture in the Contemporary Spanish Novel*. West Lafayette, Ind.: Purdue University Press, 2010.

Fernández Porta, Eloy. "Poéticas del Prozac: Tres líneas en la novela española de los noventa." *Quimera* 145 (1996): 35–37.

Ferrari, Enrique. "¿Hubo una Generación X en España?" *Siglo XXI: Literatura y cultura españolas* 2 (2004): 259–263.

Ferrero, Carmen. "Review of *Veo veo*, by Gabriela Bustelo." *España Contemporánea* 12, no. 1 (1999): 113–115.

Folkart, Jessica A. "The Ethics of Spanish Identity and In-difference." *Philosophy and Literature* 35, no. 2 (2011): 216–232.

Fouz-Hernández, Santiago. "*Generación X?* Spanish Urban Youth Culture at the End of the Century in Mañas's/Armendáriz's *Historias del Kronen*." *Romance Studies* 18, no. 1 (2000): 83–98.

García Galiano, Ángel. "Review of *Tocarnos la cara*, by Belén Gopegui." *Reseña* 264 (1995): 29.

García Galiano, Ángel, and Andrés Sánchez Magro. "Narrativa española de los noventa: La sociedad literaria." *Reseña* 277 (1996): 2–7.

Gavela-Ramos, Yvonne. *El espejo de Perseo: Cultura visual en la narrativa y el cine español*. Vigo: Editorial Academia del Hispanismo, 2015.

———. "La retórica de lo icónico en la narración fílmica de *Veo veo* de Gabriela Bustelo." *Revista de Estudios Hispánicos* 45, no. 2 (2011): 307–328.

Gibbs, Robert. *Correlations in Rosenzweig and Levinas*. Princeton: Princeton University Press, 1992.

Gil Casado, Pablo. "Tetralogía Kronen: Realismo, dimensión críticosocial y postmodernidad." *Ojáncano* 26 (2004): 77–102.

Gillespie, Richard, Fernando Rodrigo, and Jonathan Story, eds. *Democratic Spain: Reshaping External Relations in a Changing World*. London: Routledge, 1995.

Ginart, Belén. "Anagrama publica *Sentimental*, tercera novela de Sergi Pàmies." Review of *Sentimental*, by Sergi Pàmies. *El País*, September 10, 1996. Accessed October 3, 2017. https://elpais.com/diario/1996/09/10/cultura/842306403_850215.html.

————. "Blanca Riestra describe una iniciación a la vida en su novela *Anatol y dos más.*" Review of *Anatol y dos más*, by Blanca Riestra. *El País*, December 5, 1996. Accessed October 5, 2017. https://elpais.com/diario/1996/12/05/cultura/849740407_850215.html.

Girgus, Sam B. *Levinas and the Cinema of Redemption: Time, Ethics, and the Feminine.* New York: Columbia University Press, 2010.

Gómez Navarro, José Luis. *El régimen de Primo de Rivera: Reyes, dictaduras y dictadores.* Madrid: Cátedra, 1991.

Goñi, Javier. "'Sólo creo en los escritores que son lectores fanáticos.'" Review of *Varadero* and *Arde lo que será*, by Juana Salabert. *El País*, January 14, 1996. Accessed September 18, 2017. https://elpais.com/diario/1996/01/14/cultura/821574001_850215.html.

González Calbet, María Teresa. *La dictadura de Primo de Rivera: El directorio militar.* Madrid: El Arquero, 1987.

Gopegui, Belén. *Tocarnos la cara.* Barcelona: Anagrama, 1995.

Graham, Helen, and Jo Labanyi. "Introduction. Culture and Modernity: The Case of Spain." In *Spanish Cultural Studies: An Introduction*, edited by Helen Graham and Jo Labanyi, 1–19. Oxford: Oxford University Press, 1995.

————, eds. *Spanish Cultural Studies: An Introduction.* Oxford: Oxford University Press, 1995.

Grande, Guadalupe. "Review of *Arde lo que será*, by Juana Salabert." *El Urogallo* 120 (1996): 75–76.

Guenther, Lisa. *The Gift of the Other: Levinas and the Politics of Reproduction.* Albany: State University of New York Press, 2006.

Gullón, Germán. "Cómo se lee una novela de la última generación (Apartado X)." *Ínsula* 589–590 (1996): 31–33.

————. "Introducción." In *Historias del Kronen*, by José Ángel Mañas, v–xxxviii. Barcelona: Destino, 1994.

Guthrie, W. K. C. *A History of Greek Philosophy.* 3 vols. Cambridge: Cambridge University Press, 1962–1969.

Gutiérrez Resa, Antonio. *Sociología de valores en la novela contemporánea española.* Madrid: Fundación Santa María, 2003.

Hamblet, Wendy C. *The Lesser Good: The Problem of Justice in Plato and Levinas.* Lanham, Md.: Lexington Books, 2009.

Hammond, Michael, Jane Howarth, and Russell Keat. *Understanding Phenomenology.* Oxford: Basil Blackwell, 1991.

Hand, Seán. *Emmanuel Levinas*. London: Routledge, 2009.

———, ed. *Facing the Other: The Ethics of Emmanuel Levinas*. Surrey: Curzon Press, 1996.

———, ed. *The Levinas Reader*. London: Blackwell, 1989.

———. "Shadowing Ethics: Levinas's View of Art and Aesthetics." In *Facing the Other: The Ethics of Emmanuel Levinas*, edited by Seán Hand, 63–86. Surrey: Curzon Press, 1996.

Handelman, Susan. "Facing the Other: Levinas, Perelman, Rosenzweig." In *Divine Aporia: Postmodern Conversations about the Other*, edited by John C. Hawley, 263–285. Lewisburg, Pa.: Bucknell University Press, 2000.

Hansel, Joëlle, ed. *Levinas in Jerusalem: Phenomenology, Ethics, Politics, Aesthetics*. Amsterdam: Springer, 2009.

Heidegger, Martin. *Being and Time*. Translated by John Macquarrie and Edward Robinson. New York: Harper & Row, 1962.

Henseler, Christine. *En sus propias palabras: Escritoras españolas ante el mercado literario*. Madrid: Torremozas, 2003.

———, ed. *Generation X Goes Global: Mapping a Youth Culture in Motion*. New York: Routledge, 2013.

———. "Pop, Punk, and Rock & Roll Writers: José Ángel Mañas, Ray Loriga, and Lucía Etxebarria Redefine the Literary Canon." *Hispania* 87, no. 4 (2004): 692–702.

———. *Spanish Fiction in the Digital Age: Generation X Remixed*. New York: Palgrave Macmillan, 2011.

Henseler, Christine, and Randolph D. Pope, eds. *Generation X Rocks: Contemporary Peninsular Fiction, Film, and Rock Culture*. Nashville: Vanderbilt University Press, 2007.

Hernando, Violeta. *Muertos o algo mejor*. Barcelona: Montesinos, 1996.

Hodge, Joanna. "Ethics and Time: Levinas between Kant and Husserl." *Diacritics* 32, nos. 3–4 (2002): 107–134.

Hooper, Kirsty. "Alternative Genealogies? History and the Dilemma of 'Origin' in Two Recent Novels by Galician Women." *Arizona Journal of Hispanic Cultural Studies* 10, no. 1 (2006): 45–58.

Horowitz, Asher, and Gad Horowitz, eds. *Difficult Justice: Commentaries on Levinas and Politics*. Toronto: University of Toronto Press, 2006.

Izquierdo, José María. "Narradores españoles novísimos de los años noventa." *Revista de Estudios Hispánicos* 35, no. 2 (2001): 293–308.

Jordan, Barry, and Rikki Morgan-Tamosunas, eds. *Contemporary Spanish Cultural Studies*. New York: Oxford University Press, 2000.

Katz, Claire Elise. *Levinas and the Crisis of Humanism*. Bloomington: Indiana University Press, 2013.

———. *Levinas, Judaism, and the Feminine*. Bloomington: Indiana University Press, 2003.

Kellner, Menachem. "Jewish Ethics." In *A Companion to Ethics*, edited by Peter Singer, 82–90. Oxford: Blackwell, 1991.

Kietrys, Kyra A., and Montserrat Linares, eds. *Women in the Spanish Novel Today: Essays on the Reflection of Self in the Works of Three Generations*. Jefferson, N.C.: McFarland, 2009.

Klodt, Jason E. "'Nada de nada de nada de nada': Ray Loriga and the Paradox of Spain's Generation X." *Tropos* 27 (2001): 42–54.

LaFollette, Hugh, and Ingmar Persson, eds. *The Blackwell Guide to Ethical Theory*. Chichester: Wiley Blackwell, 2013.

Langa Pizarro, M. Mar. *Del franquismo a la posmodernidad: La novela española (1975–1999)*. Alicante: Universidad de Alicante, 2002.

Legido-Quigley, Eva. "Conversación con Belén Gopegui: La necesidad de una vía política." *Ojáncano* 16 (1999): 90–104.

———. "La superación de una 'episteme' posmoderna saturada: El caso de Belén Gopegui en *Tocarnos la cara*." *Monographic Review / Revista Monográfica* 17 (2001): 146–164.

Levinas, Emmanuel. *Discovering Existence with Husserl*. Translated and edited by Richard A. Cohen and Michael B. Smith. Evanston, Ill.: Northwestern University Press, 1998.

———. *Entre nous: Thinking-of-the-Other*. Translated by Michael B. Smith and Barbara Harshav. London: Continuum, 2006.

———. *Ethics and Infinity*. Translated by Richard A. Cohen. Pittsburgh: Duquesne University Press, 1985.

———. *Existence and Existents*. Translated by Alphonso Lingis. 1947. Reprint, Dordrecht: Kluwer, 1978.

———. "Martin Buber and the Theory of Knowledge." In *The Levinas Reader*, edited by Seán Hand, 59–74. Oxford: Blackwell, 1989.

———. *On Escape*. Translated by Bettina Bergo. Stanford: Stanford University Press, 2003.

———. *Otherwise Than Being, or Beyond Essence*. Translated by Alphonso Lingis. Pittsburgh: Duquesne University Press, 1981.

———. *Outside the Subject*. Translated by Michael B. Smith. London: Athlone, 1993.

———. "Reality and Its Shadow." In *The Levinas Reader*, edited by Seán Hand, 129–143. Oxford: Blackwell, 1989.

———. *Time and the Other (and Additional Essays)*. Translated by Richard A. Cohen. Pittsburgh: Duquesne University Press, 1987.

———. *Totality and Infinity: An Essay on Exteriority*. Translated by Alphonso Lingis. Pittsburgh: Duquesne University Press, 1969.

Lin, Yael. *The Intersubjectivity of Time: Levinas and Infinite Responsibility*. Pittsburgh: Duquesne University Press, 2013.

Lincoln, Bruce. "Revolutionary Exhumations in Spain, July 1936." *Comparative Studies in Society and History* 27, no. 2 (1985): 231–260.

Lingis, Alphonso. *Libido: The French Existentialist Theories*. Bloomington: Indiana University Press, 1985.

Linhard, Tabea Alexa. "The Maps of Nostalgia: Juana Salabert's *Velódromo de invierno*." *Revista Hispánica Moderna* 60, no. 1 (2007): 61–77.

Llewelyn, John. *The HypoCritical Imagination: Between Kant and Levinas*. London: Routledge, 2000.

López-Cabrales, María del Mar. *Palabras de mujeres: Escritoras españolas contemporáneas*. Madrid: Narcea, 2000.

Loureiro, Ángel G. *The Ethics of Autobiography: Replacing the Subject in Modern Spain*. Nashville: Vanderbilt University Press, 2000.

MacIntyre, Alasdair. *A Short History of Ethics*. London: Routledge, 1966.

Malka, Salomon. *Emmanuel Levinas: His Life and Legacy*. Translated by Michael Kigel and Sonja M. Embree. Pittsburgh: Duquesne University Press, 2006.

Mañas, José Ángel. *Historias del Kronen*. Barcelona: Destino, 1994.

———. *Mensaka*. Barcelona: Destino, 1995.

Mañas Martínez, María del Mar. "Juana Salabert o la persistencia de la memoria." In *Mujeres novelistas: Jóvenes narradoras de los noventa*, edited by Alicia Redondo Goicoechea, 59–78. Madrid: Narcea, 2003.

Mancha San Esteban, Luis. *Generación Kronen: Una aproximación antropológica al mundo literario en España*. Alcalá de Henares: Universidad de Alcalá, 2006.

Marr, Matthew J. "Generation X and Its Discontents: The Girl Aggressor and Youth Subjectivity in the Cinematic Adaptation of *Mensaka*." *Revista de Estudios Hispánicos* 42, no. 1 (2008): 131–155.

———. *The Politics of Age and Disability in Contemporary Spanish Film: Plus Ultra Pluralism*. New York: Routledge, 2013.

Marrugat, Jordi. *Narrativa catalana de la postmodernitat*. Barcelona: Universidad de Barcelona, 2014.

Martín, Sabas. "Narrativa española tercer milenio (guía para usuarios)." In *Páginas amarillas*, edited by Martín Sabas, vii–xxx. Madrid: Lengua de Trapo, 1997.

———, ed. *Páginas amarillas*. Madrid: Lengua de Trapo, 1997.

McCaffery, Steve. *Prior to Meaning: The Protosemantic and Poetics*. Evanston, Ill.: Northwestern University Press, 2001.

Mensch, James R. *Levinas's Existential Analytic: A Commentary on Totality and Infinity*. Evanston, Ill.: Northwestern University Press, 2015.

Molina, Víctor. "De textura y talante tan distintos." *Quimera* 145 (1995): 61–64.

Molinaro, Nina L. "The Art of Time: Levinasian Alterity and the Contemporary Spanish Novel." In *Levinas and Twentieth-Century Literature: Ethics and the Reconstruction of Subjectivity*, edited by Donald R. Wehrs, 255–277. Newark: University of Delaware Press, 2013.

———. "Facing Towards Alterity and Spain's 'Other' New Novelists." *Anales de la literatura española contemporánea* 30, nos. 1–2 (2005): 301–324.

———. "Looking for the Other: Peninsular Women's Fiction after Levinas." In *Women in the Spanish Novel Today: Essays on the Reflection of Self in the Works of Three Generations*, edited by Kyra A. Kietrys and Montserrat Linares, 133–151. Jefferson, N.C.: McFarland, 2009.

———. "Watching, Wanting, and the Gen X Soundtrack of Gabriela Bustelo's *Veo*." In *Generation X Rocks: Contemporary Peninsular Fiction, Film, and Rock Culture*, edited by Christine Henseler and Randolph D. Pope, 203–215. Nashville: Vanderbilt University Press, 2007.

Montetes Mairal, Noemí. *Qué he hecho yo para publicar esto: XX escritores jóvenes para el siglo XXI*. Barcelona: DVD Ediciones, 1999.

Moran, Dermot. *Introduction to Phenomenology*. London: Routledge, 2000.

Moszczyska, Katarzyna. "Entre '*Cuatro Calles*': Hacia el análisis sociodiscursivo de *La fiebre amarilla* y *El somier* de Luisa Castro." In *Gonzalo Torrente Ballester y los escritores nacidos en Galicia*, edited by Manuel Ángel Candelas Colodrón and Magda Potok, 197–208. Vigo: Editorial Academia del Hispanismo, 2009.

Naharro-Calderón, José María. "El juvenismo espectacular." *España Contemporánea* 12, no. 1 (1999): 7–20.

Narbonne, Jean-Marc, and Wayne J. Hankey. *Levinas and the Greek Heritage, Followed by One Hundred Years of Neoplatonism in France: A Brief Philosophical History*. Leuven: Peeters, 2006.

Navajas, Gonzalo. *La narrativa española en la era global: Imagen, comunicación, ficción*. Barcelona: EUB, 2002.

Navarro Martínez, Eva. *La novela de la Generación X*. Granada: Universidad de Granada, 2008.

Nelson, Eric Sean, Antje Kapust, and Kent Still, eds. *Addressing Levinas*. Evanston, Ill.: Northwestern University Press, 2005.

Núñez Seixas, Xosé Manoel. *Los nacionalismos en la España contemporánea: Siglos XIX y XX*. Madrid: Hipòtesi, 1999.

Odartey-Wellington, Dorothy. *Contemporary Spanish Fiction: Generation X*. Newark: University of Delaware Press, 2008.

Ortiz, Morella. "Espacios para la subjetividad femenina en *Veo veo*, de Gabriela Bustelo." *Céfiro* 11, nos. 1–2 (2011): 84–95.

Pàmies, Sergi. *Sentimental*. Barcelona: Quaderns Crema, 1995.

Pao, Maria T. "Sex, Drugs, and Rock & Roll: *Historias del Kronen* as Blank Fiction." *Anales de la literatura española contemporánea* 27, no. 2 (2002): 245–260, 531–546.

Payne, Mark. *The Animal Part: Human and Other Animals in the Poetic Imagination*. Chicago: University of Chicago Press, 2010.

Peinado Abarrio, Rubén. "La narrativa minimalista de Luisa Castro." *Corrientes* 1 (2011): 92–111.

Pereiro, Peregrina. *La novela española de los noventa: Alternativas éticas a la postmodernidad*. Madrid: Pliegos, 2002.

Pérez, Janet. "Belén Gopegui, la nueva novela femenina y el neo-realismo postmoderno." *Letras Femeninas* 31, no. 1 (2005): 42–48.

———. "Review of *Tocarnos la cara*, by Belén Gopegui." *España Contemporánea* 10, no. 2 (1997): 117–119.

———. "Tradition, Renovation, Innovation: The Novels of Belén Gopegui." *Anales de la literatura española contemporánea* 28, no. 1 (2003): 115–138.

Pérez, Jorge. *Cultural Roundabouts: Spanish Film and Novel on the Road.* Lewisburg, Pa.: Bucknell University Press, 2011.

———. "Suspiros de España: El inconsciente político nacional en la narrativa de José Ángel Mañas." *España Contemporánea* 18, no. 1 (2005): 33–51.

Perpich, Diane. *The Ethics of Emmanuel Levinas.* Stanford: Stanford University Press, 2008.

Pertierra, Tino. *El secreto de Sara.* Barcelona: Alba, 1996.

Preston, Paul. *The Spanish Holocaust: Inquisition and Extermination in Twentieth-Century Spain.* New York: W. W. Norton, 2012.

Rabanal, Hayley. *Belén Gopegui: The Pursuit of Solidarity in Post-transition Spain.* Woodbridge: Tamesis, 2011.

Rademacher, Virginia Newhall. "Playing for Real: Simulated Games of Identity in Spain's Gen X Narrative." In *Generation X Goes Global: Mapping a Youth Culture in Motion*, edited by Christine Henseler, 193–211. New York: Routledge, 2013.

Redondo Goicoechea, Alicia, ed. *Mujeres novelistas: Jóvenes narradoras de los noventa.* Madrid: Narcea, 2003.

Reed, Lou. "I'll Be Your Mirror." *The Velvet Underground & Nico.* Produced by Andy Warhol. Released March 12, 1967. New York: Scepter Studios.

Reverte, Jorge M. *La División Azul: Rusia 1941–1944.* Madrid: RBA, 2011.

Richardson, Nathan. "The Art of Being Forgettable: Ray Loriga's *Lo peor de todo*, the *Generación X*, and the New Cultural Field." *Arizona Journal of Hispanic Cultural Studies* 9 (2005): 207–217.

Riestra, Blanca. *Anatol y dos más.* Barcelona: Anagrama, 1996.

Rivera de la Cruz, Marta. "Belén Gopegui: Cada vez hay menos gente que quiere asumir la responsabilidad de saber más que otro." *Espéculo* 7 (1997). Accessed June 4, 2004. https://webs.ucm.es/info/especulo/numero7/gopegui.htm.

Robbins, Jill. *Altered Reading: Levinas and Literature.* Chicago: University of Chicago Press, 1999.

———, ed. *Is It Righteous to Be? Interviews with Emmanuel Levinas.* Stanford: Stanford University Press, 2001.

Robles Ejea, Antonio, ed. *Política en penumbra: Patronazo y clientelismo políticos en la España contemporánea*. Madrid: Siglo XXI, 1996.

Rodríguez, Béatrice. "Luisa Castro o la escritura doble." In *Mujeres novelistas: Jóvenes narradoras de los noventa*, edited by Alicia Redondo Goicoechea, 97–107. Madrid: Narcea, 2003.

Romero Marco, Álvaro. "Melodrama, laberinto y memoria en la novelística de Juana Salabert." In *La pluralidad narrativa: Escritores españoles contemporáneos (1984–2004)*, edited by Ángeles Encinar and Kathleen M. Glenn, 107–118. Madrid: Biblioteca Nueva, 2005.

Romero Salvadó, Francisco J. *Twentieth-Century Spain: Politics and Society in Spain 1898–1998*. New York: St. Martin's Press, 1999.

Rosen, Bernard Carl. *Masks and Mirrors: Generation X and the Chameleon Personality*. Westport, Conn.: Praeger, 2001.

Rubin, Corey Michael. "Rats in the City: Mapping a Space-Character Interface in the Narratives of Spain's Generation X." PhD diss., University of Iowa, 2014.

Rushkoff, Douglas, ed. *The Gen X Reader*. New York: Ballantine, 1994.

Salabert, Juana. *Arde lo que será*. Barcelona: Destino, 1996.

Sandford, Stella. *The Metaphysics of Love: Gender and Transcendence in Levinas*. London: Athlone, 2000.

Santana, Cintia. *Forth and Back: Translation, Dirty Realism, and the Spanish Novel (1975–1995)*. Lewisburg, Pa.: Bucknell University Press, 2013.

Sanz, Marta. *El frío*. Madrid: Debate, 1995.

Sanz Villanueva, Santos. "Así pasaron veinte años." *República de las Letras* 50 (1996): 19–24.

———. "El archipiélago de la ficción." *Ínsula* 589–590 (1997): 3–4.

———. "Review of *Veo veo*, by Gabriela Bustelo." *Cuadernos Hispanoamericanos* 559 (1997): 117–118.

Schneewind, J. B. "History of Western Ethics: 8. Seventeenth and Eighteenth Century." In *Encyclopedia of Ethics*, vol. 1, edited by Lawrence C. Becker and Charlotte B. Becker, 500–509. New York: Garland Press, 1992.

Schroeder, Brian. *Altared Ground: Levinas, History, and Violence*. New York: Routledge, 1996.

Schroeder, Brian, and Silvia Benso, eds. *Levinas and the Ancients*. Bloomington: Indiana University Press, 2008.

Schroeder, William R. "Continental Ethics." In *The Blackwell Guide to Ethical Theory*, edited by Hugh LaFollette and Ingmar Persson, 461–486. Chichester: Wiley Blackwell, 2013.

Sealey, Kris. *Moments of Disruption: Levinas, Sartre, and the Question of Transcendence*. Albany: State University of New York Press, 2013.

Severson, Eric. *Levinas's Philosophy of Time: Gift, Responsibility, Diachrony, Hope*. Pittsburgh: Duquesne University Press, 2013.

Shankman, Steven. *Other Others: Levinas, Literature, Transcultural Studies*. Albany: State University of New York Press, 2010.

Simmons, William Paul. *An-archy and Justice: An Introduction to Emmanuel Levinas's Political Thought*. Lanham, Md.: Lexington Books, 2005.

Singer, Peter. *Animal Liberation: A New Ethics for Our Treatment of Animals*. New York: HarperCollins, 1975.

———, ed. *A Companion to Ethics*. Oxford: Blackwell, 1991.

———. *Ethics in the Real World: 82 Brief Essays on Things That Matter*. Princeton: Princeton University Press, 2016.

———. *The Life You Can Save: Acting Now to End World Poverty*. New York: Random House, 2009.

———. *The Most Good You Can Do: How Effective Altruism Is Changing Ideas about Living Ethically*. New Haven, Conn.: Yale University Press, 2015.

———. *Practical Ethics*. Cambridge: Cambridge University Press, 1979.

Smith, Angel. *The Origins of Catalan Nationalism, 1770–1898*. Basingstoke: Palgrave Macmillan, 2014.

Smith, Carter E. "Social Criticism or Banal Imitation? A Critique of the Neo-realist Novel Apropos the Works of José Ángel Mañas." *Ciberletras* 12 (2004). Accessed March 18, 2016. http://www.lehman.cuny.edu/ciberletras/v12/smith.htm.

Smith, Michael B. *Toward the Outside: Concepts and Themes in Emmanuel Levinas*. Pittsburgh: Duquesne University Press, 2005.

Solano, Francisco. "Review of *Arde lo que será*, by Juana Salabert." *Reseña* 271 (1996): 35.

Soldevila Durante, Ignacio. "La obra narrativa de Belén Gopegui." In *Mujeres novelistas: Jóvenes narradoras de los noventa*, edited by Alicia Redondo Goicoechea, 79–95. Madrid: Narcea, 2003.

Song, H. Rosi. "Anti-conformist Fiction: The Spanish 'Generation X.'" In *A Companion to the Twentieth-Century Spanish Novel*, edited by Marta E. Altisent, 197–207. Woodbridge: Tamesis, 2008.

Soufas, C. Christopher, Jr. "Origins and Legacy of the Spanish Literary Generation." *Anales de la literatura española contemporánea* 36, no. 1 (2011): 209–223.

Spires, Robert C. "Depolarization and the New Spanish Fiction at the Millennium." *Anales de la literatura española contemporánea* 30, nos. 1–2 (2005): 485–512.

Staehler, Tanja. *Plato and Levinas: The Ambiguous Out-Side of Ethics*. New York: Routledge, 2010.

Tahmasebi-Birgani, Victoria. *Emmanuel Levinas and the Politics of Nonviolence*. Toronto: University of Toronto Press, 2014.

Taylor, Mark C. *Altarity*. Chicago: University of Chicago Press, 1987.

Toumayan, Alain P. *Encountering the Other: The Artwork and the Problem of Difference in Blanchot and Levinas*. Pittsburgh: Duquesne University Press, 2004.

———. "Levinas and French Literature." In *Levinas and Nineteenth-Century Literature: Ethics and Otherness from Romanticism through Realism*, edited by Donald R. Wehrs and David P. Haney, 126–147. Newark: University of Delaware Press, 2009.

Tsibulsky, Danielle. "Análisis pragmático de *Mensaka*." *Gaceta Hispánica de Madrid* 7 (2005): 1–30.

Tussell, Javier. *Carrero: La eminencia gris del régimen de Franco*. Madrid: Temas de Hoy, 1993.

Ulrich, John M. "Introduction. Generation X: A (Sub)Cultural Genealogy." In *GenXegesis: Essays on "Alternative" Youth (Sub)Culture*, edited by John M. Ulrich and Andrea L. Harris, 3–37. Madison: University of Wisconsin Press / Popular Press, 2003.

Ulrich, John M., and Andrea L. Harris, eds. *GenXegesis: Essays on "Alternative" Youth (Sub)Culture*. Madison: University of Wisconsin Press / Popular Press, 2003.

Urioste, Carmen de. "Cultura punk: La 'Tetralogía Kronen' de José Ángel Mañas o el arte de hacer ruido." *Ciberletras* 11 (2004). Accessed March 18, 2016. http://www.lehman.cuny.edu/ciberletras/vii/urioste.html.

———. "La narrativa española de los noventa: ¿Existe una 'Generación X'?" *Letras Peninsulares* 10, nos. 2–3 (1997–1998): 455–476.

———. "Narrative of Spanish Women Writers of the Nineties: An Overview." *Tulsa Studies in Women's Literature* 20, no. 2 (2001): 279–295.

———. *Novela y sociedad en la España contemporánea: 1994–2009*. Madrid: Fundamentos, 2009.

———. "Punk y ruido en la 'Tetralogía Kronen' de José Ángel Mañas." *España Contemporánea* 16, no. 2 (2003): 29–52.

Valle Detry, Mélanie. "Belén Gopegui o *contar lo que viéndose no se mira*." In *Convocando al fantasma: Novela crítica en la España actual*, edited by David Becerra Mayor, 57–106. Madrid: Tierradenadie, 2015.

Vargas, Javier. "*Anatol y dos más*, de Blanca Riestra: La insuficiencia del cuerpo como expresión identitaria." *Letras Femeninas* 28, no. 2 (2002): 35–47.

Villalba Álvarez, Marina. "Dos narradoras de nuestra época: Gabriela Bustelo y Marta Sanz." In *Mujeres novelistas: Jóvenes narradoras de los noventa*, edited by Alicia Redondo Goicoechea, 123–130. Madrid: Narcea, 2003.

Wahl, Jean. *Le choix, le monde, l'existence*. Grenoble: Arthaud, 1947.

Waldenfels, Bernhard. "Levinas on the Saying and the Said." In *Addressing Levinas*, edited by Sean Nelson, Antje Kapust, and Kent Still, 86–97. Evanston, Ill.: Northwestern University Press, 2005.

Wehrs, Donald R., ed. *Levinas and Twentieth-Century Literature: Ethics and the Reconstruction of Subjectivity*. Newark: University of Delaware Press, 2013.

Wehrs, Donald R., and David P. Haney, eds. *Levinas and Nineteenth-Century Literature: Ethics and Otherness from Romanticism through Realism*. Newark: University of Delaware Press, 2009.

Wyschogrod, Edith, and Gerald P. McKenny, eds. *The Ethical*. Malden: Blackwell, 2003.

———. Introduction to *The Ethical*, edited by Edith Wyschogrod and Gerald P. McKenny, 1–11. Malden: Blackwell, 2003.

Index

memory (*continued*)
  La fiebre amarilla, 140, 142; in *El frío*,
    79; in Levinas, 124, 132, 163n55; in *El
    secreto de Sara*, 95, 101; in *Tocarnos la
    cara*, 114; in *Veo veo*, 67
Merleau-Ponty, Maurice, 17, 19, 161n36
metaethics, 7–8
metaphor, 26, 44, 60, 64, 77, 91, 92, 93, 102,
    137, 141, 187n7, 198n34
metaphysics, 1, 2, 5, 6, 17, 17, 58, 61, 62, 72,
    91, 94, 120, 146, 154n12, 158n25, 196n16
mirror, 65, 66, 68, 71, 72, 112
monarchy, 3, 31, 33, 34, 35, 41–42, 44, 47,
    166n11, 168n25
morality, 5, 12, 14–16, 27, 38, 152n5, 157n18,
    160n31
mother, 85, 95–102, 129, 130–131, 139–140,
    197n34. *See also* maternity
music, 59, 81, 83, 97, 170n36, 175n49,
    181n22, 181n23
mystery, 23, 61, 105, 122, 138, 140, 142,
    163n55, 182n24

neighbor, 25–26, 29, 39, 120, 124
neorealism, 63–64, 87, 177n60. *See also*
    dirty realism; hard realism
nomos, 11, 12
nostalgia, 63, 66, 105, 157n18, 190n32, 195n15

obligation, 1; in *El frío*, 76; in Levinas, 8,
    27, 94, 122, 123, 124, 126, 146, 160n31; in
    El secreto de Sara, 95; in *Sentimental*,
    133; in *Tocarnos la cara*, 116. *See also*
    duty

paradox, 2, 12, 25, 31, 35, 67, 90, 92, 100,
    119, 135, 137
paranoia, 68, 70, 71, 84, 85
paternity, 96, 99, 137, 140, 142. *See also*
    father
perception, 2, 13, 19, 21, 58, 59–60, 68, 79,
    87, 93, 103, 110, 134, 145
persecution, 27, 39, 120, 124
phenomenology, 6, 13, 15–20, 21, 22, 91, 121,
    146, 159n28, 159n30, 161n34, 161n36

pity, 100, 193n61
Plato, 7, 9–10, 11, 12–13, 19, 59, 121, 124,
    155n16, 156n17, 159n28, 192n60
poetry, 9, 97, 192n60
postponement, 90, 92, 94, 100, 106, 120,
    145. *See also* deferral; delay
power, 2, 32, 33, 35, 43, 45, 46, 51, 68, 90,
    102, 124, 130, 132, 166n7
practical ethics, 7, 8, 11, 153n10
Primo de Rivera, Miguel, 31–35, 167n11
priority, 67, 119, 120, 121, 123, 125
prophecy, 124, 125
prose, 60, 90, 104, 124–125
Protagoras, 11
proximity, 77, 78, 93, 120, 123, 125, 126, 129,
    131, 133, 136

rationality, 1, 2, 8, 12, 13, 15–16, 27, 61, 121,
    142. *See also* reason
reason, 1, 12, 14, 15, 59, 72, 121, 122. *See also*
    rationality
reciprocity, 18, 64, 79
relativism, 8, 11, 12
religion, 43, 167n17
repetition, 4, 62, 63, 69, 72
resistance, 24, 26, 34, 68, 104, 106, 115, 145
response, 1, 10, 11, 13, 17; in *Anatol y dos
    más*, 108; in *Arde lo que será*, 127, 129, 131;
    in *El frío*, 76; in *La fiebre amarilla*, 139,
    140; in Levinas, 24, 26; in *Mensaka*, 86;
    in *El secreto de Sara*, 97, 101; in *Tocarnos
    la cara*, 113; in *Veo veo*, 65, 70, 72
Rosenzweig, Franz, 160n33

said, 25–26, 78, 91, 120, 123, 124, 125,
    126–127, 133, 156n17, 194n6
Sartre, Jean-Paul, 17, 19, 159n30, 161n36
Saussure, Ferdinand de, 22
saying, 9, 25–26, 118, 119, 123–127, 143, 146,
    153n11, 156n17, 194n6
Scheler, Max, 16–17, 19
Second Republic, the, 3, 35, 37
secret, 95, 98, 99, 100. *See also* enigma
self: in *Arde lo que será*, 126, 129; in *El frío*,
    76, 78, 81; in *La fiebre amarilla*, 138, 139;

About the Author

NINA L. MOLINARO is an associate professor of Spanish at the University of Colorado Boulder. She has published *Foucault, Feminism, and Power: Reading Esther Tusquets* (Bucknell University Press, 1991) and *Policing Gender and Alicia Giménez Bartlett's Crime Fiction.* Together with Inmaculada Pertusa-Seva, she has coedited *Esther Tusquets: Scholarly Correspondences,* and with Nancy Vosburg, she has coedited *Spanish and Latin American Women's Crime Fiction in the New Millennium: From* Noir *to* Gris. Her scholarly areas of expertise include postwar Peninsular literature and culture, Hispanic women's literature, literary theory, and contemporary Peninsular film.